His

His

BRILLIANT NEW FICTION BY GAY WRITERS

edited by Robert Drake with Terry Wolverton

Faber & Faber   **Boston · London**

Introduction, Collection, and Notes copyright © 1995 by Robert Drake and Terry Wolverton

The acknowledgments on p. 241 constitute an extension of this copyright notice.

Library of Congress Cataloging-in-Publication Data

His: brilliant new fiction by gay writers / edited by Robert Drake
    with Terry Wolverton.
       p.   cm.
     ISBN 0-571-19866-X
       1. Gay men—United States—Social life and customs—Fiction.
     2. American fiction—20th century.   3. Gay men's writings, American.
     I. Drake, Robert.   II. Wolverton, Terry.
     PS648.H57H57 1995
     813'.01089206642—dc20   94-45997
                                                                  CIP

Cover design by Susan Silton
Cover photograph by Robert Flynt
Printed in the United States of America

To Scott

Contents

Introduction

It has always seemed to me a great injustice that the artists of the world
are expected to produce, along with their "great" works, the commodities
for consumption which all non-artists are expected to produce.

—Jack Kerouac, January 10, 1943

Jack Kerouac was twenty years old when he penned those words in
a letter to a friend. I was startled when I read them, for they
echoed the thoughts of a favorite author of mine who referred to
himself as a "hermaphrodite"—half poet, half philosopher. This
hermaphrodite spoke of the responsibilities of the artist when he
said, also in a letter, "Work for your contemporaries, but create
what they need, not what they praise."

Similar letters, similar thoughts, yet Friedrich Schiller wrote
his letter in 1795. Since the popularization of the printed word,
since the first impressions of popular literature made it into the
world to sit on bookshelves beside "classic" texts and vie for the
attention of the purchaser, there has endeavored to exist an un-
easy collaboration between art and commerce. This notion rears
its head perhaps most vividly in our present day, with CD-ROM
multimedia texts entering the marketplace to compete for the
consumer's dollar, and what many, rightly or no, presume is the
concurrent de-emphasis of the printed word. However, there remain books aplenty on the shelves of bookstores and homes; my
own home is filled with books, some of which I know I shall die
not having read. I pick up new volumes monthly to add to my

private library and I react enthusiastically to a new, intriguing title on the shelf of a public library, often bringing it home to read before all the other books that sit quietly in line before it.

In developing this anthology, I struggled with thoughts of how best to define literary fiction for myself and those who might read this book, how to possibly create a collection that was vibrant and wholly new. Fortunately, I had Terry Wolverton to help me resolve these questions, and to meet me, effort for effort, in the work required to pull together the stories—the book—you now hold.

We had said from the beginning that literary quality would be our sole criteria for stories included in *His* and its companion volume, *Hers*. This would separate them, we felt, from other anthologies that tended to narrow their focus along lines of identity politics or category writing. In our books, transgressive writers would rub shoulders with old-school authors, to the benefit of every reader. Yet as time passed—as we invested more and more labor into gathering the writing in these volumes—I found myself contemplating the meaning of "literary quality." As Kerouac and Schiller were so well aware, writing does not exist in a vacuum. Writing is created by people, working to transmit ideas, images, and stories from their heads into a medium readily graspable by an Other, the reader-at-large. Literature is created by people living in a time whose influences are felt—are acting upon the writer—as every word is set upon the page, as every attempt is made to reach for something known by themselves—and, in their heart of hearts, Others—as Art. Writers want to be published, but even more, they pursue an ineffable immortality: They want to leave their mark. I believe that even the soul of the most dispassionate hack harbors a desire to render with the shaping of words something new and remarkable; even more so for them, perhaps: Their Art is shaped from a medium so many others have made serve only the ordinary.

Before I can move toward an estimation of what literary quality may be, I must pause to question further cultural differences, particularly with regard to the assembling of anthologies. I firmly believe that a commitment to cultural diversity is a crucial aspect of Art as pursued by any editor who hopes to assemble a lively, vital, honest anthology. This commitment is no way in conflict with literary quality.

Any editor, then, must set for him- or herself the task of self-education with regard to what quality might mean when seen in different cultural representations. An editor must ensure that writers working at this level are aggressively sought out within the culture at large, and, importantly, within various subcultures. To do anything less does a disservice to talented writers and the literary community.

This argument is perhaps especially valid when we take into consideration *His* and its companion volume. I have been sickened by fawning pseudo-intellectuals who eagerly pin the badge of "cultural difference" on shoddy writing and, in so doing, deny these artists the criticism they seek—the educational experience all writers seek in exposing their work to the world. This is inexcusable, and the literary community continues to pay a price for it. Talented writers are perhaps done the gravest disservice, being praised more for their subcultural relevance than for the quality of their work.

We need to acknowledge that literary quality is something that can be realized on its own, without having to fit neatly against a previously or newly established entitled paradigm. It is a grave error to assume any such entitled model as "best," for that assumption means that we have failed to realize a Central Artistic Truth: that difference in itself leads naturally toward a qualitative "bestness" unique and whole and valid within each culture and outside of it as well, when fed and nourished.

This is the criterion, then, that we have employed in assembling these anthologies, the brass ring we have tried to grip and hold.

Literary quality, in its best possible understanding, reflects the diversities of excellence present within the minds and talents of good and true writers. Yet this is subjective; is it possible to raise the thought of objective literary quality?

No; not outside the realm of the canonical. No commercial anthology will satisfy every reader, every time, for within its pages ensues the war of commerce and art: We seek, as writers and editors, to create what readers need, but we also hope to create what they will praise—if only for the reason that such praise tends to lend more readers to avail themselves of the work. This combination of two conflicting impulses, of course, violently bloodies Schiller's ideal, even as it seeks to bandage those wounds.

Be the writing collected within the covers of a book, or digitally impressed upon the spinning silver surface of the CD-Rom disc, what is hoped is that, when all is read and done, an editor's instincts will have worked well enough during the process of selection to draw together stories that individually satisfy and collectively prove no less rewarding: what Kerouac refers to as the authors' "'great' works" that, gathered as *His*, become "commodities for consumption."

—ROBERT DRAKE, 1995

His

Queerbait

MARK A. SHAW

for Darby Crash

"The word gay is becoming oppressive."
Camille Paglia, "The M.I.T. Lecture,"
Sex, Art and American Culture

Snake and I didn't hijack a gay bar because we shared a secret sorrow. We were not fascist skinheads (as reported in the regional *lesbigay* press), homophobes, closet cases or confused.

We hijacked the Arabian Nights because we were pissed-off teenage fags who wanted to dance. We were pissed-off teenage fags who knew that if we heard "It's Raining Men" just once more there would be a horrible price to pay. Four hundred mindless disco queens watched in open-mouthed horror as two boys in Converse high-tops, Catholic girls' skirts, ripped T-shirts and spiky flattops danced together to the Cramps, played at gun-point by a d.j. in fear for his life.

As a teenage fag in the all-white suburbs of Kansas City, Missouri, I developed a theory to explain the aggressive banality of the populace. During the great migration, before the wagon trains headed west to massacre indigenous peoples and steal their land, they gathered in Kansas City to load supplies and unload the more spectacularly idiotic members of their party. These orphaned half-

wits remained behind to found a culture that worshiped the food
source with an alarming fervor.

While my peers in Eastern Jackson County, Missouri, were listening to the Carpenters and the Captain and Tenille, I devoted
myself to the Velvet Underground, Bowie, Brian Eno, Roxy Music
and the Stooges. I spent many hours in front of the mirror in my
bedroom listening to Bowie's "Rebel Rebel," imagining myself in a
tight skirt, trying to dance like the cool black girls on "Soul Train."

My salvation arrived in early 1976 while watching "Saturday
Night Live." A boy with an angelic face and curly blond hair
pounded out a few chords on a piano. A rail-thin figure of inde-
terminate gender in black jeans and a white shirt clutched the microphone and sang in a flat, matter-of-fact voice, "Jesus died for
somebody's sins, but not mine."

The world ended, a new world was born and I was remade.
Patti Smith was performing an incantation on national television,
impersonating Shiva, calling forth a new world, creating a new
range of possibilities on the show most revered by my peers. I
knew, come Monday morning, that I would face a generation
transfigured, inflamed.

At school on Monday, I wore black jeans and a white shirt. My
classmates joked nervously about "the dyke" they saw on television. In the locker room after gym class my eyes lingered tellingly
on the thick, dark thighs of a boy who beat up his girlfriend after
she got pregnant. His dick thickened before he blushed, called
me a faggot and dressed hurriedly. I smiled and wore the epithet
as a badge of honor, an accessory to the shame I felt in desiring
such an asshole.

During the three years between Patti's appearance and my escape from the suburbs, I devoted myself to erasing any trace of
wholesomeness. By avoiding the sun, I significantly reduced any
vestigial Midwestern pigmentation, leaving me with a glamorous
pallor, assisted by cropped hair dyed platinum and eyes ringed
with thick black eyeliner. I combed through bookstores downtown
looking for magazines like *NME* from London, *New York Rocker* and
Punk from New York and *Slash* from Los Angeles. These magazines
chronicled the tiny segment of my generation who refused to accept the limitations of contemporary youth culture.

Late in the summer before my senior year, I found a flyer ad-
vertising a record store called Rock Therapy that stocked releases

from independent record labels, product made by thousands of teens around the world who started bands and produced seven-inch pieces of plastic to communicate with each other. Dave, the man who owned the store and dressed like my father did in 1958, insisted I buy singles made by local bands. He directed me to a new club, the Downliner, where local bands like Hitler Youth, the Embarrassment, DuChamp and Get Smart played on weekends.

I met Snake in 1979 at the Downliner, a punk club in Kansas City located in the basement of a cowboy bar. The parking lot behind the bar was full of disaffected Midwestern youth milling around ignoring the cowboys who, with some regularity, leaned out of the upstairs door to yell "faggot." Quite often, this epithet was directed at women who either ignored them or screamed "That's dyke, you asshole," or "Suck my dick, you stupid cowfucker." The bearded, shaggy-headed, pot-bellied cowboys would disappear for a moment, only to return armed with empty PBR bottles, which they tossed at our heads.

Although I had made a diligent study of the photos of punks in New York and England, I had profound doubts about my ability to capture the punk fashion ethos. I had stolen a suit from my father's closet, purchased by him in 1956 when he married my mother. The shoulders of the jacket were enormous and tapered to a tight waist. The long coat came to mid-thigh, covering the high-waisted, voluminously pleated baby blue trousers. I wore a gray rayon shirt I had acquired in a downtown thrift store, with a skinny, dark blue silk tie with a lurid Vargas girl now faded to yellow. I adorned the bimbo on my tie with a safety pin through her huge, leering red lips.

I teased my platinum hair into a fifties pompadour, ringed my eyes with black eyeliner and coated my lips with pale pink lipstick. Every part of me was brightly colored, except my face, which looked cadaverous in contrast.

No one at the Downliner seemed to think I looked ridiculous. The skinhead at the door commented, after glancing at my fake I.D., "I get it, Jerry Lee in Hell. Cool."

I noticed Snake my first night there. He was hanging out with two women wearing men's suits. He wore enormous, long khaki shorts and a T-shirt with a silk-screened image of Iggy clutching his thick, greasy dick. He performed a shuffling dance in the dirt while

the sound system from the club blasted the Specials's "Do the Dog."
The two women, both pale with blue-black hair and bright red lipstick, wore tailored suits with white shirts, broad floral ties, suspenders and black wingtips. They held their joined hands over
Snake's head, creating an arbor under which he danced—his feet
shuffled and raised the dirt while his hips moved in a circle. His
baggy shorts whipped around his legs, resembling a skirt.

Get Smart, a trio from Lawrence, Kansas, began to tune up and
Snake's protectors lowered their hands. He stood and wiped the
dirt from his face as they made their way into the club. I leaned
against a wooden pillar and finished my cigarette. Snake stopped
as he passed and grinned at me.

"What's your name, pretty boy?" He drawled.

"Doug," I answered, meeting his leer.

"You sure got a pretty mouth, Drug."

"Have you been taking cowboy lessons from our friends upstairs?" The smoke from my cigarette curled into my eyes, forcing
me to squint in what I hoped was a menacing manner.

He wiped the leakage from my eye with a long brown finger,
which moved from my face to his mouth. He licked the teardrop
from his finger with a flick of his tongue. "They call me Snake."

"Why do they call you Snake?"

He moved his hips in a slow grind and grinned. "Because of
what I can do with my tongue." The women held their fingers in V
shapes in front of their mouths and moved their tongues quickly
between them.

"This is my cousin Magdalene and her girlfriend Marlene."
The women nodded in unison. "Give me a drag of your cigarette."

I handed the unfiltered Camel to Snake, who inhaled deeply.
He dropped the cigarette on the ground, reached over and pulled my mouth open. He leaned in until we were staring at each
other from an inch away and blew the smoke into my open
mouth. The girls smirked. "I'll look for you inside, Drug."

Get Smart played clever pop music that both criticized and em-
braced the pop idea. During their first set, I caught only occasional glimpses of Snake, who was either at the bar or on the
dance floor with Magdalene and Marlene dancing in a space always cleared of other dancers because of the danger of being
struck by their flying elbows and knees. They were joined by a

young man with a blond crew cut and a jaw so square he could have been a poster child for ethnic purity. They performed a dance that most closely resembled a ritual sacrifice. I often found myself dancing with a young woman with a short black helmet of hair, a smart black cocktail dress and opera-length gloves.

Snake joined me at the bar during the break between sets. The heat of a hundred thrashing bodies had plastered his short black hair to his head and molded the image of masturbating Iggy to his thin chest. Amphetamines made his black eyes glitter maniacally and his mouth grimace.

"I think Dolly likes you."

"Who's Dolly?" I asked.

He pointed at the elfin girl with whom I had been dancing. She smiled and raised an enormous martini glass and waved it at us conspiratorially.

"Don't get the wrong idea about our little scene outside." He waved his fingers at the woman behind the bar, dressed in near perfect replication of Lulu, who placed four beers in front of us. "I'm not gay or nothing." Snake handed one of the beers to me without meeting my eye. "You just looked so uptight I couldn't help fucking with you."

I picked up a napkin from the bar and leaned over to wipe the sweat from his forehead and whispered in his ear. "This place is everything I ever wanted."

He grinned and looked at me out of the corner of his heavily lidded eyes. "There's a party after closing. Dolly will show you where it is."

The party was held in some band hovel north of the river. The three-room shack in the middle of a cornfield was sparsely furnished with someone's Early American discards. The wooden floor was stained with liquor and its after-effects. A powerful sound system setup in one room provided for the dancers in the next.

After hours of dancing to pounding, minimalist, dark music, all of the men and most of the women had removed their shirts. Exhausted and very drunk, I left the throng in the middle of the floor to lean against the wall and watch. In the next room, Snake was arguing with the ersatz d.j., who cued up Screaming Jay Hawkins's "Constipation Blues" before he walked away. Snake removed the record and placed another on the turntable. When the music ceased abruptly, the mob stopped moving and screamed "Turn it back on" in one voice. As the record cued, Snake entered the room. "This is for the *real* dancers." He grabbed me by the belt loop as the first blast of horns sounded and I recognized the Ohio Players's "Rollercoaster," an oft-heard selection on "Soul Train."

I wasn't sure how uncool an appreciation for black music was to this crowd, so I was unwilling to perform my private ersatz-black-girl mirror dance. Magdalene and Marlene, still in semiformal attire, performed an elegant dance that involved bending at the waist, twisting at the hips, and jerking up and down like pistons. Dolly sort of twisted off to the side. At first, Snake and I performed a similar ritual. Halfway through the song, he scooted his plump little butt into my groin and moved my arms around his waist as we swiveled and bopped as one.

He moved my hands from his sweat-soaked abdomen, up the line of dark fur ascending from his shorts, to cover his small hard nipples. I remembered he had told me he wasn't gay, so I just placed my open palms on his chest.

He leaned his head back and whispered in my ear. "What's the matter, Drug? Don't you want to make these poseurs drip cum in their shoes?" ·

I licked the sweat from the back of his neck, moving my tongue over the salty rough stubble remaining from his most recent haircut. I moved my palms in circles over his tits and I placed my teeth around the tendons at the base of his neck. As I pinched his nipples, I ground my front teeth on the cord of tendons. Snake yelped and twisted under my grasp until my dick nestled between the cheeks of his hard, round butt.

Snake moved my hands down to grip the fat dick trapped in the folds of his voluminous shorts. I worked his dick while he bucked against me. He sang, in a dark baritone, words from Patti Smith's song "Horses."

A few of the boys on the sides of the room looked uncomfortable and aroused. One or two, either very brave or uncontrollably moved, furtively rubbed their crotches and gaped. Most of the women appeared merely amused. Magdalene and Marlene stopped dancing to snap their fingers at us and toss pennies at our feet.

Snake's dick throbbed and both my palm and his khaki shorts were wet. I smeared my hand over the expanding stain, squeezing drops out of his dick like toothpaste. Snake turned his head and licked the side of my face as he moved my hand to my mouth.

"Taste me, Drug." I licked my palm, tasting something like school paste and vinegar. He grabbed my dick and I shot off in my black jeans.

Magdalene and Marlene tossed cigarette butts at us and shouted brava. A fat blond skinhead muttered "faggot" as he shoved his way past us, and the girls followed to torture him.

Snake attempted to play the song again but the crowd objected by hurling empty beer bottles at him. He relented and drifted off outside. The d.j. returned and played Joy Division. I lined up to get into the filthy toilet.

The man in front of me, who had been taking pictures all evening, was older than most of us. He must have been almost thirty, but he was okay in a sort of banker-on-the-skids kind of way.

"Quite a show you and your friend put on out there." He studied my crotch speculatively. "Got some good pictures."

"What are you going to do with them?"

He made the international masturbation gesture. I noticed he wore a wedding ring.

"Where's your wife?" I asked, sneering.

"She's home with the kid." His turn in the toilet arrived. "Wanna share?" he asked me, daring me to join him. I did.

He shut the door and leaned against it. "Do you mind if I watch?"

"Just don't take any pictures." I was desperate enough not to mind an audience. I ignored him until I realized he was pressed against my back, looking over my shoulder.

"Nice piece of meat, boy." His language alone made me squirm.

"Um, thanks." It hardly seemed something for which I could take credit.

He whispered in my ear. "You're much prettier than my fifteen-year-old son."

I tried to finish as quickly as possible, but it was not an activity that could be hurried.

"I should get you and your boyfriend to baby-sit sometime." He unzipped and moved to join me moments before the door opened and Snake stuck his head in.

"Hurry up, Drug. Dolly wants to take you home with her."

"He's not my boyfriend!" I shouted at the perverse married man as Snake dragged me out of the bathroom.

"Why am I going home with Dolly?" I asked Snake.

"She likes you."

"What about you?"

"She likes me too, but I've got to make an intervention. The girls are punk-fucking Buster with a beer bottle. I think they're taking revenge on Fatty Arbuckle. They keep screaming 'Squeal like a pig, fatty.'"

"Who is Buster?"

"That fat blond skinhead. Go on Drug, Dolly's waiting." He pried my mouth open and inserted his tongue in what was less a kiss than a cavity search.

I woke up the next morning in bed with Dolly and the Aryan poster boy. Dolly's ancient wind-up alarm clock said two o'clock but wasn't necessarily trustworthy. The insufferable humidity left an oily sheen on Dolly's small freckled breasts and the blond boy's small pink butt, which served as a powerful jolt to memory and my dick.

I remembered fucking him while he lay on his back with his knees neatly tucked under my arms. Dolly lay behind me, watching as intently as an anthropologist at her fieldwork, her seriousness of purpose only occasionally undone by her giggles. Each time I rammed into him, the blond boy scowled and grunted, "You goddamn son of a bitch."

As we all awakened he got out of the bed, picked up his clothes, and went into the bathroom. Dolly put on a robe and disappeared into the kitchen. She returned with coffee and cognac at the same time as the blond boy, once again dressed. He frowned and rubbed his butt through his tight black jeans.

"You'd better not tell my wife about this," he grunted before he slammed the door.

"He has a wife? What's his name?" I asked Dolly.

She handed me a mug filled more generously with cognac than coffee. "His name is Dwayne, but we all call him Hansel."

"Who is his wife?" I lit a cigarette and handed it to her before lighting my own.

"Her name is Vicky. Of course, we call her Gretel. She's my best friend. If she finds out about this, and he'll tell her tonight when they have a fight, she'll probably beat the two of you up. She's a mean drunk."

"How did we end up here?"

"Snake orchestrated the whole thing. He insisted I give you two boys a place to sleep, and once I put the two of you in the back-seat, the little Dutch boy began to puke out the window. Between pukes, he kept saying, 'I want to fuck your brains out' to you, al-though that wasn't what he wanted at all."

"Did you get what you wanted?"

"Oh, child, I find nothing more entertaining than watching you boys combat natural law." She shoved me out of bed. "Now drink your coffee and get out of here before my lover comes home. She does not share my affection for boyflesh in action."

"You're a lesbian?"

"No. I'm definitely not a lesbian. I'd categorize myself as a man-hating-dyke-from-hell." She gave me a quick peck on the cheek. Before she hustled me out the door, she handed me a piece of paper. "This is your boyfriend's number. You're supposed to call him this evening."

"He's not my boyfriend."

"Yes he is. Now run along, I'll see you on Friday."

That evening, I called the number Dolly had given me. A woman answered and I asked to speak to Snake.

"Who?"

"Um, Snake."

"Who is this?"

"My name is Doug Sanders. I'm looking for a guy named Snake. He's got black eyes and short black hair. We met at the Downliner last night."

Her voice became icy. "My son's name is Vincenzo Vendetta. I will bring him to the phone."

I heard him in the background yelling "Who is it, Ma?"

She bellowed in response. "Some boy named Doug who asked to speak to a snake." She dropped the receiver and continued to bellow. "Did you cut your hair with my pinking shears again? You look like a Neapolitan orphan, some low-life *ragazzo*. . . ."

He yelled "At least I'm not some long-haired Deadhead asshole

like your nephew Angelo...." He was interrupted by a loud slap
that resounded powerfully across the wires, her incoherent curses
and his cries of "Cut it out, Ma," as her voice finally drifted away.

"Hey, Drug, what's up?"

"Hey, Vinny."

"Don't fucking call me that. You know my name."

"Hey, Snake."

"You have fun last night with little Hansel?"

"I'm not looking forward to meeting Gretel, but Dolly's all
right."

"Yeah, I knew you and her would hit if off. What are you doing
Friday?"

"Nothing, why?"

"The Cramps are playing."

"Cool. Where?"

"In the basement of a church in Raytown. Wanna go?"

"Yeah, sure. You mean, like a date?"

"What? You mean, like, do I wanna go steady? Do I wanna fucking hold your hand? Fuck no. I don't play those stupid-ass high-
school games."

"Sorry, I misunderstood."

"That doesn't mean I don't wanna ride your dick for a
few hours," he whispered so his mother wouldn't overhear.
"Magdalene and Marlene are going with us."

He said he'd pick me up at ten and asked me if I could sing.

"I suppose so; I've never tried."

"Cool, we'll talk about it on Friday with the girls. I gotta go.
Talking to you gave me a hard-on and now I've gotta go have a
wank. See you Friday."

One of the blessings of the punk aesthetic was that I didn't need
to agonize about fashion. Black jeans, a black or white T-shirt and
a leather jacket allowed me to remain on the cutting edge.

Once I was adorned with the face and demeanor of the
damned, the buzzer sounded only half an hour later than expected on Friday evening.

"Yeah," I answered.

"It's Magdalene. Get your sweet boymeat down here and bring
whatever drugs you have."

I grabbed a bottle of my mother's heart pills and ran downstairs. The girls, once again dressed in menswear with black pork-pie hats added, leaned against the car smoking cigars.

"Hurry up lad, our reptilian chum is meeting us there." Magdalene ushered me into the front seat, as she climbed behind the wheel. "He had to pick up Hansel and Gretel."

Marlene noticed my look of horror at the prospect of meeting the feared Gretel. "Fear not child, you are under our protection," she promised.

"At least for tonight," Magdalene added, and they joined their pinkies in front of my face and shook them. They began to hum the theme from *The Godfather.*

"Sorry we're late," Marlene apologized. "We had to stop at the hospital to visit a friend."

Magdalene giggled. "Buster's having his piles trimmed."

"What goodies did you bring us?" Marlene asked before I could get details on their mission of mercy.

"If you brought Percodan we'll kill and eat you. I hate downers," Magdalene added.

I produced the bottle from the inside pocket of my leather jacket. "My mother's heart pills."

"Look it up," Magdalene commanded.

Marlene turned and pulled a huge beaten-up volume from the backseat. I dropped one of the small pink pills on her palm and she began comparing it to those pictured in the book.

"Crystodigin, point one milligram. It is a crystalline-pure single cardiac glycoside obtained from *Digitalis purpurea.* Digitoxin is a cardiotonic glycoside. It is indicated in the treatment of heart failure, atrial flutter, atrial fibrillation and supraventricular tachycardia. Anorexia, nausea and vomiting have been reported."

"What will it do to us?" Magdalene asked.

"It will either make our hearts beat faster or slower," Marlene warned.

"It always makes mine beat faster," I assured them.

We each swallowed one, with plans to take more if the effects were not immediately evident.

We parked outside a small white church next to a graveyard, teeming with young men and women dressed to repel. A girl with a shaved head and a safety pin through her nose, dressed in a blood-stained prom dress from the fifties, leaned against a tombstone with a boy in a crew cut, yellowed long underwear and an orange tulle square-dance skirt. They tossed their cigarettes aside and leaned over to snort speed off the squared-off top of the memorial sculpture.

I was so grateful for finding my peers in such a pastoral setting, I wanted to kiss them both for daring to exist. Previously, this yearning for communion was so strong that a photograph of a young woman in a trash bag, adorned with safety pins and a sneer, brought tears to my eyes.

Snake, dressed in tight black jeans, a tattered white T-shirt and an enormous biker jacket, shuffled across the lawn toward us.

"How's Buster's butt?" He asked the girls.

"It's seen better days," Magdalene answered.

"I'm glad I never had to see it." Snake turned and faced me. His pupils were enormous. "Suddenly..." he leered at me. "I get the feeling..." He rummaged in the pocket of his black jeans, stroking his dick. "I've been surrounded by..." He pulled a baggie with sugar cubes out of his pocket. "...horses." He placed one of the sugar cubes on his palm, and extended it to the girls. Magdalene leaned down and licked the cube into her mouth. The cube was replaced and Marlene accepted the offering. Snake held his open hand out to me.

"What is it?" I asked him.

"A reward for my favorite little pony." He placed his arm around my waist and nuzzled my neck while holding the small white cube in front of my face. He moved his hand up my back and left it on my neck as I buried my face in his palm, lifting the sugar cube with my tongue and lips, grimacing at the overwhelming sweetness, then savoring the salty taste of sweat on his fingers.

"Do you know how to pony?" He wriggled his thick black eyebrows at me. "Do you know how to twist? Well, it goes like this."

Snake pulled my face to his and slid his thick tongue into my mouth, sharing with me the taste of dissolving sugar, cigarettes and beer. He pulled back and stared into my eyes, a string of saliva still connecting our lips.

A group of stocky suburban boys in Stiff Little Fingers T-shirts laughed and pointed until one of them was brave enough to shout, "Faggots."

Snake smiled at them. "You sure seemed to like the taste of my butthole last week, Jimmy. I thought I'd never get your fat face out of my hairy crack."

They walked toward us grimacing, making threatening noises. The girls moved in front of us and Magdalene displayed her switchblade. "If one of you useless pieces of meat gets any closer I'll cut your tongue out."

Marlene offered her matching knife for their inspection. "And I'll cut off your pudgy little boy-paws."

"Then no more circle jerks for you wankers," Magdalene warned. The girls moved their blades over and under one another, sharpening them, smiling at one another while keeping watch on the small mob. Magdalene moved her hand to rub Marlene's small hard breast as they kissed deeply.

"Fuckin' dyke cunts," Jimmy muttered as he and his friends moved away to sit under a tree.

Snake bowed to the girls. "Shall we go inside and worship?"

"You two get the beer out of the car and we'll find you before the ceremony begins," Magdalene commanded, wrapping her arm around Marlene, leading her to the steps and into the dark basement of the ramshackle church.

Before descending, she turned back to us with a threat. "Don't get carried away and squirt all over my backseat or I'll make you lick it up later."

"While dressed as cheerleaders," Marlene suggested.

Snake decided we needed to kill a couple of beers each before the show. He sat in the backseat, with me between his legs.

"You'd look really cute in a cheerleader's skirt," I suggested.

"Well, Drug, I'll tell you. I'm not particularly interested in looking cute, you know."

"It'd work for me."

"Yeah? What makes your dick hard? What do you think about when you wank?"

I thought for a moment, unwilling to confess an admiration for the thick thighs on my classmate who beat his pregnant girlfriend. "Patti Smith's dick turns me on."

"You fucked a lot of guys?"

"No."

"How many?"

"None." This seemed a loathsome confession, and I felt the blood creep into my face.

"What about little Hansel? He told me his butt hurt for days."
"That doesn't count. I really don't remember it."
"You'll remember it when you fuck me."
"When will that be?"
"Very soon, Drug. Very soon."

The Cramps's degenerate repertoire included songs about canni-
balism, grave robbing, flying saucers, teenage werewolves and a
song about a man who was part fly.

Nick Knox played drums, Bryan Gregory and Poison Ivy Ror-
schach played guitar and Lux Interior screamed, pleaded, ranted
and wept. The Cramps did not rock—they throbbed, and we
oozed. They created the party music of the damned, music to accompany one's nightly ascension from the grave through layers of
mud, gravel, maggots and worms.

The band set up in the corner of the basement lit by a single
bulb, underneath an unfinished ceiling with falling insulation.
Ivy, dressed in unholy tight gold lamé pants, with a cigarette dangling from her bright red lips, struck a chord and a wall of noise,
like an imminent tornado, filled the basement. This was the
music of my parents' fifties youth, turned inside out, exposing its
slimy interior.

Snake, standing behind me, grabbed my hipbones as Nick
began pounding a primal rhythm. The crowd began to thrash and
gyrate. Our stomping feet awakened clouds of dust from the dirt
floor, while the infernal noise loosened disgusting, ancient matter
from the basement's unfinished ceiling, which stuck to everyone's
sweating faces as the temperature in the unventilated room rose.

Snake moved his hot hand under my T-shirt and slid it over my
sweaty stomach and up to my right tit. His free hand pulled my
butt into his crotch and held it in place between his thick thighs
while he moved our hips in the small circle allowed by the tightly
packed crowd.

Lux Interior—part Bela Lugosi, part teenage werewolf—
stalked the front of the crowd like Elmer Gantry with a hot poker
up his butt, ranting.

While her partner provided a dark facsimile of a Pentecostal
service, imitating a snake-handling preacher hijacked by Satan,
Ivy merely strummed complacently, bemused by the enormous
noise she could make with such a simple gesture.

A little before midnight we climbed the stairs to discover frost on the ground. All of us who had spent the last two hours in the black, hot basement of the desanctified church stood around the parking lot looking at the horrifying spectacle of one another. The dirt from the floor and the spider webs and insect carcasses from the ceiling had covered our hot, sweating bodies, which now steamed upon exposure to the early autumn chill. Our faces were dark brown, streaked by rivulets of sweat, and adorned with little puffs of pink insulation.

Snake and I crawled in the back of Magdalene's green Delta 88, sharing one of the last of the two beers. I sat in the corner with Snake jammed against my shoulder alternately tilting the warm Pabst Blue Ribbon to my lips before replacing it with a kiss and a drag from his cigarette. Magdalene and Marlene passed the other beer back and forth in the front, singing along to an eight-track of Nico doing the Doors's "The End," sounding like a pair of particularly somnambulistic Marlene Dietrichs.

"Wasn't that more fun than your average night at the Arabian Nights?" Snake whispered in my ear.

"I've never been there."

"Girls," he yelled over Nico's lugubrious monotone, "Drug has never visited the Sultana's Privy."

"It's still early..." Magdalene observed.

"And we're still tripping..." Marlene offered.

"Let's," Snake commanded.

"I don't mean to complain, but, where the *fuck* did you get this useless acid, Snake?" Magdalene asked.

"From Angelo."

"Goddamn waste-of-flesh hippies." Magdalene tossed the now empty beer can at a passing pickup, and sped away before they could follow us.

"We can't go to a cha-cha palace looking like this, even if we are bull dykes." While we were stopped at a red light downtown, Magdalene leaned over to Marlene and removed a thin layer of brown dirt from her cheek with her tongue.

Marlene squirmed away and wiped the spit residue from her face. "Mom's Altar Guild is meeting at our house tonight, so your house is free."

Glancing briefly behind her, Magdalene spun the steering wheel to the left and the enormous green car squealed through a

U-turn that tossed Snake and me on the floor, the last of the warm beer pouring over my face. Magdalene missed a row of parking meters on the other side of the street with only a few inches to spare. Once we had recovered, Magdalene spoke to Snake, meeting his gaze in the rearview mirror.

"This means we get to dress you boys."

We didn't have time for all of us to shower since the bars would be closing in an hour and a half, so we splashed away the dirt from our arms and faces and changed clothes. The girls merely changed their suits while they left Snake and me alone in Magdalene's bedroom to put on the pile of clothes the girls had yanked from long drawers, laughing maniacally.

Snake made me dress first. I was worried he'd make some smartass remark about my long, skinny white legs or the boner I'd had on and off all night, which was clearly visible once I'd stripped down to my underwear. Instead, he walked over and gripped my dick through my shorts. "Does your mamma make you wear these Drug?" He yanked them down, knelt and ran his hands up my thighs. He looked up at me, the whites of his eyes unnaturally bright, and ran his rough tongue around the head of my dick, collecting the juice that had begun pouring out as soon as he touched me.

"You taste like a boy, Drug." He stood and kissed me, so I could taste it too. He pulled the tight skirt up over my hips, tugged the Sacred Heart T-shirt on over my head, and ripped the shoulder of it so my nipple showed. "I like your dick, Drug." He said this right in my face. I could feel his breath in my eyelashes. I dropped my head to his shoulder while he jacked me off.

"Whoa. I don't want you squirting yet. We'll save that for later. I've got a show to put on for you."

He moved across the room and pulled off his T-shirt so I could see the parts of him I'd only touched. His chest wasn't heavily muscled, just solid. The line of curly black fur that climbed from his jeans spread up his torso to his chest. His skin was light brown, his flat nipples were darker. He unsnapped his jeans and pulled them off quickly; his short, fat, dark brown dick had leaked a trail of juice to his thigh that wobbled while his dick swung between his furry thighs.

"The only good thing about having to get up early every

Saturday to play soccer was it made my legs kinda big." He turned around, moving his hand over his butt. "And my butt's really hard." He spread his feet apart and moved his hands to spread his cheeks; one finger playing with the dark fur lining his crack. "I want your dick in here, Drug."

I moved toward him, my skirt tented, sucked on my finger, and slid it into his hot, furry butthole while I licked his ear. "Can I fuck you now, Snake?"

He spread his feet further apart and moved his ass, pulling my finger deeper into him. "Can you sing, Drug?"

"What?"

"Can you sing?"

"I told you I don't know. Why?"

"I want you in our band."

"What band? Who's in it?"

"It's called Queerbait. I play guitar and sing a little. Magdalene plays bass—oh, yeah, keep moving your finger in and out of my butt—Marlene plays keyboards and Hansel plays drums. So, can you sing?"

"Everybody can sing. Listen, Snake, I've got to come."

He yanked my finger out of his butt and shoved it in my mouth. "You get to come after band rehearsal tomorrow night." He pulled on another Sacred Heart T-shirt, ripped it, and messed up his hair.

"You ready to scare the shit out of some brain-dead queens?"

"What are we going to do?"

"Follow me, Drug, and do exactly what I tell you. The girls will watch our backs."

"Come on, cocksuckers, or we'll miss last call!" Magdalene stuck her head around the door, and whistled. "Very sexy legs, Drug. Shave those things and you'd make a pretty fair Dietrich."

"Is the bag ready?" Snake asked her.

"In the trunk. Come on, I found a fifth of Jameson under the sink."

Magdalene drove more cautiously, watching for cops, taking huge swigs of the Irish whiskey. I had to struggle to keep Snake's hands from under my skirt. I knew, wherever we were going, I didn't want to walk in with a big boner.

"So, where are you taking me?" I asked.

"The Arabian Nights," Magdalene explained.

"The Sultana's Privy," added Marlene.

"The tackiest gay bar on the Plains." Snake gestured toward a nondescript, sooty brick building standing alone in a parking lot. "Most gay bars have to redecorate every two years to stay in business. Not the A-rab. No design queen has come near the place since Armistice Day."

"We'll get the bag and meet you boys inside." Magdalene opened the trunk, removed a battered leather bag, and tossed the empty whiskey bottle under a nearby pickup.

Gay bars in the Midwest usually hire bodybuilders to guard the door, in the mistaken assumption that a queen with really big tits will intimidate those who are inclined to behave poorly and encourage others with mammary fixations to drink more. The great big queen at the door, dressed in tiny little shorts and a pink spaghetti strap T-shirt, seemed to be horrified by two boys in miniskirts. As we moved through the bar, the same look of horror followed us, shining from each perfectly groomed face. Almost every gentleman present was adorned with a perfectly symmetrical mustache.

They weren't horrified by the sight of men in skirts. The many drag queens decorating the place were easily assimilated. They were confused by our unwillingness to approximate femininity. Their discomfort was probably not helped by Snake repeatedly flipping up my skirt, exposing my perpetually hard dick.

When the girls crossed the room, the men recoiled and averted their eyes.

The main room of the bar was shrouded in ancient, filthy, red velvet fabric, strung from the center of the ceiling. No one was sitting on the huge pillows pockmarked with cigarette holes. Miniatures of Michelangelo's *David* were strewn about the floor, destroying the Persian motif.

Snake would have been happy to cruise the room, outraging every single man present. I made him stand with me in a dark corner, drinking Budweiser after Budweiser, trying to get drunk. The acid we had dropped hours earlier, in front of the Downliner, prevented intoxication.

I caught occasional glimpses of the girls, pogoing in the middle of the dance floor to Donna Summer. Magdalene crossed the

room every fifteen minutes, stripped to her now damp and cling-
ing gabardine trousers, white shirt unbuttoned to her waist, exposing her corset and red suspenders.

One outraged muscle queen stormed up to us. "Why don't you
straight boys stay in your own bars? We don't appreciate your kind
coming in here and making fun of us."

Snake smirked at him and lifted my skirt.

"You like my friend Drug's dick?"

The man's eyes flitted nervously from Snake's face to my very
hard dick, which Snake milked slowly. Snake collected the dripping goo in the palm of his hand, which he brought to his face
and cleaned off with a broad swipe of his tongue.

"Don't call me a straight boy, faggot."

The muscle queen retreated to a cluster of bosomy companions, gesticulating wildly.

An older gentleman in a Brooks Brothers suit stopped in front
of us and smiled indulgently. "I don't suppose a few hours alone
with the two of you would be in my price range?" he asked.

Snaked patted his sagging cheek affectionately. "Not tonight,
sugar. But we're going to need to buy band equipment in a couple
of weeks, so why don't you give me your number, and we'll give
you a call."

A card was produced and pocketed by Snake, who again lifted
my skirt, providing the gentleman with a sneak preview.

Magdalene appeared, purchased and downed three shots of
whiskey. "Marlene wants to dance."

"Where's the bag?"

"She's performing a dance of adoration around it. The queens
are transfixed. They've never seen a dyke worship a handbag."

Snake grabbed my skirt and tugged me across the room to the
dance floor. "Come on Drug, time for the floor show."

Some moronic gay bar music was blasting in 4/4 time, and I
was reduced to performing my private mirror dance, twisting my
skirt and whipping my hips in a circle, occasionally flashing my
butt. Snake and Magdalene's flailing elbows quickly cleared a
space for us to dance. I hoped Snake wouldn't grab me, because
the last thing I wanted was to flash a hard-on on the dance floor,
which was exactly what he wanted. He moved behind me and ran
his hands up and down my thighs while we swiveled.

The song ended abruptly and the d.j. played a slow song, the one played after last call has been announced to clear the bar.

A very drunk queen screamed in my face, "Go away! You're ruining everything."

Snake grabbed my hand and all four of us climbed the three stairs to the d.j. booth. "My friend here has a request."

Magdalene opened the bag. She handed a record, the first Cramps E.P., to the d.j., who wouldn't touch it.

"My friend wants you to play 'Human Fly.'"

The d.j. put his hands on his hips. "I'm not playing that punk-rock shit. I think you'd all better leave. You're upsetting people."

"We're upsetting people, huh." Snake winked at Magdalene and she held the bag open again. "I sure wouldn't want to upset a bunch of gym and disco queens." Snake pulled out a handgun. "Just play the song and we won't upset anyone else."

"Oh, my God. What are you, some kind of criminal? Do you want money?" The d.j. scurried into the corner of the booth, waving his hands in front of his face. "Go away! Just go away!"

"That's a nice gun." They all turned to face a statuesque black drag queen in ratty Andrews Sister drag. "But those skirts are beyond the pale of respectability."

Magdalene shook the drag queen's hand. "That snood is to die for. I'm Magdalene, this is Marlene and those two are Snake and Drug."

"I am Franzelle. What's the problem?"

Snake kept the revolver targeted on the d.j. "We want this asshole to play the Cramps's "Human Fly" so I can dance with my boyfriend. He's not being cooperative."

"Give me the gun." Snake handed the revolver to Franzelle, who aimed it once more at the hysterical d.j.

"Okay, asshole, I've been trying to get you to play the Brides of Funkenstein for weeks now and if you don't play these kids' request, I'll shoot your fingers off, one at a time."

"I could lose my job!" the d.j. shrieked.

Franzelle cocked the gun. "Just play the fucking song or you'll never lift a needle again."

The d.j. took the record, holding it at arm's length, and placed it on the empty turntable.

Franzelle gestured toward the dance floor. "You kids go dance. I'll cover her."

The ominous throb of Ivy's guitar filled the room.

Nick Knox's drums began to pound and Snake and I began to thrash. We had the dance floor to ourselves. We throbbed, twisted and jerked, occasionally crashing into each other.

Most of the patrons cowered on the side of the floor, cringing at the music, covering their ears, watching us.

One particularly burly chap grabbed my arm, trying to drag me off the dance floor, but Franzelle waved the gun in his face and he let me go. She moved to the back of the bar as the song ended, holding the emergency exit open. Marlene ran outside to start the car while Franzelle covered us. As we walked toward the exit, Franzelle grabbed Snake.

"You boys aren't gay, are you?"

Snake smiled at her. "No, we're not." He pulled me to him and kissed me very gently. "We're Queer."

Arson

BERNARD COOPER

From the moment I learned about come-as-you-are parties, I wanted to throw one. Birthday parties, picnics, and costume balls paled in comparison. I couldn't shake the image of people—relatives, teachers, friends from junior high—converging on my house in candid states of dress. I pictured them coming from all directions, from apartments and parks and places of business, drawn from every type of routine. One person lifted a cold forkful of dinner to his lips. Another raised a flyswatter, though a fly was nowhere in sight. The vain cashier from Woolworth's wore curlers. The authoritarian crossing guard was wrapped in a baby-blue bath towel. Propriety, modesty, and just plain embarrassment made them move as slowly as sleepwalkers, and still they came, some of them grumbling, some of them pointing with glee at one another, a dowdy battalion in underwear and housecoats who forged through the city streets toward my door.

The image of this party was so vivid and gratifying that, several times a day, I imagined picking up the telephone and dialing prospective guests. "Hello," I'd intone, as though nothing were out of the ordinary. And then I'd blurt the startling news, "I'm having a come-as-you-are party!" I suppose it was a kind of egotism or wishfulness to assume that people, regardless of their outfit or grooming, would drop what they were doing and appear in public, shedding their inhibitions just for me.

In retrospect, I can't help but see this obsession as the odd blossom of my loneliness. My mother was preoccupied with

housework, my father with the practice of law. Most of the neighborhood kids were on vacation or attending summer school. The
light that summer was direct and unrelenting, the afternoons vast.
Left to my own devices, steeped in a restless imagination, my solitude was nearly constant.

The come-as-you-are feeling often welled up in me as I was getting ready for bed, brushing my teeth or staring at my naked body
in the bathroom mirror. What, I wondered, were other people
doing or feeling at that moment? Were they mesmerized by the
weight of their limbs, by the heat of their skin, by the sight of their
wrinkled genitalia? Why did my particular mind exist in my particular body? It was difficult to believe that anyone else beheld themselves with such abject and melancholy astonishment. In the
bright isolation of the bathroom, as the neighborhood around
me settled into the anonymity and silence of the night, I most desperately wanted a glimpse into the privacy of others.

That summer I began making regular visits to the model homes
of Los Feliz Estates, a nearby tract in the Hollywood Hills. None of
the real estate agents seemed to notice or mind a thirteen-year-old
wandering through the rooms. Sometimes there would be a lull in
the number of prospective buyers and I would find myself virtually alone, able to part the drapes or furtively flush a toilet. But no
act thrilled me as much as coaxing open a desk or bureau drawer.
I knew these houses didn't belong to anyone real. I understood
that the rooms were furnished to give the illusion of home. Yet
every time I opened a drawer—heart racing, breath held in
check—I expected to find some contraband, some evidence of a
stranger's life: a rubber, a Tampax, a diary, money stuffed in a
sock. What I found instead was emptiness and the faint, escaping
scent of wood.

In the bottom drawer of the built-in bureau in my bedroom, I
kept hidden a small collection of pornography, magazines with almost apologetically innocent names like *Pony Boys!* and *Buddies.*
The young men between the covers, with their glistening pec-
torals, backs, and thighs, appeared to have been marinated in oil.
One sunned on a rock. Another sprawled on a plaid couch, his
nakedness accentuated by the banality of his surroundings. A few
studio shots featured moody lighting and classical props—a plaster column, a Grecian urn—and in case there remained any question of artistic intent, each model's crotch was sheathed in a

loincloth. Only rarely were two men shown in the same photograph, and even then they never touched; any heated contact between them was something the viewer inferred. For the most part,
each man waited for admiration on his solitary page. Arms tensed,
stomachs sucked in, they invited the camera's scrutiny. Their bra-
zenness excited me as much as their physiques.

Not a day went by without my fretting that the magazines, and
therefore my desire for men, might be discovered. Finding a fool-
proof hiding place became nothing short of a criminal pursuit,
and before I'd finally decided on the bottom drawer of the built-in
bureau, my illicit library had been wedged beneath the mattress
and stashed in an old Monopoly box. No sooner would I find a
new hiding place than I'd picture that place being violated.
Suppose my mother decided to air the mattress one day? Suppose
my brother, home for a visit, got the urge to play Monopoly? The
dread of being discovered seeped into my dreams; I'd be blithely
chatting with a policeman, say, when I'd realize to my horror that,
instead of wearing my usual clothes, I was wearing the pages of
Pony Boys!.

Eventually, even the drawer of the built-in bureau seemed like
a risky hiding place, and I thought it might be safer to keep the
magazines *behind* the drawer. I took hold of the brass knobs and
slid the drawer out with the stealth of a burglar, nervous that my
mother, puttering in the kitchen directly below, might hear me
and become suspicious. It's entirely possible that I took further
precautions, like locking my bedroom door or turning on the
transistor radio, so thoroughly did the fear of exposure control
me like a marionette in those days. My anticipation mounted as
the lowest drawer inched toward me on its tracks. When it finally
popped out of the wall and landed with a muffled thud on the
carpet, it left behind a rectangular hole. I bent down, peered inside. It was as if I'd pulled back the skin of the house and could
glimpse the bones and organs within. Two-by-fours and rolls of tar
paper lined the floor. Here and there, drips of plaster and paint
were preserved in a secret museum. Dry rot had turned patches of
wood velvety and uneven. The surface of a pipe a few feet away
glinted in the sudden flood of sunlight, and from it issued the
sound of water like a sudden rush of breath.

From then on, every time I removed the drawer and reached
for my cache of naked men, I saw the darkness at the core of our

house and suddenly doubted the white walls, the tidy rooms in which I lived.

To be homosexual was to invite ostracism and ridicule, and I would have done just about anything to escape my need to masturbate to images of men. I bargained with myself, made promises not to, devised equations of abstinence and reward. *Today is Monday; if you don't touch yourself till Saturday, you can go to Woolworth's and buy that model of a sixty-five Corvette.* But no sooner would I muster my resolve than I'd find myself in a haze of amnesia, a couple of magazines spread before me, opened to my favorite pages. Sometimes it seemed that the only antidote for constant shame was the forgetfulness of orgasm, my body crumpled in a fit of overflowing, every sensation obliterated except for pleasure.

In an effort to control once and for all my helplessness in the face of lust, I retrieved from the same bureau where I stashed the magazines a pair of plastic handcuffs I hadn't played with in years. Somehow, I got the idea to hook them to my wrists whenever the impulse to masturbate was about to overwhelm me. The reasoning that followed my literal self-restraint went something like this: *OK. You've done everything you possibly can to prevent it. If it happens, it happens, and you can't blame yourself.* And then I went at it while wearing the handcuffs. In this way I policed my own desire, kept guilt and shame at bay with a toy, and stroked myself with impunity. But it wasn't long before this ritual lost its power to ease my conscience, and soon I started to feel absurd, as though I were wearing a set of matching bracelets, and the plastic links seemed pitiful and weak, and I imagined someone barging in my room and finding a boy, bound by the wrists, unable to resist himself.

I bought the pornography at a store that sold candy, key chains, batteries, dusty artificial flowers, and tabloids in foreign languages. I discovered it by accident one afternoon while walking up and down Western Avenue in search of a Mother's Day card. The place was run by a woman whose eyes, magnified by thick glasses, seemed to follow you wherever you went like the gaze in certain portraits. Her eyes were deceptive, though, because she never seemed to care what happened in her store. Perched atop a stool behind the counter, she rarely moved except to sigh, her posture wilted by boredom. There were times I thought it would be a breeze to sneak past her into the alcove that contained the

pornography and simply steal the magazines I wanted. That way I
wouldn't have to endure the humiliation of having to buy them,
terrified she might ask my age, my hands shaking as I counted out
change. Instead, I tried to ignore her, to act nonchalant as I strode
toward the shelf where women licked their lips and played with
their nipples. My habit was to peruse at least one or two of the
girlie magazines before I moved on. I flipped through a blur of
bleached hair, arched backs, and breasts rising from frothy lace
bras. I probably even convinced myself that, blood humming from
sheer fright, I was actually kind of excited by women, but drawn to
men just a little more. Once I'd looked at girlie magazines long
enough to give the impression—to whom, I wonder, since there
was rarely another customer in sight—of genuine interest, I'd drift
toward the rack where I invariably wanted the first magazine I laid
eyes on. Whoever was on the cover—a man washing his car in the
nude, sweat beading on his tattooed chest, soapy water dripping
down the fenders—he was too beautiful a vision to contain. I
couldn't look for long before my mouth went dry and my skin
began to itch.

The mechanics of the sale were clouded by panic. But the last
thing I saw before I left the store were the big omniscient eyes of
the proprietress, like the eyes of God, brilliant with judgment,
peering from a mortal's head.

Back in the silence and privacy of my room, I noticed that one
corner of the brown paper bag that held my purchase was moist
and soft from the sweat from my palm, as though it had turned to
suede. Only then would it occur to me how ferociously I must
have hugged, gripped, shifted the package from hand to hand as I
hurried home, frightened the bag might rip wide open, afraid I'd
run into someone I knew. Sitting cross-legged on the floor, I extracted the magazine from its wrapping and turned the pages,
only a little more calmly than I had in the store. Once I'd gained
an overall sense of the contents—how many men were featured,
were they smooth or hirsute, husky or thin, was there some sort of
story or theme involved?—I began again from the first page. This
time I went more slowly, evaluating, savoring, finally choosing the
most beautiful man as though I were holding a harem. By then I
couldn't stand more excitement and, faint from the whole clan-
destine ordeal, peeled off my pants. Climax came quickly, and the
instant it did, the mass and shadow of the model's physique

seemed to bloom into three dimensions, and my own body, in a fever-dream of want, became more real along with his.

After masturbation there was room for remorse; it flooded in to take the place of satisfaction. Every time I so much as glanced at one of those magazines my appetite for men was confirmed, and it stung me to think that the price I'd have to pay was the world's condemnation. How could such an awful penalty result from such exquisite sensation? I can't, to this day, imagine what childhood would have been like without the need for secrecy, and the constant vigilance secrecy requires. The elaborate strategies, psychic acrobatics. You ache for a way to make sense of your nature. You dive headlong into the well of yourself. And no matter what plans you hatch, promises you make, no matter what you do to erase your desire, you feel incorrigible and aberrant before you even know the meaning of the words. Every day you await disgrace. You look for an ally and do not find one, because to find one would mean you had told. You pretend to be a person you are not, then worry that your pretense is obvious, as vulnerable to taunts as the secret itself. In a desperate attempt at self-protection, you shrink yourself down to nearly nothing, and still you are there, closed as a stone.

One Saturday toward the end of summer, a few days before school started, my parents were invited to a brunch in Orange County. My mother baked a chicken breast and left it in the refrigerator in case I got hungry while they were gone. My father cleaned out the car and checked the yard a couple of times to make sure he'd turned off the sprinklers. They departed with an unusual amount of ceremony, telling me they might not be back till late, asking me if I'd be OK. This show of concern might have been what made their leaving seem especially momentous. And opportune. Seconds after the Oldsmobile pulled out of the driveway, it occurred to me that I could purge my life of tempting possessions. Start from scratch in the eighth grade. Wipe clean the slate of longing.

Most of the bonfires I'd seen were from beach blanket movies, teenagers doing the twist and the watusi while flames raged and crackled on the sand. A bonfire seemed as effective a way as any to do the job; heat would scorch the photographs, turn the pages to flecks of ash. My first thought was to set the fire in the middle of the backyard, away from the plump hibiscus bushes and wooden lawn chairs. But the grass was still wet from the sprinklers and I figured the flames wouldn't take. I could grill each magazine on the barbecue, then pour the ashes into a trash can. But suppose a neighbor poked his head above the fence to see what curious meat was cooking. The whole outdoors seemed too...overt. I needed a more protected place.

The garage made sense mostly because my father's car was no longer in it, and it seemed logical—if a boy's tormented, over-eager inspiration could be called logical—to take advantage of the Oldsmobile's absence. The floor of the garage was cement, after all, and wouldn't burn. I could close the heavy wooden doors, yet still see what I was doing because of the two small windows on opposite walls. Except for my father's workbench and the Kenmore freezer my mother no longer used, the high-ceilinged garage was practically empty.

Match; magazines; empty garage! I waited fifteen or twenty minutes to make sure my parents were good and gone. As I walked from room to room, the house seemed huge and plush with quiet—and I grew more resolute with every step.

When the moment was right, I dashed upstairs with a grocery bag and yanked the drawer out with such force it slammed into my knees. I groped around, grabbed the seven or eight magazines I owned, and crammed them into the bag. Should someone see me in my journey across the narrow breezeway that separated the house from the garage, I could tell them I was taking out the trash. On my way to the back door, I stopped at the kitchen cabinet where my mother kept a veritable gallery of ashtrays—weird shapes like glass taffy—and several boxes of wooden matches. I snatched an entire box, but made a mental note of its exact position on the shelf so that I could replace it without causing suspicion. How proud I was of my foresight, glad that my knack for deception had finally come in handy.

Standing inside the garage, facing outward to pull closed the double doors, I could see the crest of the Hollywood hills rising against the horizon. In the midday sun, the windows of distant houses glowed like yellow embers. As soon as the doors were shut, the cavernous room grew sheltered and cool. I waited for my eyes to adjust, and then my renewal was under way. I piled the magazines in the middle of the room where puddles of oil, left by the Oldsmobile, stained the floor; in the dim light, they looked deep and primeval as pools of tar. I paused a moment to contemplate how best to start the fire, and it was then I noticed the men at my feet, their bodies seductive, tight, exciting. But I'd gone too far to stop what I was doing. When I struck the match on the side of the box, the rasp and stench of sulfur made me shudder.

For the first second, everything went according to plan. Touching a match to the first magazine, I felt a sense of profound relief that I wouldn't know again until years later when I actually touched a man. The *s* at the end of *Pony Boys!* caught fire and flared, igniting in turn another magazine on which a sailor wore only bell-bottom trousers. I thought he too would go up in flames, but instead a trail of smoke curled lazily and disappeared. The fire went out before it had begun, and I had to rethink my approach.

On his cluttered workbench, my father stored the can of lighter fluid he used to start the barbecue charcoal; I found it without the slightest trouble, as though some prodding, superior force had placed it smack in my path. I removed the cap, aimed the metal spout toward the pile of pornography (which seemed to grow larger the longer it took to destroy) and squeezed a thin jet of fuel on top, saturating every page. Vapors assailed me, and with them came associations of afternoons in our backyard, Mother molding the hamburger patties my aproned father would flip with aplomb, his aluminum spatula catching the light. What a disappointment to return to my senses in a dank garage, the doors shut tight against prying eyes, the most incriminating objects I owned heaped in an acrid, sopping pile.

This time I stood back and tossed the lit match, having wits enough to understand that, unless I kept my distance, my eyebrows and hair were in danger. But nothing could have prepared me for the whoosh that followed, a whisper of swift consumption. I recoiled from the blast of heat, walls around me tinted red. Flames shot several feet into the air, some of them as tall as I. From their flickering tips coiled strands of black smoke that streamed toward the ceiling and spread across it, ominous as thunderheads. Even if the fire eliminated my collection of men, what if there remained a thick black telltale smudge on the ceiling of my parent's garage? I floundered by firelight, plucked from the realm of possibility a dozen useless excuses, *a can of insecticide had exploded; I had tried one of Mother's cigarettes,* and while I was at it, the puddles of oil began to burn, and my bonfire reached its peak.

The first scrap of anatomy was a man's arm. It fluttered down like a molted feather, part of a picture singed at the edges. Legs and shoulders and buttocks came next. The magazines were burning to pieces, and the pieces, lifted on sudden updrafts, were raining everywhere. I swiped at the stifling air, trying to catch a couple of muscles. When it finally dawned on me that things were getting worse instead of better, I leapt in and out of the fire in a sorry effort to stomp it out. In the periphery of my vision, I saw my shadow loom up on the walls, all wavering agitation. I slapped at my smoldering shoelace, plucked at the cinders landing in my hair. The more I stomped on the hot spots, the more the bodies multiplied, a flurry of glowing male flesh. And just before I managed to smother the fire, in a single wracking spasm of guilt, I imagined my picture on the evening news and the blackened rubble of our former home.

Even after the flames had been extinguished, there was smoke to contend with. The garage was hazy, unbreathable. Throwing open the double doors, I half expected to see fire trucks arriving, or the neighbors lined up in a bucket brigade. I was stunned to realize that it was still a Saturday afternoon, the sky clear, the hills unsinged. Smoke billowed over my head and drifted into the placid air. I ran to the edge of our driveway and breathed deeply, as though I were preparing to dive into water, then ran back inside. I flung open the two small windows and used the grocery bag to fan away the remaining smoke. Coughing, eyes watering, I came out for air once more, turned on the spigot and wrestled the garden hose around the side of the house and into the garage. Though fairly certain the fire was out, I doused the mound of burnt magazines.

Getting rid of the smoke was a cinch compared to the bits of men's bodies. My dread of the magazines being discovered in my bedroom was nothing compared to the dread that I'd never locate all the fragments of anatomy lurking who-knows-where in the garage. A handsome head had landed near a jar of nails on my father's workbench. A naked gladiator, nearly complete, wedged himself in a terra-cotta pot. I imagined my parents pulling up in the Oldsmobile, quizzically sniffing the stale air, and finding pieces of male physique inexplicably stuck to their shoes. My hands were black by the time I finished scrutinizing every square inch of the garage, groping behind the freezer, hoisting myself up on a stepladder to check the high shelves of the workbench. I scooped every stray appendage into the grocery bag, which I stuffed at the bottom of the garbage can. Examining the ceiling with a flashlight, I convinced myself that my father wouldn't notice the vague gray shadow that, if pressed, I could blame on car exhaust. I considered spraying the garage with the can of air freshener my mother kept in the guest bathroom, but wouldn't lilac smell as suspicious as smoke? I swept the wet ashes into a dustpan. Then I had to scour the dustpan. Then I had to wash the bristles of the broom. Then I had to bleach the kitchen sink.

My clothes were permeated with smoke and smudged with soot, and I decided to stuff them behind the drawer where I'd hidden the pornography until I could figure out how to clean them without risking my mother's questions. My tennis shoes required an entirely different, but equally anxious, set of ablutions, and after I cleaned them I wadded the paper towels in such a way that the black smears were concealed. Even the washrag with which I cleaned my face had to be examined for traces of soot. It was as if I were leaking a dark persistent misery, as if I tainted everything I touched. For the rest of the afternoon and into the evening, every time I closed my eyes I saw a phantom of the conflagration, as if I'd been branded by its afterimage. Trying to divert myself with records and books, I would periodically stop what I was doing and, as though jarred awake by a bad dream, sniff the clothes into which I'd changed, or search my skin for particles of ash, seized by the apprehension that I hadn't covered my tracks.

My parents were oblivious to the crisis when they returned home after dark. They must have had a couple of drinks at dinner; my mother's cheeks were flushed, and my father blinked slowly as he told me what they ate. I listened intently, asked several questions. Who else was there? Did they play any games? I wanted to distract them from my act of arson, but I was also soothed by the details of their party, a tale of mingling, ease, and indulgence.

That night, while getting ready for bed, it became clear to me that attempts to reform myself would prove every bit as disastrous as

staying the same. The ruined clothes behind the drawer; the grocery
bag at the bottom of a trash can—now I had even more to hide.

The guest list for my party consisted of Jack Perlstein and Richard
Levine, two boys I knew from synagogue and junior high. Though
unrelated, Jack and Richard might have been mistaken for brothers; they both possessed alert brown eyes and wavy hair. They also
lived in the same stucco apartment house. Athletic and friendly,
Jack and Richard were slow to exploit their physical power. We
sometimes ate lunch together in the school cafeteria or walked
home in a raucous trio. Jack and Richard shared a repertoire of
phrases. "Yes, Mother dear," one of them would drone whenever
the other offered advice. "Pip pip," in an arch English accent,
greeted any pretentious remark. They both called me Cooper instead of Bernard, this formality having the paradoxical effect of
tenderness.

Because we'd once studied Hebrew together in preparation for
our bar mitzvas, Jack and Richard considered me, in the broader
context of the junior high, an equal member of our ethnic subset,
though I was nothing like them in temperament or strength. They
teased me good naturedly about my tendency to daydream and
equivocate—"Earth to Cooper, come in Cooper"—and for the
first time my reticence seemed like an eccentricity rather than a
flaw. A boy, for once, among boys, I relied on their attentions—
back slaps, mock blows, gross jokes—for a taste of normalcy, attentions made especially tenuous and sweet because I suspected that
Jack and Richard, like everyone else, would turn their backs if my
secret were revealed.

I'd hardly seen either of them that summer. They'd been working together as counselors at a camp for Jewish youth outside Los
Angeles. Figuring they'd be home by now, I dialed Richard first.
"Uh-huh," he answered the phone, as though it were the middle,
and not the beginning, of a conversation. We caught up on news
of the summer with the halting, blasé phone persona of adoles-
cent boys. And then, unable to restrain myself, I sprang my surprise. "A what?" asked Richard. After I explained the premise of
the party, he told me that he was wearing shorts and a T-shirt. In
my zeal to get the party underway, it somehow slipped my mind
that, if I wanted to have the guests arrive in compromising
clothes, it would be pointless to call them at two in the afternoon.

I had to improvise, to bend the rules, and in what Richard himself might have called "a save," I asked him to come to my house the next day, but to wear what he wore to bed that night. "Whatever," he said. Then I phoned Jack and asked the same.

The sheer intensity of my anticipation embarrassed me long before the guests showed up. The day of the party, dressed in a pair of powder blue pajamas, I set up my hi-fi in the living room and recruited my mother to make a platter of sandwiches, aware that the outfit made my fuss seem all the more fruity. Circling the living room, I searched for something to touch or rearrange that would make the prospect of fun more likely. Wax apples were adjusted, pillows plumped. I chalked my excitement up to the fact that this was the first party I'd given on my own, and not to the fact that two boys I idolized were due to arrive at my house any minute, looking like they just rolled out of bed. Over and over, I imagined the hilarity that would ensue once the doorbell rang, Jack in his underwear, Richard in his bathrobe. Even if I couldn't have put it into words, the metaphysics of the party weren't lost on me: wrenched out of context, together in our bedclothes, we would be more alike than ever before.

The sound of the bell made my heart pound, and I had to take a moment to compose myself before opening the door. Standing side by side, the Hollywood Hills rising behind them, Jack and Richard wore the same chinos, short-sleeved shirts, and scruffy Keds they wore to school. The effect was as jarring as a bride in a bikini. "Did we wake you?" asked Jack, the two of them doubling over with laughter. I forced myself not to show any signs of anger or disappointment. "Very funny," I said, ushering them inside. They made a beeline for the sandwiches. Hot with shame, I raced upstairs to change. "Cooper," Richard shouted after me. "We came as we are."

"Yeah," I yelled back, "a couple of jerks."

"Honey," I heard my mother call from the kitchen, "I think your friends are here."

Jack and Richard's snickering was muffled by mouthfuls of tuna.

The few seconds I'd spent in their presence were almost as bad as the dream in which I wore the pages of *Pony Boys!*, proof I was skewed, forever out of synch. I threw on my school clothes, but the change seemed futile, like dressing a chimpanzee in a

suit to make him look human. Returning to the living room, I be-
rated myself for going through with such a stupid idea in the first
place, and wished I'd never opened the door. Could I make them
think it was all a bad joke? What I'd wanted all along, it occurred
to me too late, was a girl's party, with lots of gossip, dancing practice, and lolling about in pretty pajamas. Worried that the slightest sound or movement might give away my girlish urges, I sat on
the sofa and turned to stone. Ten minutes into the festivities and
it was already obvious that laughter and astonishment weren't
likely to materialize. The sandwiches were almost gone. The
prospect of fun had deflated like a balloon. The wheels of the
party spun in a rut.

Jack and Richard asked what we were going to do besides listen
to records. Every so often one of us would throw out an idea that
the others would instantly veto. No, I protested a little too loudly,
when one of them said, "Monopoly?" Our indecision lumbered
on and on, and I thought I could see, through the picture window, the deepening light of afternoon. It was one of those still
and smoggy summer days. We finally decided to venture outside,
snatched a pack of my mother's cigarettes, and left the house.

Refugees from a defunct party, we roamed the neighborhood.
The heat made us too listless to accomplish anything more than
petty mischief. Jack threw a rock and chipped the flank of a plaster deer. Richard flipped up the red flags on a few mailboxes. I
showed them how you can squeeze the buds of drooping fuchsias
to make them pop like cap guns. After a while we sat down on the
grassy bank of someone's front yard, beneath the shade of a
carob tree. The three of us lit cigarettes and pretended to smoke
like veterans. Richard blew loose, short-lived smoke rings. Jack
picked flecks of tobacco off his tongue and flicked them into the
air. I took a long, labored drag, then held up my cigarette. "Filter
tips," I said in a disgruntled baritone, "you could get a hernia
from the draw." This was something I'd heard on TV, but Jack
and Richard laughed in approval, and I felt the remark had re-
stored me to their graces. Soon our cigarettes collapsed into ash.
Dizzy from smoke, unable to speak, the three of us lay back on
the lawn and stared at sunlight swimming through the leaves.
Pressed against the turning earth, I felt dry grass crackle behind
my ears. My friends breathed deeply on either side, two strap-
ping, affable boys.

Life in the eighth grade was not very different from life in the seventh. Jack and Richard and I stuck together at school, yet no matter how well we got along, agreed on pop tunes, or copied homework, my secret remained a threat to our allegiance. My parents began to seem like people whose love I'd lose if they really knew me, and I viewed their habits—Mother washing dishes in the kitchen, Father rushing off to work—with a premature nostalgia. In the absence of pornography, I could ferret out the male flesh in *Reader's Digest, Look,* and *Life:* ads for after-shave, Vapo-Rub, vacations in Bermuda.

I no longer thought about throwing a come-as-you-are party, but my wish to see into private lives, to witness what the world kept hidden, would not disappear. I pored over a book at school that showed layers of anatomy—tissue and organs and skeleton— lifted away as the pages were turned. Pat Collins, the "Hip Hypnotist," was my favorite act on TV; she persuaded her subjects to shed their inhibitions, and they bawled like babies, barked like dogs. Charles Atlas, maker of he-men from weaklings, flexed his muscles in comic books, and there were times I stared with such fixity I could see the tiny dots of the printing, as if I were glimpsing the man's very atoms.

The more fiercely I guarded my inner life, the more I loved transparency and revelation. I wanted the power to read people's minds. Radar hearing. X-ray eyes.

Tar Pit Heart

TIM MILLER

It hit me in the heart. Right here. Only later it hit me in the head. Well, a lot of things have done that. The election of Ronald Reagan. AIDS. The first time I got fucked. My only date with a boy in high school.

There is a **bed** here. Right here in front of me. It has a big old pine headboard painted Pin-N-Save Antique Green. The Vitalis hair tonic on my father's head has rubbed a hole right through the paint to the maple wood underneath.

My mom's Noxema is still on the bedstand. I always tried to use that Noxema to beat off with, but it never seemed to get up a good slide. This is the bed. The bed I was conceived on. The bed where I would be born once again. Uh oh. We're digging into the past now. I brought my shovel. You can use it to clear the shit away or to knock a hole in your own argument. Be sure to put on your hard hat so that no jagged piece of yesterday bruises your brain. I remember. I remember.

When I start to remember things, I think it's kind of like the Old Mine ride at Knott's Berry Farm. Everyone agrees to pile into the rickety prospecting train and go deep into the red red red and highly unpredictable earth. There is excitement and fear because you know at some point there will probably be a choreographed disaster of some sort. The roof will cave in. The water will overflow. A dynamite explosion will bury everyone. But we get on the ride anyway. I'm here to tell the tale. I remember. I remember.

I **offer** this story as a tribute to the first time this meat and bones got close to other flesh and blood. It is the story of the only date I went on with a boy in high school.

I met him. **Richard**. The guy I would go on the date with. I was seventeen years old. He was seventeen. My senior year of high school. Seventeen. Oh, my god. This is almost seventeen years ago. I will be thirty-four this year. I am old enough to be my own father in this story. It's a stretch, I know, but it's possible. I think maybe I *am* my own father in this story. Trying to give birth to myself?

Would you buy that? No, it's been done.

I'm not my father. I'm just me looking back. Trying to conjure my queer self at seventeen when my entire body was a hard-on. Oh, I had a hard-on for Dostoevski. A hard-on for Patti Smith. A hard-on for many of the boys in my gym class.

Richard went to a different **high school** in Anaheim near Disneyland. He grew to his seventeen years in the shadow of the Matterhorn bobsled ride. He was slight and fair, cute, and wore glasses, always a plus. He was the lead singer in a proto-punk rock band in Tustin. They mostly did songs taken from texts of the Marquis de Sade. My friend Kathy introduced us. She had been charmed by him at one of those Bohemian hangs in Fullerton, the Left Bank of (hyper-conservative) Orange County.

She loved him first. But once she figured he was a fag, she decided to pass him on to her friend Tim.

I asked him out. "Hey, you wanna go to the beach with me and then we'll go into L.A. to the Shakespeare on Film retrospective at the County Museum of Art?"

He said he did.

I picked him up in Anaheim in my **sixty-five VW** blue Bug. This car was the most important thing in my life. My initiation. My symbol of growing up. Source of my freedom. I drove the streets of Hollywood listening to Roxy Music and feeling the future inside my body.

Richard and I went to **Diver's Cove** at Laguna Beach. I had been to this beach many times before with my Congregational church youth group. But now everything was different. On my date, the sand was epic, like in *Lawrence of Arabia*. My body was new and grown up. Each word of conversation was golden and hung crystalline and perfect in the cool fall air before it was blown by a gentle breeze toward the mini-malls of Costa Mesa.

We found a secluded nook and talked. I noticed that he was building a **barrier** of sand between us with his doodling fingers as he told me he always felt that he built walls between himself and other people. I listened. Feeling like I was having the first adult conversation in my life. I said, "Richard, this is so intense. It's such a coincidence. I know exactly what you mean. I feel like I do that too. But, Richard, we have to find the way to break through those walls."

Our hands moved through the sand and our fingertips touched. Our eyes locked and there was this "Star Trek" laser beam of awareness and feeling in the moment. We leaned in and kissed. The Big Bang. **YES!!!** The **triumph** over all the times I was chosen last for football. YES!!! The **tears** down my face when my cousin would knock me down, hitting me in the face, calling me "Half-man! Half-man! Half-man!". The **times** my sister dressed me as a girl—I looked like Jackie Kennedy in my pillbox hat and bouffant wig—and introduced me to our neighbors as her distant cousin Melinda from Kansas. That confusing ping-pong of **feelings** when I watched David Cassidy on "The Partridge Family." I think I love you. But what am I so afraid of?

Our lips parted and I tasted his mouth. The roof of his mouth tasted like cigarettes. His tongue tasted like a child's. His gums tasted like my own. We kissed for a long time.

He pulled his high school ring off his finger and slipped it on mine. The Valencia High Panthers. And we began the feast.

I wear this ring around my neck. I treasure it because I really think this will be the only high school ring that I'm gonna get in this lifetime. The wave crashed on a California beach and the page has turned.

We **drove** blissfully back through traffic on the Santa Ana freeway past the theme parks. Our hands intertwined. Talking about things. I was in love and he was in a punk rock band and the world was new in 1976 because soon Jimmy Carter was going to be president. We drove by Knott's Berry Farm and a cloud hung over my VW. Richard told me about this affair he had been having with Ricky Nelson, who had been reduced from his "Ozzie and Har-

riet" glory to performing gigs at the Knott's Berry Farm amphi-
theater. They had had a very bad sex scene backstage. This scene
seemed to include a large amount of LSD and several enormous
summer squash. Did I believe him? Was he making this up? I'm
not sure. What was he telling me? That he's scared of sex? Scared
of me? I could relate. I was afraid of everything. WE WERE
YOUNG QUEERS IN LOVE AND SCARED SHITLESS!!! Some
things don't change.

We picked up my friend **Kathy** at her house in Whittier. She was
going to go to the movies with us. Now this might seem strange to
you, that we would go on a romantic date with my friend Kathy.
But let's face it. Kathy wasn't a dyke, but she was definitely the
queerest of the queer, and we queer kids have to look out for each
other.

We were going to see the **Zefferelli** film of *Romeo and Juliet* at
the County Museum. SHAKESPEARE ON FILM! I had seen it as a
little kid when it first came out with my sister and her best girlfriend, who had the unfortunate name of Kay Hickey. I remembered being nervous what with all the kissing and naked bodies
and heavy breathing. It was all a little bit much for me, so I covered my face. But then there was that long shot of the beautiful
Romeo played by Leonard Whiting naked and facedown. The
camera slowly pulled away revealing that butt in all its fabulous-
ness hovering there lunar-like in the soft Verona light. My fingers
opened over my eyes. My hands reached toward the screen, casting a panavision shadow of searching fingers onto that perfect ass.

And right then...at that moment I enlisted.

I signed up. And today I am career officer.

Because I knew someday I would get to see that butt again except this time I would be watching that perfect ass with my new
boyfriend from Anaheim.

We got to the County Museum of Art and found a free parking
place on Sixth Street. (It's a magical story, alright?) We had a romantic walk (just the three of us) past the La Brea Tar Pits. Now,
for those of you that don't know, the La Brea Tar Pits are primor-
dial pits of petroleum sludge. They have been there since the
dawn of time, or at least since our field trip in first grade. For tens
of thousands of years, prehistoric animals, people, tennis balls

and coffee cans have fallen into these pits and been sucked to the center of the earth.

The feeling of eternity that was there in my heart and in my head was so strong. All of those beasts and that one woman that got pulled into that tar, thousands of years ago. They were like me. Feeding and fucking. And then they got sucked to a tarry death. This put us in the proper mood for the movie.

We walked down Wilshire and into the movie theater. We sat in the **front row**. The lights dimmed slowly. Slowly. The movie began.

I sank down in my seat. I slowly reached over and grabbed Richard's hand. I had never watched a movie while holding someone's hand before. It was so nice! I saw why people like it so much. That feeling of connection. A lifeline back into the world as the movie rolls and rolls.

And what a movie to watch on your first date with a boyfriend. **It had everything. Big feelings.** Poetry. Swordplay. Passion. Doomed love. Kisses. Michael York. Now, what is it when a coupla fag teenage boys hold hands and watch *Romeo and Juliet* at the County Museum of Art? What is actually going on? There is a survival technique about how we manage to see how we are. I figured out how to put myself in the film. I took in the images. Became them. Used them. Sure, I enjoyed all the cute Italian boys stuffed into their tights and bulging codpieces. But I also watched this movie and projected myself into those scenes. Sometimes I was Romeo/Tim hanging with his friends. And then I was Juliet/Tim throwing herself on Romeo/Richard's chest. And sometimes I was Mercutio/ Tim, so obviously in love with Romeo/Richard and ready to die for him. I dreamed I was Romeo/Tim running away with Mercutio/ Richard. I wanted to save him from his pain, so haunted by Queen Mab. We would run off to someplace safe and fine...like the Renaissance Faire in the San Fernando Valley. We would make a life together there at the Pleasure Faire in Agoura. We'd get a little duplex over a tallowmaker's shop. There'd be a big fluffy bed with feather comforters. We would take our clothes off and slip our bodies between the cool sheets, just like I would when I was a little boy. I would come home from church and take off all my clothes— the suit, the tie and the tight shoes—and put my naked little boy's body between the polyester sheets. Loving the feelings. Making them mine. Reclaiming my body from church and state.

I remember. I remember.

But then the shit happened. The sword is pulled and there is a plague on both our houses and everyone is torn from each other.

The movie ends and all are punished.

The lights came up. It was very quiet. We left the movie theater and **walked** quietly out past the tar pits. I went off by myself through the trees down to the chain-link fence surrounding the pits. I looked at the moonlight sheen of water hovering over this eternal, life-filled goo. Gazed at the giant plastic sculpture of the woolly mammoth stuck there across the pit. Then I saw something. The woolly mammoth started to move. Opened its eyes. Lifted one massive leg. A rapier pierced through the tar. There were these shapes by the mammoth. Tybalt and Mercutio and Romeo and Juliet rose out of the heavy sticky stuff, hovered a bit and whispered to me....

"Live these days.

Love well.

Value every kiss.

And savor your body's blink between being born and dying."

They waved at me and **sank** slowly back into the unforgiving tar pit. Only the woolly mammoth was left. I thought for a second that I saw him wink at me as he curled his trunk and tusks back in a permanent plastic death trumpet. I shook my head and the vision was gone.

My friends called to me. I ran to join them. I was so happy. I danced in front of them down the path past the bone museum. I leapfrogged over the bronze saber-toothed tiger. I crowed to the wind. I jumped on top of the mastodon...and shouted to the night.

And yet I wish but for the thing I have:

My bounty is as boundless as the sea (I know these lines because I had the film soundtrack LP),

My love as deep; the more I give to thee,

The more I have, for both are infinite.

We fell on each other and **ran** galumphing toward my VW.

I opened the passenger door and Richard got in the back and Kathy in the front. We laughed and screamed and joked about stuff. We were just so glad to be together in a car in Los Angeles in 1976 and not in Verona in 1303. I drove a little bit too fast down Sixth Street toward La Brea. I kept trying to catch Richard's eye there in the backseat. I wanted to keep the connection going. Stay the link. He said something I couldn't hear, and I looked way over my shoulder to hear him and our eyes met and we smiled and...

THEN IT HAPPENED.

It was a wild, panic-filled slo-mo. The crunch of metal. The breaking of glass. Rubber spinned. We were thrown forward. I was hit in the heart... the steering wheel knocked the wind out of me, and then my head became stars as I hit the windshield here... just in time to see Kathy break the glass with her forehead as Richard was thrown between the front seats and cut his face on the rearview mirror. The horn was stuck blowing. The woolly mammoth in the tar pit heard it and struggled to escape and come save me but he just sank deeper toward death. Gas leaked from the tank. And I thought to myself, **"Why, God?** Why on my only date with a boy in high school did I have to rear-end a hopped-up maroon El Camino at forty-five miles an hour thus totalling my beloved Bug?" Questions careened. Can I get the car home somehow? Was anybody killed? How will I explain this? Do I look like I have been kissing a boy all night long???

We got out of the car. We were OK. People began to gather.

My car was dead. The woolly mammoth could not help. Who will save me now? **I'll call my father.**

I walked, about two inches tall, to a phone booth on Fairfax and told my dad what had happened. He arrived shortly after, followed by a tow truck. I don't think he did a big **shame** thing on me... but I definitely could be repressing that. We began the drive home. We piled in my dad's Datsun. My mind raced. I plotted to myself. How could I salvage this evening? I looked at Richard. All I wanted to do was lie down with him and kiss him. The unfairness of these circumstances was fucked. I started to improvise plans and strategies. Finally, I had it. I said, "You know, Dad, it's very late, isn't it? It really doesn't make sense to drive Richard all the way back to Anaheim. Maybe he should stay at our house tonight and then we can drive him home in the morning."

Creative, huh?

My Dad raised his eyebrow. Seventeen-year-old boys do not do sleep-overs. But he was beat and it was almost two A.M. and what can you do? He grunted an OK.

We got to Whittier and dropped off Kathy. We drove to my house, silent as somnambulists as we arrived. We climbed out of the car. As my Dad tried to open the door, my Mom kept locking it on the other side, and I said to my father, "Gee, Dad, we're both pretty upset from what has happened. I think we wanna sleep in the same room tonight."

My Dad raised his other eyebrow and gave me a funny look, but then just sighed and said, "Whatever." Which was as close as we were going to get to a blessing that night.

Now, I know I said "same room," but I really should have said **"same bed,"** because there was only one bed in my room. **One bed.** This was **THE bed.** The bed I had been conceived on. My parents had gotten a new giant double king and I, ever the drama queen, liked the idea of sleeping on "The Bed I Was Conceived On."

Richard and I shut the door to my room and I locked it. He sat on the bed and looked nervous. Then it happened. The miracle of life. He stood and walked toward me and we kissed.

This is the best thing we get in life on the planet Earth. The finest thing. I felt it in my **heart,** where the steering wheel had taken my breath. I felt it in my head, where my face had smashed the glass. And now I felt my love and desire for this boy rise up from those two places on my queer body.

We took off our clothes but kept our underwear on and got into the cold bed. I felt as my skin hit those sheets and I naturally moved to hold my friend's body that at that moment maybe I became a **man.** This might have been the moment. Maybe I am a man now with a man's ways. I will comfort my boyfriend as we lie down at the end of a hard day. I will **soothe** Mercutio, who in this story does not die from his wide and deep wound. I will **honor** the little boy I was who had the good sense to wiggle his body naked between the sheets after church. I will **take** this boy and that man to my heart.

We **touched.** He looked at me and said, "You know I'm still pretty fucked up from that bad sex scene with Ricky Nelson at Knott's Berry Farm. Is it OK if we just hold each other and kiss?"

Well, I didn't care. This was enough of a miracle for one night.

The woolly mammoth had taught me that.

I was happy to smooth that rough touch with a gentle kiss. That out of the crash. The explosion of metal on metal. The face breaking the glass. Now, to be there in that bed at the end of a hard day with a scared and (except for his J. C. Penney underwear) naked punk rock boy filled me with such feeling.

He looked me in the eye.

We kissed. And kissed. **And kissed again.**

His senior ring on my finger.

His body next to mine.

His hand on my heart.

I slept with him on **THE BED**.

And I was conceived once again.

Heroes

GIL CUADROS

I let the shower run hot over my back till it hurts just a little, the skin tensing, muscles irritable then surrendering. Steam rises in the tub around my large feet and toes, swaddles my calves and thighs. In clouds, the vapor lifts toward the cell-like window, out through the screen to a cooler freedom. I imagine that the moon hovers like a voyeur, observing my movements, watching intensely my more intimate procedures. My hand cups warm water under my scrotum, splashes against my anus. The face of the moon appears unchanging tonight, its crater eyes peer through the pittosporum tree's branches, that are laden with small white flowers. The flowers exude a thick, oily aroma that buries Fountain Avenue. I lift my arm as if to push aside those branches, a violent summer wind myself, shamelessly exposing the voyeur. I rub clear blackberry soap in the pits of my arms, washing away the odor that has built up during the hundred-and-six-degree day. The wiriness of my pubic hair traps globes of lather as I clean the shaft of my dick. The folds of skin around my balls smell of my body's unctuous sweat, a medicinal odor, metallic from the various medications meant to protect my one remaining T-cell. My chest, back, and neck shiver uncontrollably in the shower. At first I assume it is somehow my body at fault, that I have caught some new illness, carelessly exposed myself to an airborne virus that will eventually kill me. It is moments before I notice the shower's water temperature has suddenly plummeted. I continue to clean after I've adjusted the faucet. Pumice is embedded in the bar of soap; the head of my cock, the crack of my ass tingle with the abrasion. I stick a tentative finger in my asshole, afraid my finger might come out with shit or my asshole explode diarrhea. I press a little past the sphincter; I will the muscle to relax, then tighten again. My body obeys. I rub the bar of soap quickly between my palms. With one hand I start to pull on my dick; with my other hand I spread open my cheeks, again pushing my middle finger inside my ass, loosening the muscle then placing another finger beside.

All my sex fantasies begin with my being owned by an older white man, large-chested, gray-haired, an intelligent writer of essays and opinions, someone not afraid to put bruises on my body or to kiss me on the lips, his arms pulling me in a suffocating embrace. I read *Mr. Benson* at the age of twenty-one, reciting it to my sex partners before bedtime; some were too embarrassed by its explicitness, asking me to take the book home when I left their apartments. I imagine my *Mr.* ———— grabbing my balls and hard dick, pulling them roughly out from behind me toward my own asshole, my cock straining from its stiffness, him slamming my face up against the shower walls, his hand pressing down where neck and spine meet. He calls me by my first name, the shortened version because he thinks it's more masculine. His voice conveys anger, excitement, pleasure, or tenderness just by the way he says *Gil.* When he comes he howls like a blood-thirsty animal under the full moon, waking timid neighbors, too afraid to pound the common connecting walls of our apartments. They think of limbs and torso bruised, a spouse with blackened eyes, a lover stabbed repeatedly, a dark man jailed for his rage, released into a quiet, ignorant neighborhood. They hear the crack of his hand against my ass, my scream he muffles with his fist as he shoves his still stiff and cum-dripping cock into my hole. He says he loves his white dick up my dark-brown ass. My hand stops jerking for a moment, my body spasms as I turn in the shower and the tin-tasting water runs into my mouth; the moon moves away from the window.

I wipe my body with sun-dried towels fetched from the clothesline out back; the black towels are stiff and scratchy. The ends I grab like a shoe polishing rag and rub across my back, down my legs, finger in between toes. The towels are now slightly damp; they smell of detergent and my flesh. I swab the bathroom mirror, one moment showing a blur of brown skin, black hair, then through clear bands on the glass I can see my eyes, large white saucers surrounding dark maple orbs. Above my pierced nipple is a scar shaped like an animal's paw, pink and raised. I touch it more gently than any other part of my body; I'm still afraid that the skin where the Hickman catheter had been might break open like a sacred heart. It was a simple procedure to remove the attachment—local anesthesia, a clipping of the surgical thread that tied the white tube to a secure part of skin. Afterward, the doctor withdrew the long white tube that led into my heart. He asked if I could feel the Hickman being extracted. I said, "Not really." What I did feel was a small sensation where the doctor placed his cold, latex-covered hands near the opening, a numb feeling of the insides of my chest being rubbed by the small bulbous ending.

For months I had the Hickman. The infusions I had to take while fighting the cryptococcal meningitis wrecked my veins; regular IVs were hard to put in. I'd fought against the Hickman, uncomfortable about this added jewelry. Hickmans used to mean certain death. Soon. My first lover died just after he had one installed. The doctors convinced me to sign papers to allow the procedure, telling me how much easier it would be for John's veins, and all the while I kept on thinking how ugly his broad chest would look from now on, freakish. The truth is, staring at my own scarred chest, I am the first person I know who survived one and had it removed. I imagine an invisible tube sewn onto my chest, the other end attached to John; and I am too afraid to pull away and tear our skin, and all I can think is he is dead.

I dry under my arms, notice as I raise them that there is a bulkiness I'm not used to, my shoulders and lats larger than yesterday. My body changes shape rapidly. Before the meningitis, I weighed close to two hundred pounds, all fat for my five-foot-six-inch body. While I stayed in the hospital, the medications caused me to shit endlessly, till it was no longer controllable, my bowel movements pure liquid. My weight dropped steadily, and for the first time in my life I was underweight, one hundred and thirty eight. I began to fit into clothes I had always wanted to, having to try things on excitedly at the stores at least three times to find the right smaller size. My stomach showed the muscles that make the abdomen, the curving lines that lead to my crotch. Every time I passed a mirror it was like a new person there, and I liked him

much more, how small and unassuming he'd become, even a bit
sexier than I remember him ever being.

My skin had changed color too, slightly orange from a MAC
prophylactic medication I took. My fevers subsided, the mycobac-
terium having been reduced. People constantly stopped me on
the streets or in the stores, asking where I was from, staring at my
glowing skin. The black tattoo designs slipping out from under
my short-sleeved shirts suggested the Middle East, Turkey, India.
They would be amused with my answer—California. They would
speak slowly to me as if English weren't my first language, "No, really, where are your parents from? Grandparents?"

I flex my arm in the mirror and impress myself, the steroids
I've been taking are working; their only drawback, the possibility
of encouraging a cancerous growth. The diarrhea is slightly con-
trolled by a twice daily injection of another drug. I turn to look at
my backside; my flattened, saggy AZT butt is now growing round
and firm again. I believe all the risks are worth it.

Craig sits splay-legged on the floor, his large tablet of watercolor
paper in front of him. He uses a pencil to fill in some small details
in the background of a portrait he's done of me; lush green leaves
grow out directly from the surface. The TV's glow makes the white
paper change hues; on the screen, flesh is blurred pink and
spotty, a dick pumping into a shaved white ass, a prison scene in a
lower metal bunk bed. The stereo is also on, what I left as I went
into the shower. A Bowie CD shuffles, then the opening sounds of
electronic violins, whining and cold. I notice on Craig's thigh a
small mark, darker than a bruise, lighter than a birthmark. It was
what had started the small fight between us—me not understanding why his doctor wouldn't biopsy the spot right away, Craig
telling me how uncaring County Hospital is, how it does not com-
pare with my private insurance. His real concern is the pain he
feels, a numbness shooting up his calves, concentrating in his
knees. He says his doctors don't believe he's in that much pain,
that because he's on Medi-Cal/Medi-Care (or, as we call it, Medi-
apathy) they won't prescribe anything stronger than Tylenol with
codeine. For something stronger, he would have to pay for the
prescription himself. He asks me, "With what money?" Craig rubs
his legs like an old man, says "fuck" under his breath. His fingers
run over what I fear is the beginning of lesions covering his body.

I try not to let the two-centimeter mark, the color of red and blue melted candle wax, upset me too much again. I wonder, are there cancerous growths hidden in the walls of his lungs, on the surface of his brain? Will he be one of the ones who go quickly? There is nothing I can do for him. I am not his doctor. If I could, I would buy him health insurance, would change the whole world so that it would be I who died first.

It comforts me to think he will survive after I've gone, he is the part of me who will continue. I don't want to believe anything else, except I worry who will love him after I am gone, will he become as bitter and lonely as I became after John died? Will he take care of himself, or let everything fall apart? John's death is still close enough that I can feel the thought change the muscles in my face, my cheeks tighten, the corners of my mouth frown. Craig looks up, tilts his head at my expression, trying to decipher what I am thinking. I want to release him, to end this relationship before either one of us gets sicker. Bowie sings "Heroes" in the impassioned and crestfallen tone that I feel.

I slide underneath the striped black-and-white sheets of my bed, my warm skin touching the cool fabric. I curl onto my side, facing the TV screen, and recognize the video Craig is playing. The story is about a speed trap on a highway in the South. Truckers and buff young hitchhikers use the road, pulling over to the side to fuck in the back of big rigs. After they've just come, patrolmen bang with nightsticks on the metal back doors, calling them "homos, queers!" Large muscular arms are pulled back and handcuffed, while the merchandise in the trucks is confiscated. The men are forced into a *Cool Hand Luke*–type labor camp, where blond boys are raped and the largest-dicked man is in perpetual solitary confinement, frustrated he can't get it on with the other inmates or guards. The video's truth appears to be found in his confinement for lack of a full and useful erection.

Craig sits back and finishes the last swigs of beer in his glass. I have lost track of his drinking tonight, slightly glad of this freedom of mind. His mustache catches small droplets of fluid on the tips. He comes over to me in bed after he's put his painting away. My dick stiffens a little, another side effect of testosterone steroids. I think of his dick hardening and then sitting on it, but I fear liquid shit covering the bedsheets, his dick and my ass. His face moves close to mine and then he kisses me. His mouth is wet and tastes of beer and the ice cubes he places in his glass. My father drank warm beer from cans he stored in the garage, so to me Craig's habit of putting ice in his beer seems luxurious. The TV is flickering the last scenes of the video, the guards and inmates in a final orgy. Craig reaches under the sheets, grabs the hair of my crotch roughly. I return his kisses, biting fully his lower lip, not wanting to extract blood but feeling compelled to. It becomes a contest of who will wince first. He turns his hand, fingers twined in my hair. I let go of his lip, afraid I'll bite through. He holds on. His tongue sidles down my torso and he lifts my legs up. I start to push away, can tell he wants to eat my ass. He turns me on my knees and I can feel his tongue pressing into my hole and again I move away. I can hear Craig sigh in frustration. I look over at the screen and see a man squatting over two cocks. Craig slips his white T-shirt off and I pull his boxers down over his ass. His dick is musty next to my nose. He says, "You're all clean and I'm dirty." I tell him I like it that way. The tip of his dick is moist with urine. I lick at the small droplet, let my tongue linger in the small slot at the head of his penis. Somehow, the camera shows the man's ass-hole expanding to fit the two dicks. I lift the weight of Craig's limp and growing cock with my tongue. I breathe in deeply. I take his dick all the way into my mouth, putting my hand at the base, willing it to become hard by trapping pressure. Craig responds with deep-throated moans, sighs. It doesn't seem to take long to suck him off, my mouth enjoying the work it's performing, my hands curved around Craig's thighs. The TV screen hisses a snow field, the end of the tape. His fluid lies over my tongue, salty and full of potential life. It invades my body like love.

I am in my old home in Pasadena, in the bathtub. The walls around the tub crumble plaster into tepid water. I am slightly surprised when John's hand moves to the water faucet, letting the tub fill with more warm water, silky with baking soda. At once I smell shit, the kind of shit John had while he'd been sick in the hospital. The smell at once overwhelms then dissipates as I look into his face, his blue eyes. In his eyes I see myself, much younger and naive. My face looks less haggard, smooth and without care, college my only concern. John looks as he did, young again, his cheeks full and ruddy, his blond hair neatly combed to the side.

On his ring finger a small gold wedding band, one of a pair we had exchanged at Christmas. The gold glimmers as his hand squeezes a sea sponge. The texture of the sponge is not rough, but soapy as he runs it over my arm, not yet tattooed; water trickles as tears would. I imagine I can taste the bitterness of the water. I begin to cry as I notice the sponge moving over small marks raised on my skin. The odd shaped badges are dark as bruises and covered with thread-like red veins. I try to pick on one, to dig out the imperfection with my nail. John holds my hand steady, doesn't let me finish what I've started. A trickle of blood oozes from under the scar. As it hits the water, the color widens like melted wax dripping into a warm pool. The blood floats like thin petals of lotus flowers on the surface, constantly moving and in flux. The blooms land on my legs and mark them permanently. John says, "Try not to cry." And I fail. Embarrassed at my weakness, I sink underneath the water and all sound is muffled. I shake my head under the water, come up for air gasping like a young boy. I smell gasoline, the sulfur from a match. Around the tub's ledge are votive candles. Under the shower head and the chrome enema hose is a crucifix of Jesus. Red oil drips from the small marks in his forehead, palms, and feet. As his blood touches the water, steam plumes upward; it is like lava flowing into the ocean. The marks on my legs and arms fall away in the water, they become rose petals. John tells me if I drain the water, he can read the future by the petals lying in the tub. I stand up and Craig is there now, naked, with a large bathsheet. He pats me dry. I kiss him but he turns away, which only makes me more determined to bite through his lips. Craig turns back into John and then John disappears. The towel floats, invisibly held by open arms.

To Nam
and Bac

HENRI TRAN

Years later, whenever I read about another bombing in Beirut, it immediately reminded me of Saigon—another act of terrorism, another random casualty of war, another mass of innocents blasted into oblivion. After a while an outsider could not help but wonder, what is left there to bomb, destroy, maim and annihilate? The natural reaction is to dismiss the picture altogether, for sooner or later one assumes it would be reduced to total nothingness. I came to understand (for lack of a better word, if understanding doesn't imply acceptance) the American perspective toward postwar Vietnam: It is better forgotten, as it has become too preposterous, too inconvenient a memory to graft onto one's conscience, to say nothing of being a wound that time alone cannot heal for those involved. Reality proves otherwise: Life goes on, however crippled it has come to be.

My memories of Saigon are those of a continental city. After having taken political control of the entire Indochina peninsula in the late nineteenth century, the French colonialists chose Saigon to be the focal point of their life in transit. They affectionately nicknamed it "the Pearl of the Orient" and strove to cultivate a nostalgic miniature of Paris. Turn-of-the-century architecture mingled with art deco motifs to grace the stately buildings that lined the broadly paved, uncluttered boulevards. Where the

Place de la Concorde should have been stood the Marine Memorial guarding the Ben Thanh Market. Less than a mile away down
Le Loi Boulevard—a much shorter and skimpier version of
Champs Elysees—at the traffic hub where the Arc de Triomphe
should be located, one found the Soldiers' Square facing the
Building of Congress. On this square the South Vietnamese government later erected the infamous Comrades-in-Arms statue,
which was the first thing the Communists pulled down when they
entered the city.

As a young teenager, I used to go swimming at the Club Sportif.
This recreation center was nothing less than the Jardin de Tuiler-
ies with the poshest facilities in the Orient at the time plunked
down in the middle, including a tiny casino on the top floor, of
the administrative building. The swimming pool was located on
the "deck" of a mammoth aquatic complex built to look like an
ocean liner, and topped off with an open-air restaurant that
sprawled across the terrace. I used to walk among the graveled
paths that circled the base of the building whose walls were
draped with wisteria in bloom, and to listen to the tireless buzz of
the cicadas that sought refuge from the summer heat.

Whenever I went there to swim, it was because my would-be
stepfather, whom I called Uncle Lu, was in town. He would park
the car a block from our house on Sunday mornings and wait for
me. He was a married man, though not to my mother; and since I
did not live with her but with my father and my stepmother, Uncle
Lu preferred to keep a low profile. My parents understood and
did not take offense that he would not show up at our front door.
He would drive me to the club in his Volvo just like any normal
parent driving his kid to the pool.

Sometimes he would leave me there on my own. I didn't mind
being by myself since it was already a treat to be there. After all, it
was an elitist club, primarily catering to the legion of French civil-
ians who had put down roots in Saigon. Later the club would
admit the American military officers who were stationed in the
capital, but membership was never open to the general public.
So it was there that I picked up Groucho Marx's credo, to apply
throughout my adulthood: I don't want to belong to any club
that accepts me as a member—open admission would simply take
away the thrill of getting in. The Sportif also whetted my appetite

for a more cosmopolitan life, where one would always sit at tables covered with white cloth and be served by waiters in starched uniforms, where one could order a "beefsteak" with salad and french fries at every meal and eat them off smooth silverware and cool china.

Before long I decided that Saigon, or Vietnam at large, was not the place for me. Uncle Lu used to say after each meal we had on the Sportif terrace—I once watched in disbelief while he ate a banana without ever touching the fruit with his fingers; the whole process looked to me like surgery, being performed daintily with knife and fork—that I ought to study hard, get a degree and then everything would come my way.

I didn't necessarily admire the man, partly out of an unsuspected streak of inherent racism among the Vietnamese toward anyone Chinese, even though I was part Chinese myself. Furthermore, I envied him for his ability to take care of my mother— he had recently bought her a condo in Hong Kong—and for his import-export business in metal that spanned both sides of the Pacific, Saigon being but one port of transaction. Last but not least, he couldn't hold a candle to my father, whose lack of prestige was more than compensated by an abundance of charm. Looking at clean-shaven, portly and balding Uncle Lu, I said to myself, boy, a man needs some charisma. But I had to admit, however grudgingly, that he set a model for the way of life that I preferred to the one I was seeing around me. Uncle Lu traveled overseas, he took my mother on exotic trips. He certainly was a member of the jet set, whereas my father could not even get in the Sportif.

So I studied hard, and hurriedly. The summer of 1974, I was preparing for my second Bac. The Baccalaureats (or Bacs, for short) were a cultural heritage from the motherland—that was how France had been referred to and revered by its Indochinese colonial outpost, up to my parents' generation. Following the school system imposed by the French Academy in Paris, there were two mandatory exams outside of class finals awaiting all students at the end of eleventh and twelfth grades. Each exam was nationwide and lasted two weeks. Each was categorically comprehensive, which meant any topic one had been taught during one's academic life up till then could well be a subject on the test. For my generation, the Bacs implicitly bestowed another value that had nothing to do with the art of learning but with the chilling art of survival: They passed as a waiver for the draft. One took the first Bac to go on to twelfth grade, and after graduating from high school, the second. A boy coming of age—that is, of the age to enlist—could not possibly fail either Bac without sensing that his future had taken a shortcut to the territories of war.

As a result, after each Bac, I watched half my friends drop out of school and enter the army. It was the only option open to them: They could neither stay in school, nor at home. The female students sobbed and moaned equally when they failed the Bac. However, their lives did not depend on it—they simply considered themselves to have missed the boat. Girls would keep going at it year after year until by hit or miss, they would eventually fall out of school. Boys did not have the luxury of time, they were not allowed a second chance. The war had already peaked. The Americans were withdrawing their last "military advisors," and the nation's army was going through its *Vietnamization* period—a euphemism for bringing the indigenous troops up to the American standard so that the South Vietnamese army would not be viewed as a sinking ship. What was lacking in the troops' leadership was made up by their capacity to swell, thanks to the abundance of young draftees. There was virtually no way any young man, if he was not passing the Bacs and proceeding on to the university in a timely manner, could either stay home or leave the country. Nor could he evade his military duty, except under extraordinary circumstances.

Some tried to defeat the system. In more ways than one, we all did. There were always undertakings to sneak teenage boys out of the country. Usually people who lived in Cholon, Saigon's Chinatown, would have relatives in Hong Kong or Taipei and therefore make arrangements for those wanting to leave. A boat would take a boy from the port of Saigon out to the open sea, where he would be transferred clandestinely to a freighter heading toward the desired destination. Entering Hong Kong was considered the easiest way, due to the gray zone outside its harbor, the docking area of the sampans, home for the contingent of the boat city. However, this route of escape was only for the most intrepid—or the most desperate—adventurers since the chances of getting ashore safe and sound were slim. In spite of the staggering amount of money one's family had to come up with, one usually disappeared on the-high seas. The tales of smuggling are always the same, regardless of the nature of the merchandise. A more effective way to survive was to go through the motions at home, get drafted, then, through well-oiled connections, get assigned to behind-the-line duty. One could get stationed right in one's hometown to handle administrative chores or work as domestic help for the local military officers. The extent of hardship or leisure depended on one's social influence and the amount of monetary grease one's family could dispense with. Naturally these conveniences were affordable only to the upper class.

Notwithstanding one's social status and the political climate of South Vietnam at the time, I viewed those conditions of survival bargaining as one of life's harshest ironies. No one should be cornered into a situation where they have to eyeball the matter of life and death so judiciously and so prematurely. We were kids still in school. I thought of the salmon who have to get back to the river where they were born, swim upstream, spawn and then die—except we never left our stream. To fight the current, I had to stay up at night, slumping on the couch but not daring to sleep. With a blackboard on my lap and a piece of chalk in my hand, I'd go over and over quadratic equations, chemistry formulas, calculus matrixes, analytic geometry and linear algebra until four o'clock in the morning each summer when school was out and the Bac race was on. Usually I fell asleep, falling on my back and staring at the electric fan swirling on the ceiling. I felt my whole consciousness sucked into the vortex of swishing whorls of air above my head, and often the faces of old friends, those whom I had not seen for some time, would appear in the fan's orbit, like meteors plummeting out of destiny's black hole onto the barren landscape of my dream.

One month after the Bac season was over, our grades were handed out. Listings were posted on wood panels hastily erected along the outer walls of each school that had been chosen as a testing site. Pandemonium broke out all through the city as thousands of students swarmed over these sites in hope of seeing their names behind the glass cases that enclosed the listings. The scene was a premonition of the chaos that seized the capital a year later when the citizens tried to flee the advancing Communists.

The rain started early that morning. I took the bus part of the way, then walked to school, the traffic already jammed blocks ahead. People gathered in groups along the streets, either seeking shelter from the rain or waiting to get news from friends. The crowd grew larger as I approached the listing posts. I began my "dive" into the mass. Someone yelled at me.

"Hey, Phu, I saw your name!" I turned around and saw one of my classmates.

"What grade did I get?" I shouted over the pushing horde of people behind me.

"I don't know. See it for yourself—"

"What grade did you get?"

"A 'C,'" my friend grinned, stretching both arms skyward as a sign of victory. He then ran off.

'C' was the passing grade. Only those with a 'C' or higher would see their names posted. I felt relief for both of us. With more confidence I fought my way into the crowd, then stationed myself somewhere in the middle near the front where I could scan the whole area without having to get too close to the panels. People literally threw themselves onto the posts. The glass was broken at some spots, but all the listings were pretty much intact. The rain had not slackened; if nothing else, it had picked up more fury from the east wind. Around me was a standing stampede where people jumped in and out, cried and yelled, no one less frenzied than another.

The downpour amid all the commotion sent mud flying in our faces. I got a 'B.' My shirt was torn at one shoulder. I made my way out of the human avalanche without further damage, sensing a deep disappointment over my underachievement. Not getting an 'A' meant that my chance of getting out of the country through a student visa would be severely limited. Nevertheless, the relief of having finally gotten over the Bacs once and for all did more than compensate for my grudge toward life at the moment.

I walked over to the school entrance. The gate was open. Looking in, I could see my old classroom across the schoolyard. It seemed to have retreated far into the corner, dark and somber, closed shut as if it had been sealed off forever. I recognized some faces among the group gathering on the steps under the awnings. They waved at me. I crossed the courtyard, skipping over rain puddles in the grass.

After greetings, which consisted mainly of one letter, our passing grade, we chatted desultorily, knowing that once more we were the survivors. The communal sigh of relief could be heard in every word that was uttered.

"So, what are you going to do?" one asked.

"Next stop: law school, for me," said another.

"My scholarship to Australia is coming any day," said Khanh, one of our 'A' students, also one of the poorest.

"I don't know, what can you do with a 'B'?" I moaned.

"Don't be too greedy," a friend advised. "Get down on your knees right now and thank God for not forgetting to put your name on that pile of trash out there."

"I'd go home and sleep for a hundred years," another sighed.

"Not a bad idea for evading the draft!"

"The war might not be over yet..."

"Don't forget you are still a virgin—"

"Not anymore, we got him deflowered in Cholon last week! You should have come with us, Phu," the one standing next to me said with a nudge from his elbow, "Trung was looking for you."

"Thanks, but no thanks. I might run into a long-lost cousin there," I answered feebly.

"Speak of the devil. Hey, Trung!"

Out of the corner of my eye, I saw somebody come in from the street on a scooter. No doubt it was Trung, one of my favorite classmates, on whom I had a crush. He was one of the more popular fellows in the class, generous and jovial, a good sport to everybody rather than a snob like other rich kids, not to mention the only person in the class who could afford to throw parties at home. I always thought Trung would make a handsome diplomat. He was a fine looking guy with bright eyes, playful smiles and silky hair that fell dreamily over his forehead. He was also quite fond of me, even though he tried not to let it show.

During the delirious lull that came after the exam, when time seemed to have stopped for those of us who were counting the days, Trung had taken upon himself the task of prepping me for the society of grown-ups, since my world had only revolved around home and school until then. We went to his tailor and had some clothes made for me. We hung out in smoky cafés listening to anti-war songs and getting high on "filtered coffee," a sort of hand-brewed espresso. I even started smoking. When I failed to get a date to Trung's biggest and last home party, our graduation bash, he even saw to it that I had a female escort. However, Trung never attempted to get me to visit the brothel. Instead, as the monsoon season began, I would come to his house. On some rainy afternoons, we stayed shut in his room— not many of our families could afford to give each child his own room. There Trung drew the shades, turned the music low and took me into his arms. The storm lashed furiously against the windowpanes, almost drowning out the rhythm by which we practiced some new steps of a slow dance. The sky peeped through the soggy clouds, filtering a bluish haze into the room. We snuggled up to the warmth of our jointly bated breath, feeling safe and unguarded like two cats in the attic. The world seemed far, far away.

The rain stopped. However, Trung did not approach our group. He got off his scooter and walked it along the other side of the court, then paused to speak to another group that had just come out on the veranda.

"What the hell is he waiting for?" I wondered aloud.

"What do you care?" one of our group asked.

"Get over here!" I raised my voice across the courtyard.

"He didn't make it," someone said, sensing my frustration. "He was here a while ago. He said he was going to another school's posting to make sure they did not omit his name. Tough luck!"

"It doesn't matter," another explained. "Trung already told me what he would do, even before school was over."

"Well, with a Dad like his he shouldn't have to worry." Trung's father was an army colonel.

I said nothing. I felt I had just lost something very dear. Trung finally turned his eyes toward us. When his glance met mine, he quickly turned away. A few seconds later, after some brief words to one of the guys on the veranda, he jumped on his motorbike and started off back to the street. That was the last I saw of Trung.

The army quickly revved up its machinery to reap the latest crop. Many of my friends were sent to boot camp in a matter of days. I managed to get out of the country not too long afterward. The following year Saigon became Ho Chi Minh City.

Affairs of
the Day

ROBERT RODI

He takes a seat beside me on the 151 bus. Like a camera with high-speed film, I take one sidelong glance and capture the totality of him. Jet-black hair, almost blue, in a razor cut that makes it look like sculpted slate. Luminous, unblemished skin—the kind of skin that never nicks from shaving. Cheekbones clear up to his temples. (All right, I snuck a longer look for that.) Dress any ancient statue of Apollo or Antinous in an Italian suit (I bend down to scratch my ankle and steal a corroborating glance—*definitely* Italian) and this is what you'd get.

I think at first he's a clerk in some tony retail wonderland, but his watch tells me otherwise. Not big and gaudy like those two-tone Rolex monsters, it's one of those thin-as-paper jobs someone like me wouldn't even know the name of. That's where the trouble lies between us, you know. He's high-rent, I'm low-wage. I check my scuffed Doc Martens from Na Na, sleeping like cats beneath the straggles of my fraying denim cuffs. He, in his sheer socks and imported leather slippers, must sniff at me in disdain. Opposites attract, of course, but such attractions are not easy to maintain. A battle from dawn to dusk, no escaping it. (After dusk, we can presume pleasanter things.) Start with breakfast—*quelle désastre!* My lover—Reggie—has a leek omelette with Gruyère cheese and a glass of unsweetened grapefruit juice, and then it's off to his club, and I don't mean health club. I grab a bowl of Captain Crunch just in time for "Ricki Lake," and spill 2-percent milk on a velvet sofa cushion. But of course I'm so charmingly guilty about it—like a pup who's wet the rug. Open my big brown eyes and cock my head, waiting with naked anxiety for the first flickering sign of my master's mood. Is it any wonder he's besotted with me? His bohemian boy-toy; his plebeian poet. This despite the admonitions of his parents, who wring their hands in their Gold Coast apartment, seated at a coffee table stuffed with Henry Moores and nautical ashtrays, wondering how they can stop the encroachment of one of *those* people into their realm, and thank *God* gays can't marry or we'd *really* be in for it, and—

The bus hits a pothole. For a nanosecond, I'm airborne. Then Reggie reaches into his briefcase—Coach, of course—and pulls out a newspaper. For a moment, I think I see the telling salmon-pink of the *Financial Times*, but that's just the reflected light from a red rain slicker worn by a woman in the aisle. The *Wall Street Journal*, then; the *New York Times*, at the very least.

Well, no. It's the *Sun-Times*.

Hmph.

Huh.

How about that.

An investor, I bet. A self-made man. From peasant stock. Got his first job as a copy editor at his hometown newspaper. Up in—I don't know. Crystal Lake. The paper was a weekly; the writing by retirees, or housewives whose kids had grown. Major stories were about craft fairs and bone fishing. That's when he—my lover—Phil—became managing editor. Suddenly he was hiring hungry young Woodwards and Bernsteins who wrote about glue-sniffing Satan cults at the junior high. National attention followed; prestigious awards. Borrowing money, he bought the newspaper—the first of a string he owned by the time he was thirty. Ever ambitious, he set his sights higher: He liquidated his assets and realized a life-long dream by buying into the consortium that purchased the *Sun-Times*. It's more than he can manage, sometimes, keeping his vision alive amidst the sharks and shareholders. That's why he needs me. As a poet, my purity of perception is invaluable to him. Every night, after wild lovemaking—even sometimes during (the exchange of ideas being, for us, an aphrodisiac)—he uses me as a sounding board. "Isn't the existence of front-page Social Security lottery—UGN—oh, GOD—mere exploitation of the working cl—GOD—YES—"

Wait a minute. What's he doing?

He's flipped the paper open.

To the comics section.

He's—

He's—

He's reading "Nancy."

And he's *laughing.*

I turn and look out the window.

And I sigh.

I can't take him anywhere, you know. He's gorgeous, he dresses well—in fact, he dresses impeccably. But breeding will out. At my last reading—with the editors of *Horizons* in the crowd, and that stern woman from the *New York Review of Books* who single-handedly ruined one young poet's career by dubbing him "the so-so sonneteer"—my lover—Johnny—embarrassed me by giggling when I read the word "tumescent." People started to turn in their seats to glare at him before realizing they shouldn't; dozens of tushes did dozens of quarter-turns, noisily rubbing against the nap of the chairs' upholstery. My pacing was thrown, my rhythm ruined. Yet Johnny was serenely unaware of the calamity he'd caused. Still, it's not his fault; I'm to blame. I let myself be swayed by his classical beauty and his nothing-off-the-rack wardrobe. I should've known it was all a *nouveau riche* pose during our first dinner date, when he asked the sommelier for "whatever you've got that's red—that's what goes with veal, right?" But by then it was too late. I was in love. And isn't it his rough edges, his lack of polish, that excite me, keep me lusting for his touch? My writing is all refinement; I winnow away at verses, rhymes, allusions, till what's left is a little miracle of soul-sharp succinctness. Johnny, however, knocks down buildings for a living. He's incredibly successful. Is there a hint of something illicit in the way he keeps getting all the city's choicest demolition jobs? I did a little dance around the subject once; I asked him which *Godfather* movie he liked best. He said he never saw any of them. I didn't have the courage to ask about *Married to the Mob.* But there are strange calls in the night. Gruff-voiced men asking me to just tell Johnny that Stinky called. Or Four-Eyes. Or Chick. And then there was that mysterious knock on the door one night, late, when Johnny sat bolt upright in bed and whispered *"For God's sake don't answer that. . . ."*

What? What's that? A woman at the front of the bus is waving at me.

No.

Waving at *him.*

He waves back.

"Heard you were on vacation," she calls out.

He nods, and calls back, "Paris."

She rolls her eyes, as if to say, *I wish it were me.* Then she says, "Who watched the kids?"

"Peg's mom," he replies. "Had to treat her to the Pump Room when we got back. Part of the deal."

The woman laughs.

Two stops later, they get off the bus together. He's busy describing the I. M. Pei pyramid that's been tacked onto the Louvre like a paper tail onto a donkey. "Peg hated it," he says as he descends onto Michigan Avenue. "Wouldn't go near it. Said it looked like something from a 'Star Trek' movie." He extends his arm and helps his woman friend maneuver the steps. "Which is probably why I dug it."

The doors hiss and flap shut again. And my lover is gone.

Thank God, I reflect with relief, that sitting here on the bus we hadn't succumbed to the currents of erotic energy that were passing between us like jump-starts. One squeeze of his knee, one grasp of his hand, and his friend up front would've seen it. And then *she* would've been told. The wife. *Peg.* Oh, sure, she probably would've left him because of it, freeing him to be with me—but do I want him that way? After all that anguish and heartache, could things ever be the same between us?

Hardly.

And yet, if not that—what future for us?

I reach an epiphany. This life—the hiding, the hypocrisy—I deserve better. I draw a deep breath; I hold it for a moment. And then I let it go. And as I let it go, I let *him* go—my lover. My Alex. I will never see him again.

Sadness—no, more cerebral than sadness; *tristesse*—settles over me like a clean, wet linen sheet. I rest my head against the bus window. Alone again! How many times—how many partings— until I get it right?

I look at my watch. Twelve minutes to nine. I collect myself, summon the courage to face the workday.

The bus stops. Someone gets on at Michigan and Streeterville.

He's got long, dirty-blond hair, a chin full of stubble like Velcro, a sweaty T-shirt that says JUST DO ME, and a pair of lycra shorts that are filled out in exactly the way lycra shorts were meant to be filled out. He's carrying a skateboard in one hand and a neon orange helmet in the other. He throws himself into the seat next to me as though trying to block a soccer goal. Then he gasps a few breaths, deposits the helmet into his lap and the skateboard between his knees, and lets his large, sunburned hands drop to his sides. One of them grazes my thigh.

"Sorry, man," he grunts, looking my way.

"No problem," I say with telling enthusiasm. But no matter how much enthusiasm I muster, I can never match his electrifying energy. My lover, Dack—the street performer. He's awed, understandably, by my comfort and success with more traditional forms of verse; but I, in turn, am awed by the spontaneity and integrity of his combustible performances. Sex between us is phenomenal. I've actually lost *weight*. . . .

The Road to Mary's Place

DAVID KELLY

The road stretched into the horizon, a twisted black arrow pointing me home. *Home.* What a hateful little word, a false talisman conjuring Norman Rockwell images of love, acceptance, and warm embraces. While the radio DJ prattled on, the smooth purr of my rented convertible lulled me into lazy musings about my current abode, three thousand miles and another reality away. Barely twenty-four hours earlier I had been lying under a perfect California sun lusting for the man/boy in the pool. He was with a group of friends, fine men all, but not a single face I could recall. I knew only one thing about him—he was the embodiment of everything I had ever dreamed. He had a coy smile, but rarely laughed. When he did it was from deep within his soul; soft black curls tumbled over eyes as endlessly blue as any sky. His body was short, tight, and muscular with just enough softness to be real. He also carried a delicious ass that made me thank God I was a fag. He actually reminded me a little of God—nearby but beyond my reach, an unattainable ideal just close enough to tease with his perfection.

My straining erection brought me back to the present. Missed opportunities make the most bitter of fantasies. My world was completely different now. There was the same oppressive July heat, but my little deity was far away, the graceful palms replaced by stolid pines, and the glittering pool traded for the damned blacktop taking me places I did not want to go. I greedily sucked in the clean air, so rich with oxygen it pained my smog-scarred lungs. It gave me a rush of energy, almost intoxicating, and my dick refused to go down. This was no good. In L.A., desire was good and natural, something to be celebrated. This, however, was Carolina, and daring to think of a man, a white man no less, even in the solitude of the open road, was pointless and dangerous. Guilt came calling like an old friend. I laughed aloud. I really was home.

I drove along noticing the trees, the wildflowers, even the roadkill, anything to divert my thoughts. It worked, and soon I fancied myself a dispassionate observer of my native land. I had to admit, it was more beautiful than I remembered. Living in the desert I had forgotten the hue of true green. Here the surrounding forest was so lush and deep it seemed a living thing that could reach out and pull me in. Rolling hills, visible only through occasional clearings, sloped gently toward the sea. I felt in awe of the amount of open space—a state maybe a tenth the size of California seemed far more vast. I had to remind myself several times why I put up with the dirt and crowds. I passed a few unhurried souls: the wizened black man and his gnarled walking stick; a dust-blackened farmer atop an ancient tractor; a mother and her two daughters, golden blonds all, out picking blackberries and wild plums. All were quick to smile and wave, and I waved back, surprised and embarrassed to be touched by a simple act of civility.

Finally a road sign, "Holland Fifty Miles". Damn, my parents lived twenty miles beyond that. Why did they have to live on the other side of East Bumfuck? Soon enough I relaxed and imagined Holland, North Carolina, towheaded girls in pigtails and boys in knickers saying "*ja-ja*, y'all" and clogging about in wooden shoes in one-hundred-and-five-degree heat.

It was nearly that hot now, and I realized how thirsty I was—"a might parched" as they said in these parts. I was also pretty hungry. I was saving my palate for Mamma's fried chicken and biscuits—the haute cuisine of trailer-trash—but with an hour's drive ahead, a quick sandwich couldn't hurt. The question, however, was where?

Then, like a biblical vision, the forest parted and revealed a large clearing, flat land connected by a concrete bridge—the interstate—the first sign of post-1950s life I'd seen for hours. As I approached, I read a small sign: "Food, Gas, Lodging," it said, with the silhouettes of a place setting, a gas pump, a man in bed—always a welcome sight—and a big rig truck. "Awwww, shit," I moaned, my mood and appetite ebbing. I still remembered the unwritten rules of the South, and darkies—even as fair as I—were not welcome in country truck stops. I was nearly past the exit, resigned to hunger pains, when my mood turned even darker. Perhaps ten years in California had made me crazy, or maybe just plain mean, but how dare any establishment—especially this backwater dump—shun my hard-earned dollar. I was every bit as good as they—hell, I even had voted Republican once. With the conviction of the righteous, I wheeled into the parking lot, maneuvered deftly between the steel behemoths, found a space, and stepped onto redneck soil. The conquering ethnic hero.

As I took full sight of the place, however, my courage nearly failed. It was old, built in the sleek, tacky "space-age" style of the 1950s, and had not worn well. Before me were lines and lines of gas pumps for both cars and rigs; to one side a grimy, formerly white diner with a crippled neon sign that weakly flickered "Mary's Place." It reminded me of a dying pulse. To the other side stood a strip of equally decrepit motel rooms patronized by dirty, mostly bearded, grossly overweight men and their female companions. The women wore an assortment of polyester halter tops, laughably short denim shorts, and, without fail, high heels. Despite copious amounts of makeup, they looked as beaten down as the property itself. No one seemingly noticed my arrival; they were far too busy talking, laughing, swearing loudly, then pairing off and going inside rooms. "Traditional Family Values," I sniffed.

"Hey man, nice car," someone drawled.

I spun around. Two spaces away stood three men—boys, really—leaning against a pick up truck, passing between them a brown paper bag. This was a motley lot, and for a second I thought of the Three Stooges. One was tall and lanky with dirty blond hair, another lumbering and swollen, his young belly already hanging over his belt. The third, the one who had spoken, was short, slightly on the soft side, a dirty baseball cap pulled over shoulder-length hair. The first two stood back, but he boldly came forward.

Fuck! Had living in L.A. not taught me anything about checking out my surroundings? I stiffened as he ran a hand over my car, keeping one eye on his companions. They did not move, but eyed us coldly. The boy seemed about eighteen, give or take a year, and at close range did not have the hardened features of the others; rather, he seemed genuinely impressed with my wheels. I had rented the convertible at the Atlanta airport specifically to impress the locals. Evidently I was successful. Still, there was something to the entire setup that smelled of more than innocent admiration.

"Forgot to get gas," I lied and jumped back inside the car, not bothering to see if he believed me or not. I drove slowly to the gas pumps, and since it was Sunday and not crowded, I found one quickly. To my shock, I noticed that one did not have to prepay. Theft, at least, was one vice not practiced here.

"Burn much gas?"

I looked around, and there was the boy again. Either he was a persistent criminal, or too naive to recognize a brush-off. It was probably the latter, but still something felt very wrong. "Nope, not too badly," I answered, my own suppressed drawl making its return.

"Is it your car?"

I tensed again. No, I'm a typical nigger and I stole it, I almost said aloud, but held my tongue.

"Where you from? Atlanta?"

Damn nosey little cuss. "No, Los Angeles." I was wary at confirming myself a tourist and thus an easy mark. I remembered, however, that it was proved already by the rental sticker on the car's bumper. Hell, a full set of teeth was proof positive of my outsider status.

The boy loosed a low whistle and continued stroking the car so gently it was almost erotic.

"Wow, man, really?" he said in awe. "Is it nice out there?"

"Yeah, I like it," I said, feeling worldly and superior.

"Do you know any stars?"

"A couple." It was only a half lie. Porn stars had to count for something.

"Are you rich?"

A shrug and coy smile were my only reply. I had lost all fear of the kid, and actually did not want to wreck any of his illusions. For the first time, I really looked at the boy and felt silly for my earlier apprehension. He seemed not only innocent, but filled with a childlike curiosity that caused me to feel an instant kinship with him. I remembered my own adolescence amidst the same piney woods, and I remembered my hunger of news of the outside world away from sleepy towns, clapboard churches, stock-car races, catfish fries, and cross burnings. For any kid here with a free spirit illusion was an essential survival skill.

As if he could read my thoughts, he looked up at me and grinned. "I like you," he said, then gestured to his friends. "They don't like black folks, but I don't care about color none. Some is good, some ain't, just like regular people."

"Regular people, huh?" I grunted. The pump clicked off and so did my good will. I knew he meant it as a compliment, but this was the South, and the old beast had arisen at last. I mumbled a "See you later," and went to pay.

An old white lady stood ahead of me, paying by credit card and chatting with the attendant, a husky, scruffy-faced redneck who did not ask her for identification. I thumbed my own credit card nervously and wondered if he would ask ID of me. He was ridiculously slow, but I was grateful for the delay. I needed to calm down. The lady shuffled off and I handed over cash to avoid any confrontation and hurry things along as I realized my bladder was quite full. I asked for the restrooms. The cashier hesitated, his eyes narrowed, then glanced over my shoulder.

"Ten minutes," he said and handed me my change. He pointed to twin blue doors by the entrance of the restaurant. As I walked over, I wondered what the hell he meant by ten minutes. And were there nicer facilities inside unofficially reserved for white customers? God, back less than a day and I was already paranoid! The door was locked, the little red sign above the knob reading "occupied." At least it was in working order, I thought as my bladder cramped with strain. I waited a minute, then two, then five. I whistled and smiled, anything to look casual and take my mind off my screaming gut. At last, at the critical moment, the door swung open and the most obese man I have ever seen waddled out and loudly belched. Oh, joy. I sighed, steeled my courage, and went inside. Miraculously, there was little stench, and the place was quite clean. There was no stall, only a sink and toilet. I stepped up and went about my business. "Blessed relief," I whispered. The door opened behind me. I cursed my haste that I had forgotten to lock it. I did not stop or look back. Whoever it was would have to wait as I had.

"Yeah, I like you a lot," said a now familiar voice. I jumped and turned so quickly I nearly wet myself. The boy stood leaning against the opposite wall in his best faux-macho James Dean pose.

I was stunned and silent for a moment, just long enough for him to turn and lock the door. My earlier fear returned. How could I have been so damned stupid? His hands, however, went neither to his pockets for a knife, nor to his waistband for a gun, but rather to his crotch, which he fondled roughly. My fear disappeared and my jaw slackened in amazement. A T-room trick at a redneck truck stop? The idea was so clichéd it seemed almost quaint. I smiled with relief that he mistook as agreement, and he fished out his dick. It was large, much more so than I would have expected from one his size, and he was quite proud of himself, stroking it firmly, his eyes never leaving mine. I found myself growing excited, then quickly ashamed. I turned back to the toilet as if to urinate, but that need was long forgotten. I was not quite sure what to do, but I refused to run away like a coward. I was the sophisticate here and I would stand my ground.

I heard the slap of his sneakers on the tile as he approached, but I did not turn around.

"What are you doing?" I asked, listening to my heartbeat thundering in my ears.

"Twenty bucks," he whispered.

"You've got to be kidding."

"Alright... fifteen," he said, again misunderstanding. I could not suppress a laugh. "Shhhhh," he gently scolded, turning me to face him. I stifled myself, but we were both grinning foolishly. Then he dropped to his knees.

"This is dangerous," I said, earnest but weak. The boy only shrugged.

"Don't worry. I do it all the time."

I knew I should have pulled back. I should have walked out and driven away as fast as I could. I should have remembered where we were and what would happen were we discovered; but as he took me into his mouth, all rational thought disintegrated. He sucked hungrily, desperately; what he lacked in technique he made up for with effort. I had no illusions that he had any feelings for me, but somehow I knew that this was more than just a simple financial arrangement. He was too eager. He pulled off for a moment. "I want it," he said, and went back to sucking.

Maybe he did want it—need it—much more than I. I looked down into his face as his eyes briefly rose to meet mine. Again, visions of my own youth rushed back. What would I have done had

a handsome stranger from mythical California arrived and offered me respite from the necessary lies of rural life—given me
the chance to touch, to hold, to taste, to be queer. I had not initiated the encounter, but like it or not, I was responsible for it, and
his well-being. I had to make sure he knew that he mattered, that I
cared, and that there was so much more to being gay than this. I
ran my hand underneath his cap, stroking his hair and moaning
softly. He jerked away roughly. "Shhhhh," he said again brusquely,
then resumed sucking.

My feelings whipsawed again and I became truly aware of the
smell and the dirt and the redneck white boy making a meal of my
dick. I realized that we had exchanged places—he was the man-of-
the-world, as hardened as any pro back on the boulevard; and I
was the country bumpkin—worse, a country nigger—placing my
trust in the calloused hands of "masser." My empathy vanished,
and so did my restraint. I grabbed his head and forced myself
roughly down his throat. He gagged, but made no effort to pull
away, masturbating himself with his right hand and urging me in
deeper with his left. I obliged him, grinding in hard and silently,
giving no thought to his comfort.

Soon enough, I felt myself losing control and tried to pull away,
but he held me fast. Oh well, I thought, and toyed with the idea of
just letting go. I do this all the time, he had said, and I doubted if
any of his other customers had volunteered their HIV status. I
knew they hadn't, but that was beside the point. This was all still to
some extent about me, and I would not be like the other beaten,
cowardly souls who used him for furtive pleasure and robbed him
of humanity. At the last possible moment, I ripped away, spraying
across his face, neck, and shirt. He followed my lead and came in
choked grunts, his face collapsed against my leg. For a moment
we were frozen together, joined by our gasps and his fingers inter-
twining with mine, when suddenly he bolted upright. "Shit!" he
cried and hurried to the sink. He wet a paper towel and wiped his
shirt, erasing the traces of our meeting. I put away my dick and
found my wallet, hand him the cash as I left. "Thanks," he said.
"See ya."

I did not look back. What a damn stupid thing to say, I thought.
Outside, the hot air rolled over me with such anger I half-expected
the smell of brimstone. My heart shuddered with each heartbeat as
my eyes scanned the area. I was trembling with fear and exhaus-

tion, prepared to greet an angry mob assembled with torches and bibles to destroy the nigger sodomite and the corrupted white trash. There was no mob, only the boy's two friends standing against the diner wall behind me. They lazily smoked cigarettes, as relaxed as if it were they who had just had sex. They dropped the spent butts and ground them into the dirt, their eyes never leaving mine. The setting sun was casting long ruddy shadows on their clearly scowling faces; my fists clenched and my mind raced furiously over every self-defense course, book, or video I had ever seen. They stood, hesitated a moment, one spit hard upon the ground in my direction, but they did not approach. Instead, they walked into the men's room and closed the door behind. "Oh, god," I sighed, so relieved my knees nearly buckled. I turned and walked quickly to my car, still by the gas pumps, my breath coming in strangled gulps, my lungs not quite ready to relax. Suddenly the realization struck me: I had driven into the home of bigotry and intolerance, committed the most egregious of sins—and was walking away unscathed. I wanted to shout, to pump my fist in the air, and maybe even dance a jig. I settled for putting the convertible's top down and giving the cashier my best "fuck you" grin.

The first sound was a large bang, and my fear instantly reappeared. A gunshot? From where? I ducked and looked about, fumbling for my keys when I caught sight of the men's room. The bang had been the door violently flung open; the boy I had been with came running out with the taller one in close pursuit. The fat one appeared soon after. "Kill the motherfucker!" he screamed. The tall one caught the short one and flung him to the ground. They were on him in an instant, the tall one holding, the fat one kicking the squirming, flailing but silent boy in his chest, face, or groin. I started my car. Drive away, my mind screamed, this is not about you. I should have, but I couldn't. I floored the accelerator and circled toward them, waiting until I was almost upon them to hit my horn. The two attackers looked up, saw me, and jumped to the side. I slammed the brakes and skidded within a few feet of the boy. "Get in, goddammit, get in!!" I screamed, knowing the two rednecks would hesitate only a moment before turning on me. I prayed that the boy was coherent enough to do what I said, and thankfully he was, half-leaping, half-tumbling over the door and into the passenger seat. His legs still dangled outside as—with a spray of dirt and gravel—I sped away. I looked about frantically, half-hoping for and half-dreading the arrival of police. How would I explain the beaten white boy, bloody and squirming to right himself in my passenger seat, and the two neanderthals chasing us. The truth would surely come out, and when it did—oh, God! I looked back a few times but did not see the truck. I was moving fast, but not fast enough to have lost them so quickly. The boy looked at me and evidently understood my confusion. He grinned, the slight smile beaming through dirt, smeared blood, and the spreading blue-black bruise.

"They ain't coming," he said. "I got the keys."

I looked at him incredulously, then broke into a gale of near hysterical laughter. I laughed until the first tears streaked my face. The boy joined in, but not with my gusto, and each chuckle echoed with sadness.

"What was that all about?" I asked.

The laughter died almost instantly, its fuel of relief exhausted. The reality of the day crashed atop us; its weight almost tangible. He did not speak for several minutes, and I, now spent, did not have the energy to press the subject. I was contented enough to simply drive. After several miles I realized I had a new problem— the boy beside me. I did not want to become further involved, but I couldn't just stop the car and say "Get out" in the middle of nowhere. The sun was rapidly retreating, the shadows from the surrounding forest were becoming more insistent. The night out here would be completely black. What the hell was I going to do?

"Some friends you got back there," I said to break the silence and ease into conversation. The boy still did not answer. Now I was getting irritated. Forget subtlety, it was time to end this foolishness.

"Where do you live? I'll take you home." Finally, the boy reacted, breathing a deep sigh, then leaning his head wearily against the door.

"I can't go home," he said. "Not for a while at least."

"Well you can't stay here," I snapped angrily, then instantly regretted it. He was a boy, beaten and afraid. Surely I could find a kinder way to end this. While I searched for something to say, the boy spoke up.

"Those ain't my friends. They're my brothers."

I wanted to stop the car, but I kept my composure. Some wall of silence was beginning to crumble, and out of sympathy, and some prurient curiosity, I wanted to listen.

"Bobby and Leroy found out I was queer a couple of years ago. There was this trucker who would come through from time to time and he and I would get together. He was so good to me...." He trailed off in thought for a moment, his voice choking. He caught hold of his emotions and composed himself.

"Bobby and Leroy caught us one morning when I'd stayed in his truck all night. They beat the hell out of both of us, and told the trucker to stay away. For a while they left me alone...except when they'd get drunk. Then they'd slap me around, and make me...do things for them. Then slap me around again. A few months ago they figured out that there were other folk who came through that would pay good money for a guy like me. So when they need some money...we go to Mary's Place." The boy sat up very straight and deepened his voice, but as he spoke, he refused to look me in the face.

"So..." I said, not trying to hide my confusion. "That's what we did. What's the problem?"

The boy shifted again in the seat, his eyes fixed on the now black distance. Again the old hesitance returned, but I refused to allow him to slip into silence. I started to speak, but he cut me off.

"Because you're a nig—because you're black. They don't like black people—I told you that before—and my going off with you. They said it didn't look right. They said if word got out that I sucked niggers then white men wouldn't want me, or wouldn't pay as much."

"Bad for business," I hissed. "So why did you do it?"

He finally turned to me, not angry, but more stern than I would have thought possible. "Because I wanted to. I told you before—I like you."

We drove on for another few miles, the only sounds being the car and his sniffles. His composure had buckled, but not given way. He would not cry, but the tears would not be fully held.

"What about the rest of your family?" I finally asked.

"There's only Ma," he shrugged, "and she don't care much—as long as she's got her bottle."

More silence. At last appeared another road sign: "Cana Five Miles." My hometown. "You can let me off here," he said softly. "I'll hang out here then hitch back. Give Bobby and Leroy time to cool off." I nodded in agreement. What else could one really do? I wanted to tell him to take off, to leave this miserable, brutal place. There is a big marvelous world outside of these woods, and anything would be better than this, I wanted to say. But was it really? Where the hell could he really go? Charlotte? Atlanta? Washington? And do what? Ply the same trade in places that were many times more dangerous then here, become one of the dead-eyed souls that wandered the back streets and hustler bars selling themselves to whatever pervert or sicko had the price of a room or a warm meal.

We drove onto the main street of Cana, the old general store, the new discount grocers, the bank, the ten-room school that served grades one through twelve, and Butler's Motel, a modest five-room red brick strip on the side of the road, a last holdover from the town's past as a crossroads. It would do for the time being. I wheeled in and the boy looked at me. "Are we going in?" he asked, his eyes dropping to the floor. He did not mean to sleep.

"No, you are," I said emphatically. "You can stay the night here and go home in the morning—if you want." He nodded and smiled sheepishly, unaccustomed to any kindness. He started to get out, but I held his arm. I was already in this; like it or not, I had to do the rest.

"I'll come back tomorrow, before check-out. If you want to stay here you can. I'll be here a week...you can decide what you want to do then."

He kept his eyes on the floor and nodded. I reached across and took his chin gently in my hand, lifting his face to mine. He kissed me slowly, awkwardly. Kissing was an act in which he was not experienced. His eyes, blue and wet, lost their hardness and he smiled. I smiled too, then we went inside.

Levi

RICK SANDFORD

I was sitting outside and reading, clad only in some gym shorts but with my black dress hat on, when Moshe and Yitzchak stopped by. Because it was the Sabbath they were all dressed up. While we were were talking, my neighbor Dan left to go teach a tennis lesson. We exchanged amenities and then after he'd gone, Moshe turned to me, "Did you fag him?"

"No, I think Dan's straight. He has a girlfriend."

Moshe mulled this over, and I tried to take in what he had said: Did you *fag* him?

Fag had become a verb! How fascinating the mental process whereby the act that defined *faggot* had become *fag*. And I wondered, could *God* become a verb just as easily?

Did you *God* him? How funny—a *proper* verb. Maybe that was it—*God* could become a euphemism for *fuck*, for the ultimate experience we have as human beings. He *God* me in the ass. They *God* their brains out.

Of course, *God* should be the same for each tense. They had *God* one another. They *God* one another. They will *God* one another.

God you!

While I was contemplating these semantic possibilities one of the guys in the *beis midrash* walked by. All dressed in black, with his hat and dark beard, he really did look quite imposing, and I wondered if he was going to give me any trouble. As he passed by us I looked him in the eye and there was a moment when I thought he might say something, but he just continued walking.

Moshe wanted to see another book of pictures and so I went in the house and brought out Don Bachardy's *Last Drawings*, the pictures he drew of Christopher Isherwood during the last six months of Isherwood's life. Some of the drawings were of Chris without any clothes on and Yitzchak was amazed at this. "He doesn't have any clothes on!"

Moshe didn't understand it either. "Why didn't he put any clothes on?"

"Well, he was very sick, and sometimes it was easier to not have to get dressed, and the artist wanted to draw his whole body, not just his face."

As the boys continued turning the pages I became aware of the bearded man approaching us again, this time from the other direction. When he was beside us I looked at him and said hello.

He answered me very formally: "Hello."

"How's it going?"

"What are you doing?" he asked, gesturing toward the book.

"I'm showing them some pictures a friend of mine did of his lover just before he died."

"He's dead?" he asked.

I nodded. "The man in the pictures is dead. The artist is still alive. They lived together for thirty years. They met on the beach when Chris was forty-eight and Don was eighteen. Don is the artist. Chris was a writer, he was really famous. Have you ever heard of the movie *Cabaret*?"

The bearded man barely shook his head.

"It was based on one of his books. He went to Berlin in 1929 and wrote about it, just before Hitler came to power."

"You know him?" he asked.

"I knew him before he died. I know the artist, he's a friend of mine—we go to movies together."

The boys had looked up at the bearded man when we started talking, but after a moment or two they went back to looking at the pictures in the book.

"Is your name Rick?" the guy asked.

"Uh-huh, what's yours?"

"Levi," he said, saying the name under his breath and pronouncing it "lay-vee."

"Like one of the twelve tribes," I proposed, making my connections, "The priestly class, right?"

He nodded a begrudging assent, and then spoke to the boys, "What are you doing here? You should go home. Where do you live?"

The two boys stood up and moved away across the yard, resentful at being ordered around and yet somehow still respectful of this elder of theirs, but a moment later they were back.

"Are you going to talk about sex?" Moshe asked. "I know all about that."

"Go away for a minute," Levi said, but when they didn't leave he asked their names.

Moshe and Yitzchak didn't answer him and walked away across the street, apparently feeling that obeying a command was less onerous than giving away their identity. Were they afraid he might tell on them?

When they were out of hearing, Levi turned back to me, "Are you a homosexual?"

I nodded. "Are you?"

"We don't believe in that," he said.

I shrugged my shoulders and sighed.

"How old are you?" he asked.

"Forty. How old are you?"

"Twenty-four."

"Really? You're only twenty-four? You look so much older, with the beard and everything. Are you a *bochur*?"

He nodded his head.

"That means you're in the *beis midrash*, right? And you study the *Talmud*?"

He nodded assent to these questions, and I indicated the book he was holding, "What are you reading?"

"A book about the Rebbe."

"It's in Hebrew?"

He nodded again.

I raised the book I was currently reading. "I'm doing *The Varieties of Religious Experience* by William James. Do you know it?"

"I've heard of it," he said.

"It doesn't say very much about the Jews, though. Is your book about a specific Rabbi?" I asked.

"It's about *the Rebbe*, Rabbi Schneerson."

I shook my head, "Who's he?"

"He's our leader."

"Does he teach at the school?" I asked.

Levi shook his head. "He's the leader of all Lubavitch. He lives in New York."

"What's 'Lubavitch'?"

"That's our kind of Judaism."

"I thought you were Chassidic."

"We are, but there's many kinds of Chassidim. We're Lubavitch, and Rabbi Schneerson is our Rebbe."

That was interesting and I said the name "Schneerson" over again in my mind several times so as not to forget it.* "Do you think there's an English version of that book you're reading?" I asked.

"Why?"

"I'm interested. I'd like to read about your religion. I've already read the *Tanakh*, and a couple of parts of the *Mishnah*. What would you recommend?"

"A book about us? Have you ever heard of Elie Wiesel?"

"He got the Nobel Prize for Peace a couple of years ago. I have one of his books about the concentration camps, *Night*."

"He wrote a book about the beginning of our religion called *Souls on Fire*. You should read that."

"*Souls on Fire* by Elie Wiesel." I noted the title down on one of the back pages of my James book. When I looked back up at Levi, I changed the subject: "Are you a virgin?"

He didn't seem particularly offended by my question, and I could sense a certain curiosity about my motivation in asking it. Maintaining his eye contact with me, he barely nodded his head.

"I'm sorry," I told him. "You know, your sexual peak was at eighteen, and that's already six years ago."

"We don't believe in sex before marriage," he said.

"Is your marriage going to be arranged?" I asked. "I mean, will you have any say in the matter about who you get married to?"

"I'll have complete say."

"Hmm," I mused, and then I thought I might as well see if I could get to the bottom of the threat I had received. "The other day two of the guys came over here and told me I shouldn't talk to the kids. They said it was my responsibility not to talk to them, but

*Rebbe Menachem Mendel Schneerson has since died (12 June 1994/3 Tammuz 5754).

they didn't tell the kids why they weren't supposed to talk to me. And so I told the kids that it was because I wasn't Jewish, I was an atheist and I was homosexual."

"There's nothing wrong about the children speaking to you on the first two grounds. It doesn't matter that you're not Jewish or an atheist. The problem is your homosexuality—it's a sickness, a disease, and when it's acted on, it becomes a criminal act."

A sickness. A disease. A criminal act.

"What about my wearing *tzitzis* or a *yarmulka* or this hat? Since I'm not Jewish, what does that mean?"

"Nothing. They don't mean anything. For you, you're not a Jew."

"Really? *Leviticus*, the laws of Moses—they don't apply to me?

"You're not one of the chosen people."

That was the first time I had ever actually heard one of them use that term.

The Chosen People. The Master Race.

"Do you think your homosexuality is right?" he asked.

"I don't believe in 'right' and 'wrong,'" I told him. "I think those things—'good' and 'bad' and 'right' and 'wrong' are just arbitrary value judgments. Something that you might think is 'right,' I might think is 'wrong.' It's completely subjective."

Levi thought about this for a moment. The more I talked to him, and the more I was able to look at him, the more he became an individual. Underneath those clothes and that beard was a young man. He had a straight nose, a white but slightly oily complexion, and buried somewhere deep within his clear eyes was a human being petrified by existence.

"Do you believe in things you can't see?" he asked.

"Well, I don't know how the phone works, but when I'm talking to a friend I believe he's talking to me on the other end of the line."

"That's not belief."

"I'm sorry, then—what is your question again?"

"Do you believe in something that is beyond everything, something that you can't see, like God?"

"I guess I would have to say no."

"What was your religion when you were growing up?"

"Protestant. American. Middle class. During my most formative years I went to a Congregational church, and then we moved and my parents went to whatever Protestant church was closest to the house." I suddenly gave Levi a big smile, "You know what I was trained to do when I was a kid?"

"What?"

"I was taught to worship a Jew."

"Who?"

I looked at Levi incredulously, "What do you mean, *who*? Jesus, of course."

Levi continued to look at me impassively, but I think he was offended at this, at this insidious and inevitable connection. Jesus a Jew?

"I think that's one of the reasons why I'm so attracted to you guys. Even though I'm an atheist now, I still have this need inside me to worship a Jew and so when I see you—"

"Did you ever believe in God?" he asked, interrupting me.

"Oh yeah, when I was a kid. And then when I was twelve I read this book called *Elmer Gantry* by Sinclair Lewis—have you read it?"

He shook his head.

"It's a book about an evangelist, and in it he doesn't believe in God, and that was the first time I had ever come across the concept that you could doubt God's existence, and so for me at twelve it was like—well, if you could even *doubt* that God existed, then— then, 'He' didn't exist."

"Is your family religious?"

"Oh yeah, they're a mess. My mother was an organist in her church, and one of my sisters turned into a Mormon and the other one became a born-again Christian."

Levi thought about this for a moment, and then he asked me, "Is your father very religious?"

"Well, I don't really know my father. When I was growing up I didn't see him very much. When I woke up in the morning for school he'd already gone to work, and I was in bed before he came home at night."

"What did he do?"

"When I was a little kid he worked in restaurants, and then later he worked in a casino in Lake Tahoe—that's where I went to high school."

"So you were never religious again?"

I shook my head. "When I was twenty, though, I became a born-again Christian for a year. It was pretty pathetic. I hitchhiked around the western United States with a bible. And then one day I realized I was unhappy. I came back to Hollywood, and I met this boy I really liked and one day we were going past that big Catholic church—up on Sunset? And we went in and this boy said he was an atheist, that he didn't believe in God, and I loved him, or thought I did, so I said I'm an atheist, too. I've been one ever since."

Levi just looked at me for a moment. I felt he was trying to use my answers to reach some preconceived notion he had, but I wasn't sure what it was.

I suddenly thought of something else, "Oh, and that boy? That boy I was in love with? Well, he was raised Catholic, but he was adopted and I think he was really Jewish. He had curly brown hair and a big nose, and it's because of him that I've always been attracted to Jewish boys. You know: big noses, big cocks."

I could sense a war going on within Levi. He was being torn by his contempt on the one hand, and his curiosity on the other. I was just about to ask him if he had a big cock when he suddenly spoke up, "So you think of us as sex objects?"

"Some of you. There's a boy named Mendel who I think is cute, and there's a beautiful boy named Mordecai..."

"When was the first time you had sex with a man?" Levi asked.

"When I was sixteen, when I was visiting my grandmother in Phoenix. I was sitting out by the pool at her apartment building, and I was getting red and this guy asked me if I had some lotion for my skin and I said no, and so we went up to his apartment and he said—what?—oh, I remember, he said: 'I'll give you a blow job if you give me one.'"

"And you liked that?"

"Well, I had never had sex before. And I'd never jacked off before—I didn't start jacking off until I was seventeen, I started late—I'm retarded."

"What do you mean—'retarded'?"

"I'm just joking, I'm not really retarded, although I still don't shave on my cheeks. But I had never had an ejaculation, and so it was a little frightening to me, I didn't know what was happening. When I came, I remember he asked me, 'Is that it?' And then when I went down on him and *he* came I thought that he had cancer: I didn't know what his sperm was. Later, when I went home, I thought about it and suddenly everything I knew and had heard about sex all came together with my experience—and then I wanted to have sex again, over and over. But he didn't want to."

"Did you like it—did you like having sex?"

"Well, it was a little scary at first. I mean, at first I didn't really like the taste of semen, so you know what I did? When I jacked off I started eating my own cum, and after a while I really came to love it, and now I'm obsessed with it—I love the taste and texture of semen more than almost anything else in the world."

Levi glanced over his shoulder, back toward the school, as if he were afraid someone might see us talking together or overhear us. "When was the next time you had sex?"

I thought for a moment. "The next time I had sex was, let's see, the next summer—when I ran away from home and went to Hawaii. I stayed at the YMCA and had sex with some guys there. And then the next year I came to Hollywood and that's when I really started having sex a lot. It's just a rough guess, but I think I've had sex with more than two thousand men."

Levi's expression was absolutely unreadable. After twenty-four years in that Jewish environment he had mastered his ability to present a totally inscrutable face to the world.

"Have you ever had sex with a woman?" he asked.

I shook my head. "No. I've never had sex with a woman, I've never driven a car, I've never smoked a cigarette, I've never had a checking account or a credit card and I haven't seen TV since 1969: I'm very pure."

"What do you do?"

"I'm an extra, I'm a stand-in on a TV show."

"No, I mean, what do you do when—"

"When I have sex? Well, I'm a cocksucker, and I like to get fucked. I don't like to fuck. I think sex is a power game and I like to be the one in the powerful position—"

"So, men fuck you?"

I nodded. "You wanna see?"

Before he could answer I got up and ran into the house and found the magazine with the interview of me and the pictures from my porno films. When I handed the magazine to Levi he held it in his hands very gravely, as I turned the pages for him. He looked at the photographs with a magnificent impassivity. I could only glean his response by the questions he asked me.

"What about—what about the shit?"

"Well, if I know I'm going to have sex, I usually douche—you know, like an enema—so it's not usually a problem."

"Aren't you afraid of getting AIDS?"

I shrugged my shoulders, "I'm forty years old. I've had a really good life—"

"Aren't you afraid of dying?"

I shrugged my shoulders again, "Levi, I just can't go around being afraid all the time. It's boring. It's different for you, you're twenty-four, you have your whole life before you—you've never even had sex, so I can imagine, you'd be afraid of dying. You want to live. You want something in the future. I don't. I don't believe in the future. I just want to have fun. I want to have as many cocks ejaculating around me as I can. Unless I'm kidding myself, and I may be, I'm more afraid of getting old than I am of dying."

Levi thought about this for a long moment and then handed my porno magazine back to me. I couldn't tell what he was thinking. And then he suddenly asked me, "Are you happy?"

"Well, I think it's stupid, but—I took the Scientology personality test and I scored a hundred percent on happiness. It freaked the guy out who was giving me the test. He tried to sell me one of their classes because I didn't get a hundred in one of the other categories, but I told him I'd be afraid to take one of those classes because then I might jeopardize my happiness."

"Does your family know you're gay?"

I nodded my head, "They read my diary when I seventeen. And you know the man I told you about, that I first had sex with? Years later, when I was talking to my grandmother, she told me she thought she knew what was going on and she said if she had been sure, she would have had him arrested. Can you imagine?"

"Do you see your family very much?"

I shook my head. "I haven't seen them in about five years. The last time I talked to them I told them that until they stopped believing in God they didn't have a son. I told them I forgave them for the way they brought me up because they were stupid, but that I would never forgive them for bringing me into the world in the first place."

"So, you don't speak to your parents? You don't see them?"

I shook my head.

"Don't you think you're acting immature?"

I looked at Levi incredulously, "Levi, look at you! You're twenty-four years old—you're in the very bloom of your youth—and you're throwing it all away! Look at the way you dress and that

beard! You look like an old man. You should be going out and
having fun—having sex. If I'm being immature, I'd say you're
being *too* mature."

I suddenly remembered something I'd read in Ecclesiastes, and
I excused myself and ran into the house and got my *Tanakh*. A moment later I came back outside and opened it to a passage I'd
marked, and read aloud, "'Rejoice young man, enjoy yourself
while you are young! Let your heart lead you to enjoyment in
the days of your youth. Follow the desires of your heart and the
glances of your eyes.'"

Levi asked to see the book and I handed it to him. He looked
down at what I'd read, and then back up at me. "You didn't finish," he said, and read the next little portion, "'—but know well
that God will call you to account for all such things—'"

Levi handed the book back to me, and with that started back
across the street.

"But there is no God!" I called after him.

He didn't respond but just continued walking.

"It was nice meeting you!"

He mumbled something, but I couldn't hear what.

Although I'd clearly lost our little scriptural confrontation, on
some deeper level I felt I'd won. Even though he'd asked many
more questions than he answered, the intensity with which he'd
pursued his questioning had revealed an interest that *wasn't* im-
passive, and I think he knew it.

Moshe and Yitzchak had been playing in the playground of the
schoolyard and when they saw Levi walking away, they climbed over
the fence and ran back across the street to me. I slipped the porno
magazine into the book of drawings of Christopher Isherwood.

"So, did you talk about sex?" Moshe asked.

I nodded.

"Do you want to fag him?" he asked.

I watched Levi turning the corner at the end of the street, and
considered that. I nodded my head, "Yes, I think I would. I *would*
like to fag him."

Moshe laughed at the incredible picture of me fagging one of
the *bochurs*, and little dreamy-eyed Yitzchak squealed with delight.

Several weeks later when I was bicycling home from the movies I
saw one of the *bochurs* walking down the street by himself. As I got

nearer I noticed it was Levi, and I greeted him. He acknowledged
me, and I circled back around in the street to talk to him.

"I just got a book on Rabbi Schneerson," I told him, "because
you were reading one."

"What?" he asked.

I told him I would show him, and I struggled with my backpack
to get the book out, but before I could he said, "*Despite All Odds?*"

"Yes! What did you think about it, do you think it's any good?"

"Some of it's good."

"So, what do you think about New York?" I asked.

"What?"

"About the riots, about the Chassidic community—"

"What should I think?" he asked rhetorically.

I shrugged my shoulders. "I don't know. I'm really asking. All I
know is what I read in the papers, and you're on the inside—"

In Brooklyn, a few days before, a car in Rebbe Schneerson's
motorcade had gone through a red light and the driver, in an effort to avoid the oncoming traffic, had swerved his vehicle,
jumped a curb, and killed a little black boy. Within hours the
black community of Crown Heights was up in arms and had
stabbed to death a Lubavitcher from Australia. There'd been ri-
oting ever since.

"Are you a liberal?" Levi asked, as he continued on down the
street—answering my question with another question.

I equivocated a bit as I walked my bike beside him, "Well, I'm
way to the left of the Democrats, if that's what you mean."

"Do you like blacks?"

"I don't know," I began, a little uncertainly.

He redefined his question for me, "Do you like them as people?"

"Well, I don't know any blacks, really. None of my friends are
black," and I ran through the black associations in my mind. "I've
had sex with three black men. I'm not really attracted to them,
though."

"Do you know who Al Sharpton is?"

"No."

"Alton Maddox?"

"No," I said. "Who is Alton Maddox?"

"He's a big fat nigger," Levi put it bluntly.

I was listening: Yes?

"He wants to kill—people," Levi said.

I nodded. Jewish people, no doubt.

"They're animals," he said.

We reached the corner and stood there for a moment in silence. I made to turn away, but Levi asked me if I was in a hurry. It
was almost midnight and I had to be up at 5:20 in the morning,
but—no, if Levi wanted to talk, I was willing to listen.

We crossed the street and headed up Alta Vista toward my
apartment, where we paused.

"You rent an apartment here?" Levi asked.

"Yes."

Levi knew that: This was a stall of some kind.

"One bedroom?" he asked.

"One *room*," I clarified.

He was just standing there, and suddenly it occurred to me that
he might want to come in, and so I asked him, "Would you like to
see my apartment? Would you like to see where I live?"

He indicated he would.

This *was* a surprise. I lifted my bicycle and carried it up the
three steps of the walkway and led the way to #1. I stood the bike
on its stand, got my key out and opened the door and turned on
the light.

It wasn't as bad as it could have been although, after the night
air, it was very stuffy. The bed wasn't made and there were books
and clothes tossed around on it. The floor was relatively clear of
stuff, and the books on it were arranged in piles. The desk was
littered with notebooks and paper but, for the most part, they
were stacked neatly. Otherwise, the room was pretty much books
and more books, piled up, two deep, and lying everywhere you
looked.

I parked my bike in its place and stepped toward my desk as
Levi came in the room. "It's kind of a mess, but this is it. That's
my bed—I sleep with my head at the end, because that's what
one of the characters in *Ulysses* did. This is my desk—and my
computer—"

"So you *do* live in the modern world," he said.

"Yes, my computer and my answering machine," I said. "But
that's it. No TV, no car."

I pointed to the books on the bed to impress him, a whole selection of books about Jews: *Tanakh/The Holy Scriptures, The Mishnah, The Indestructible Jews* by Max I. Dimont, *Judaism* by Isidore

Epstein, *The Living Talmud/The Wisdom of the Fathers* selected by Judah Goldin and *Legends of the Hasidim* by Jerome R. Mintz.

"I thought you'd have posters," he said.

"Well," and I pointed to the poster above my desk, "That's *Follies*, that's the best musical I've ever seen, and a friend of mine gave me that one, *Without You I'm Nothing*, because I really liked that movie. *Sweeney Todd* is over there and that's Dublin," I explained, pointing to a large map on the wall, "Because I read Joyce, and I wanted to see where *Ulysses* took place."

[It wasn't until I started writing this that I realized he was probably thinking there were going to be posters of naked men all over the room.]

I looked around and noticed a photograph in a clear plastic frame propped against the wall. "Oh, and this is Aaron. He was my favorite Jewish boy," and I handed the picture to Levi to look at.

Aaron really was classic: the curly brown hair, the big nose, the full lips and sensitive eyes. Those Semitic ingredients that so often end in aesthetic disaster somehow combined in Aaron beautifully: He was the best Jew I had ever seen.

"He's dead," I explained.

"How did he die?"

"AIDS." What else?

Levi handed the picture back to me. He was very noncommittal. I didn't really know what to do, so I continued pointing things out. "Those are my notebooks by the desk, my Jewish books are over there on the second shelf. Oh, and this is my book about you guys," and I took from the bed the three-ring notebook they'd given us on the show I work on, in which I had arranged all my stories. I turned to the title page: *The Boys Across the Street.*

Levi feigned (or not?) indifference.

We sort of hovered in the middle of the room. There was no place for him to sit and I didn't have anything to offer him. As he started moving back outside I realized that we might never be alone again. I'd thought about this before and I'd resolved that if I ever got the opportunity:

"Would you like me to give you a blow job?" I asked.

He stared at me with that noncommitting look of his, and I suddenly got the feeling that this proposition of mine was the inevitable consequence of *his* conception of who I was—

"No."

The question in and of itself was *our* consummation.

"Well, you can't say you weren't asked," I told him.

He looked at me as we walked out toward the street.

"Would you be interested in that?" he asked.

"Well, sure. I mean, you're nice looking and you're a virgin, so—yeah, I'd be interested in giving you your first blow job. And you know, my experience has been that the men who are the most repressed have the strongest erections."

"I'm not a homosexual," he said.

I felt like leveling with him, "Levi—all my straight friends? They all like getting blow jobs."

"So, did you think I was going to say yes?" he asked me.

"No. I mean, I was ninety-nine percent sure you were going to say no, but I wanted to give you the experience, I wanted you to at least be able to say, 'This guy wanted to suck my cock. I knew this guy once who made porno films. He was a world famous cocksucker and he asked me if he could suck *my* cock.' That's all."

"I think you're crazy," he said, and we started walking together toward the corner on Waring.

I shrugged my shoulders and sighed: "Okay. 'Crazy'—meaning what?"

"I think you're absolutely out of your mind."

I shrugged my shoulders again, "That sounds like a negative value judgment. I know it doesn't have to be...."

"You're not normal."

"'*Normal*'"—I was contemptuous.

"You're not like most people."

"Who wants to be like most people?" and I turned on him: "*You're* not like most people."

"But you're not living the way you're supposed to."

"*Supposed*? According to who? I know, the *Torah*. The *Torah* says I should be killed."

"That's just about Jewish homosexuals. That isn't about you."

"Oh, only *Jewish* 'homosexuals' should be killed. It doesn't matter who *I* have sex with." I was indignant. "In this book I read, *Tefillin* by Aryeh Kaplan, it said that the world was created for the Jews—"

Levi acknowledged this: "God made the world for the Jews."

"But I want the world to be created for me, too."

"You're a part of creation—isn't that enough?"

I shook my head no. "*I* want to be a Jew. I want God to care about who *I* have sex with."

"Then you'll have to convert," he said.

I humbled myself before Levi with downcast eyes, "But I could never believe in God."

"So you'll never be a Jew."

I threw my hands up: What are you going to do?

"It's a waste of time your reading all those books about Jews," Levi said.

"What do you mean, it's a waste of time? I learn something all the time. I read Rabbi Schneerson's biography and then I open the paper and there's a story about him, and I already know about him. How can it be a waste of time?"

"You're sick," he said.

I held out my hands: Yeah, so?

"You read books and you can talk, you're not stupid, but you're sick. So why don't you kill yourself?"

I shrugged my shoulders again: What could I say? "I'm happy—why would I want to kill myself?"

"Because you're sick."

"Well, obviously I'm not 'sick.' But, if I were sick, I think I *would* kill myself—I'm not into pain and suffering at all. So, if I ever do get sick—"

"How would you do it?" he asked me.

That was interesting, and I *had* thought about it: "Do you remember hearing about that guy who set himself on fire to protest the war in the Persian Gulf? I thought that sounded pretty good. There's getting drunk and taking the long swim to China, there's jumping off the Grand Canyon—I'm not one for guns—"

"What about poison?"

"No. I really want to experience my death if I'm going to do it."

"Being a homosexual is like being a murderer—"

"Levi!" and I started to reprimand him, "Homosexuality is nothing like..."

"Can I finish talking, please?"

I acquiesced: Of course, *please.*

"A murderer has all these feelings building up inside him, but if he wants to badly enough he can stop his desire to kill."

"Levi, I was queer since I was a little kid—I didn't *choose* to be homosexual. It's a fundamental part of who I am. Your analogy is false."

"But you're not living the way you're supposed to."

"When I was a kid," I told him, "and I realized I wasn't like everyone else, you know what that made me do? It made me question everything, *everything*—and you know what I found out? I found out that everyone was lying to me: my parents, my school, my church, my country. When something comes from so deep inside you that it is beyond your understanding, then—that is the standard by which you must judge everything else."

"But it's not natural."

"Yes, it is—and you know why? Because it comes from *inside* me. Levi, you wouldn't know anything about 'God' or Judaism unless you read a book or someone told you about it—everything you know about being a Jew comes from outside you. *That's* not natural. I wasn't taught to be homosexual: I *am* homosexual, and that's a million times more natural than your being a Jew."

"You're talking about being an animal—"

"I'm talking about being a human being! And my wanting to have sex with another man is *not* the same thing as wanting to kill someone!"

"I didn't say that."

"Yes, you did."

"You can control your feelings," he said.

"I don't know where my feelings come from," I told him, "a murderer does. A murderer is involved in very specific situations to which he responds."

Levi considered me for a moment, and then he suddenly changed the subject, "Do you like talking to me?"

"Sure, of course. You're interesting, and what's really nice, compared to most people, is that you have a very definite point of view. That's exciting."

And then Levi spoke matter-of-factly what almost sounded like the supreme compliment:

"I learn things from you," he said.

"What?"

"I learn what homosexuals are like, why they are like they are."

"That's great. I think I'm a good representative for homosexuality. I've never been in a relationship, though. I mean, that is one way in which I am not like other queers. Most of the people I know may not be in a relationship, and maybe the ones they do have don't last long, but at least they've had them. I've never been in a relationship at all."

We were silent for a moment.

"So what's the upshot?" I asked. "What are you finding out about 'homosexuals'?"

"I don't think you saw your father enough when you were a boy."

He was giving back just what I'd told him the last time we'd spoken, no arguing with that.

A cab stopped at the corner, and as it pulled away the man who got out saw Levi and they greeted one another effusively. Suddenly Levi wasn't the dour, defensive and serious young man he always is with me. His eyes lit up and I could tell he felt let off a hook of some kind and was relieved that he had access to someone who could back him up. Levi introduced us and we shook hands. The guy's name was Danny, he was a Jew in his early twenties with reddish-brown hair, a frizzy beard, wire glasses, and—as opposed to Levi—a more practical, less ethereal sensibility.

"He's gay," Levi explained me to Danny.

Danny looked at me and I shrugged my shoulders.

Levi then defined my situation in more detail: "He's sick."

I spoke to Danny in a mock-whisper, "Our argument basically comes down to this: I think my homosexuality is below my consciousness, that it is pre-rational, and Levi thinks I have a choice."

Danny seemed to agree with me. "People don't know why they're gay. You probably don't know why you're gay."

"But you don't have to be gay if you don't want to," Levi interjected.

"But why would I want to have sex with a woman when I could have sex with a man? I think the erect penis is the most extraordinary thing in the world and I think a man's ejaculation is the most spectacular exhibition of life there is—so, why would I want to deny myself that?"

The use of explicitly sexual terms must have signalled a terminus for the conversation because Levi and Danny started back across the street, leaving me rather abruptly, without even saying good-bye.

"Good-bye," I called after them in an effort to fill up the sudden silence.

They looked back at me without answering.

And then I came home.

By paring down the civilities between us—by not saying good-bye—they affirmed between them that they weren't homosexuals themselves. I felt sure that if Danny had known I was queer before we were introduced, he wouldn't have shaken hands with me. A handshake validated me in a way that was not quite acceptable.

It was late and I had to be up early, but I had a responsibility to not let Levi slip through my fingers, so I turned on my computer and started writing.

Tomorrow would just have to take care of itself.

Love Problem

MATTHEW STADLER

Because I'm a man most people don't think of me as a lesbian. Technically, or whatever, I think they're right, but I like to call myself a lesbian. That is to say, I would like to call myself a lesbian here.

When I was a boy, a twelve-year-old boy living in a big house with my older sister and two brothers, and my sister had her best friend from school stay at our house for sleep-overs, I'd lie awake in my room listening to our drug-addicted neighbor playing Hendrix with his wah-wah. Late into the night, the various dogs were barking and the occasional sound of trucks rolled along the highway. Drunk kids in cars careened closer by, and their headlights shifted across my window. I lay there in bed, in the flickering darkness, trying to ascertain what my sister and her friend were up to. Hadn't they fallen asleep yet? It was almost two A.M. for god's sake, and they'd no TV or record player to keep them awake. I lay still under my blanket and listened intently to the empty sound of our house. The parents were asleep. Of course they were, with trust and a deep, abiding faith in the good nature of their children. They slept well, soundly and deep. My brothers were away somewhere, at parties or on trips, maybe sprawled and fucking in the backseats of those cars I heard swerving past our house. Where were they going? I wasn't interested. My sister was in bed, in the room next to me, with her girlfriend from school. Why did my heart beat so? It was only just becoming apparent to me that I had a body. The blanket was heavy against me. The house settled more deeply as the clock turned to three, and even our neighbor passed out and slept.

I crept from my bed wearing just underpants, wanting a friend just like me, and repeating an incantation: "We're lesbians, we're lesbians, we're lesbians." I felt I should be included too. I'd no dreams of bare breasts or glistening crotches, no strange postures or facial contortions burning in my mind. As I crept along the empty carpet toward my sister's room, rather, I think I imagined a sort of recognition and solidarity waiting for me behind her almost-closed door. I saw them leaning up from bed, naked and entangled, welcoming me into their club. I saw a moment of affirmation in their warm smiles, and their knowing glance toward me, their secret lesbian brother.

Later, when I had a love affair with my cousin, when he was fourteen, he told me he wished he could be a lesbian too. He said so after we'd made out in the toolshed of his family's house in Brooklyn the night I decided to quit college and move there. I was constantly alarmed by his precocious mind and gasped audibly, delighted by our shared interest in lesbians, and I wondered what it was that made the ladies so attractive to us. Sirens and dogs startled us, and we snuck back inside, careful not to wake the sleeping parents. We spent the night whispering and entangled in his bunk bed, crushing the small stuffed animals that had been his bedmates until I came along, and feeling not a little nervous because, well, I imagine you know why. I'm tempted to write only about him, because I love him so dearly, but my subject is lesbians. We were lesbians together, often proclaiming ourselves as such, and desperately waiting for others to proclaim it also. No one would. Convention and appearance conspired against us.

We tried disguises, employing makeup and mannish suits to complement our feminine faces, vying for attention at lesbian bars in New York and Boston. What we got we didn't want, and what we wanted was hard to ask for. "Hey, we're just a bunch of lesbians," I heard my poor cousin assert to a puzzled dyke, as he pushed her straying hand past his dead-give-away crotch. It wasn't an arousing stroke we'd gone there for, but an elusive inclusion, a shelter in some alternative to the manly strutting that seemed our lot in any male culture, gay or straight. Dateless, we returned to his bunk bed and undid our ties.

After my uncle found out and my cousin was taken to a psychiatrist I got a job serving drinks in a psychedelic bar on the West Side of Manhattan. I was miserable, shattered by the removal of my cousin, and unable to form coherent thoughts. It was a perfect job. I played sad Sam Cooke songs on the jukebox and shoveled cash into my pockets from the drunken teenagers I served beer to. They didn't know Sam Cooke from a lesbian, and I couldn't help them, inarticulate and deaf as I was to everything but the songs and the pay phone. Somehow, I figured, my cousin would call me on the pay phone. The cocktail waitress was straight, a sassy Barnard woman majoring in dance and French theory. "I'm in a sad mood tonight," I crooned to her each evening as we lit the pathetic table candles. At four A.M. the last band would stop playing and we'd shut the place, locking the door against the sour beer smell, and we'd walk down the street to the Empire Diner for a bite to eat. One night, while still rattling the door chains, we saw a car come careening down Twenty-ninth, knocking cans across the empty sidewalks, lurching and leaping at the curb. We stood near to the door and watched. The car slowed as it approached, and a drunk or drugged heavy-metal teen leaned out the passenger window, glaring at the two of us crouching together, and he yelled "Fucking lesbians!" I've never been so happy. Later the manager told me I was too gay and he fired me. Life isn't easy for lesbians.

It may simply be that I love my sister and envy her having a girlfriend, a big house and kitchen, loud friends, and a shelf of dog-eared lesbian fiction. I had a girlfriend (after my cousin left) but we didn't have a house. We lived in the meat market above a butcher in a building that used to be The Fuck Club. Men from Florida came each weekend in leather straps and boots, clutching xeroxed guidebooks, and asking us for drinks or a date. I apologized to each of them, and pointed them toward Hell Fire, across the street, where the bar was always open and wild dates could still be had. My girlfriend was a lesbian and I was inexperienced. She had a habit of dating any man our friend Oscar fell in love with. He loved me and lived with us, and we made him miserable. On summer Sundays we'd take the train to the beach together, fumbling through newspapers on the dirty platform, breathing the heavy smells of piss and exhaust in the stifling heat. Oscar and Debby wore colorful shorts and sunglasses, but I was still in mourning for my lost cousin. They took MDA and I took photographs and aspirin, setting my towel between them on the crowded sand, wondering where my affections lay.

Boyfriend to a lesbian, I lay in bed cherishing the taste of my own forearm, imagining it was the stomach of my cousin Max. Debby understood this, but it made her melancholy nonetheless. I spent my days bicycling aimlessly across the city, plotting an accidental rendezvous with Max, imagining what I'd say when we met. "Hi" seemed likely. Or "hello." The rest was tears and saliva. Jobless, I lived off the money my parents sent for therapy.

Debby wrote a play starring Oscar in his underpants with sad music I wrote grieving over Max. It was produced at a lesbian theater/bar/nightclub/bookstore/coffeehouse and attracted a large, diverse audience. *Home*, it was called, and Oscar spent most of the time gazing through a hung window frame into black fiddling with his shorts. Periodically actress/waitresses would billow tablecloths over a row of small round tables upstage while my sad music played. I had to press the tape button at exactly the right moment. One night Max came.

The girls were fluffing their tablecloths. The room was filled with that slightly nervous art-house silence. The music was sad. I saw him standing near the door, and thought of Sam Cooke and the pay phone. He was sixteen now and taller than before. His dark eyes and blushing face were so painfully handsome, and his loose T-shirt let me see the tender hollow at the base of his throat where I used to rest my tongue. His shirt had big black letters that read "No one knows I'm a Lesbian." But I knew, and I knew more, and nervously got up and left my station to go tell him. During the desperate months, in my darkest sadness, I'd lain in bed clutching his old shoe to my face, and written a cycle of stupid poems conjuring the flower of my frustrated love in sad phrases and arch line-breaks. Fragments came drifting to mind as I stumbled toward him, bumping tables in the hushed theater. I'd meant each word so deeply, but now they cluttered and clanked in the back of my throat like bitter metal chains. Why had I ever sent the villanelle beginning "I'd live in your mouth forever if you'd have me, and you've had me..."? I knew enough to keep quiet now and trust myself to his instincts. I needed only to make it across the room and reach him. I drew near and, wise child, he looked at me in silence for one brief moment, kissed me on each eye and stuck his hand down my pants.

Debby was so mad at me for leaving that night she got a new girlfriend whom she later dumped for a tattooed boyfriend with a habit. I couldn't help myself. Oscar was made to sing the sad tune during the billowy interludes the rest of that evening, and Debby had me replaced after that. I can't say that I blame her.

Max and I whispered in our embraces and went home to my place above the butcher's and made out. We arranged to go away for a weekend to my sister's house in Boston where we could talk all this over and understand what had happened.

These days we have books with stories of tender experimentation and discovery; characters are created who explore their sexuality, emerging from ambiguity into identity, clarity, whether gay or straight. It's all very uplifting. But my story isn't like that (and it's possible yours isn't either). Max wanted a last weekend of love because he'd decided never to see me again. I was too confusing. On the day we turned the clocks back he lay beside me covered with my sweat, pressing his face into my armpit and announced his departure. Now he lives in Buenos Aires and I have a new girl-friend, a golden retriever named Soda Pop, who's not nervous about love the way most people are. I cannot say what she means to me, but I welcome her eager affection, and always look forward to the times we spend together.

As a lesbian I can both tantalize men and stand apart from them; and while I know that is not the agenda of most women, it is, perhaps, mine.

Bitter Homes
and Gardens

LUIS ALFARO

1. Daughter

There is a great deal you do not know about me.

You only know me as the hostess at a world famous casino in downtown Las Vegas. A woman with perfect posture who hands out free miniature hot dogs to the millions of visitors at an oasis in the desert.

But I am more. So much more.

True, I have worked at this posture all my life, but when I turned thirty, I went to an experimental clinic in Frankfurt, Germany. I paid a scientist my life savings and he broke my back in fifteen different places. He then reset it perfectly and I briefly worked as a model for the J. C. Penney catalogue. My operation ensured a back as straight as a line. This, of course, is enough to constitute a life fulfilled, but I have lived more.

So much more.

I had a house once.

A stationary in a trailer park that was cable accessible.

I knew I had climbed a ladder when we got the cable.

Not a big one, but a ladder nevertheless.

My husband, the day laborer and heroin addict, was ignorant about the world but smart about holding up liquor stores. I accepted him as a fact of my life because men, they need this rush, this liquor store robbing, this adrenaline. Especially if it isn't football season. I am sure that if I had not met my husband I would now be working on the Strip. But that's life. A series of choices.

I killed a chicken when I was ten.
I had a dream one night. I think it was the queen of England. Yes, it was the queen who told me to kill a chicken for England. So I did. The next morning I awoke and killed poultry. That was the beginning of my days as a murderess. Little did I know that I would kill and kill again. And furthermore, little did I know that it would make me a feminist. A feminist! Can you believe that? All my life I slept on wooden boards in my efforts to have perfect posture in hopes that one day at the height of my desirability I could become a hostess. All I ever wanted to be was a hostess. But the queen of England told me to kill a chicken and I became a feminist.

It was a cereal box.
My husband, the day laborer and heroin addict, collected cereal boxes for leisure reading. One morning I awoke to find a kitchen loaded with cereal boxes. So, I poured myself a large bowl of milk. And the rage set in. You see, the milk had been poured. There was no going back.
Cheerios. Empty. Leisure reading.
Rice Krispies. Empty. Leisure reading.
Trix, Corn Puffs, Frosted Flakes. All empty. All leisure reading. In a fit of rage I killed my husband with my bare hands. Blood on my hands. The beginnings of my feminism. How did it happen? What drove me to it? I don't know. Only that something about being a housewife led me to murder. Sweeping the same floor that dirtied itself over and over again. Washing the same dirty dishes, picking up my husband's used syringes. It was a life of lies, empty promises. Hopes that never fulfilled themselves in the form of empty cereal boxes. I killed him like I killed that chicken.

In my own defense I must say that I prayed to the Holy Virgin for guidance. She confirmed that my husband, one of society's undesirables, must be killed. I couldn't be a housewife, a feminist and a hostess all at the same time. That ended a chapter in the life of a woman with perfect posture.

I was going to talk about the murder of my second husband, the insurance broker and street mime, but I have decided not to. One of the joys of being a feminist is that I don't have to talk about anything that I don't want to talk about.

Las Vegas has been good to me.

One day I hope to work in the Roman palace on the Strip. A backless toga is what I would be honored to wear. This causes much distress in my hostess/feminist support group. But I've worked so hard on this back. It deserves to be seen.

My mother says that I've paid more attention to my back than my husbands. It's silly and it's rubbish. These are the issues that women face in the modern world. When are my life and back mine and when are they my husband's? I don't know. The vertebrae is a very special gift. A series of bones that God puts together very carefully and distinctly. I was born imperfectly. But a clinic in Frankfurt saved my life. Never as a housewife or person with an imperfect back did I think of killing myself. Did Liberace kill himself? Did Mr. Wayne Newton kill himself? Did Siegfried and Roy kill themselves? Of course not. These are leaders in our community. Pillars in the entertainment industry. Of course they have not killed themselves and believe me, they have lots of reasons to want to kill themselves.

There are but three things that I have been in my life: a murderess, a feminist and a woman with perfect posture. Look at my back. Straight as a line. The vertebrae. A delicate little gift inching up our backs. I have always been poised for perfection.

2. Father

Has anybody ever killed a moose with their bare hands? Well, neither have I. I grew up in the middle of East L.A. and they don't have mooses over there. I don't even know what the hell a moose looks like.

Has anybody read *Iron John*? It's one of those men books. Sort of a *Fear of Flying* for us guys. I bought it because it's a best-seller. I wouldn't know what to buy if they didn't have those best-seller lists.

So, I've been having a dream about this book.

I'm killing a moose with my bare hands.

This moose is just a moose. Just one of the many stupid mooses in the wilderness and I'm killing it with my bare hands. And standing behind me are those ethical animal people and they're all white. And so of course, I pay them no mind, cause you know I work on a printing press and that's all I got on my back all day is white people. I ain't saying white people are bad. I'm just saying that all the Mexicans at work got white people on their backs. And maybe it's just coincidence but you just don't pay them no mind.

So, I'm tearing the moose apart and standing there in front of all the white people are John Bradshaw and Robert Bly. People healers. White Indians, I call them. Just standing there watching me. And they're crying. Sad tears rolling down their cheeks. And Bly looks at me and says, "Boy, you've really changed." And Bradshaw says, "Yes, you're a different man." And I feel real guilty for a few minutes there, but I finish killing the moose anyway. Cause the truth of it is, you have to make choices, and I know they're healers and all, but they're white people.

So, I don't know if the moose is the environment or white people or what. But what I do know is that things have changed. The woman I married is not the same woman I live with now. Changed.

The house I built. Built it with my own hands. Changed.

And this world. This world is changing. I don't understand it and I most certainly don't agree with it, but I know we have to live with it ONE-DAY-AT-A-TIME.

But I can see it.

I'm alive and I know what's going on. Okay?

I'm alive, I can see it and I know what's going on.

3. Mother

I wanna talk a little bit about desire.

Desire is memory. A time bomb that ticks with the kind of power that can blow up buildings. And one day it just fizzles out. Nothing.

And you forget just when it blew or how. and it doesn't really matter because all that really mattered was that it was ticking.

Yesterday, I turned forty.

I thought getting older meant getting wiser, but that's simply not
true.
Because it doesn't matter. when you're a housewife nobody cares
that you're smarter.
Not your husband.
Not the kids.
Not the Betty Crocker cake mix.
No one.

I thought that my body was changing in the way it looked at the
world, but I was wrong.
The change is in the way the world looks at my body.

Well, I just want to say that somebody lied.

Somebody promised that being a housewife, being a mother, has
its payoffs. But it doesn't.

I tried so hard not to be a broad and now I can't wait to be one. be-
cause the only women with real control in their lives are the broads.
The women with the tube tops.
The no makeup.
The no pedicure.
The no Summer's Eve.
The broads who kick in the T.V. set when that asshole, that role
model for all women, Sally Jesse Raphael, tells me I think too
much, I haven't cared enough, I haven't cleaned enough.
I bet you she's never made tortillas.
Well listen Sally fucking Jesse, Maybe you've got the pulse on how
rotten your life is, but you don't know shit about America.

Look at these hands.
Look at these.
Do you know what I've done with these hands?
I made a house with these.

Did anybody notice?
Not my father.
Not my husband.
Not my God.
None of those *men*.
These hands have done a lot. They used to make love to my husband. The other day I took one of these fingers deep inside of me and gave myself a Fourth of July fireworks in the living room at four o'clock in the afternoon. Right in the middle of "Geraldo."

These hands made these tortillas. Do you know how hard I worked on these? Do you know how many dozens of these I've made in my lifetime? DID ANYBODY NOTICE MY TORTILLAS? Just feel these things, goddamnit. I've got nothing to else to show for my life but these tortillas.
Well, my kids but ... never mind.
Tortillas are my biggest accomplishment and, believe me, I know that this body doesn't make them like she used to.
Can you hear the ticking time bomb?
What about you, Miss America?
What are you going to do when it all starts to droop?

Well I turned forty yesterday and my body is dying to be a broad. I guess I wouldn't be feeling this way if I hadn't married my childhood sweetheart. But I'm not bitter. Do you hear me? I'm not bitter. I'm miserable. That's a big difference. The difference between being a woman and being a housewife. Never forget that.

It's all here. Traces of America everywhere in this house. Talk show hosts and T.V. evangelists are deeply woven into the fabric of this house. "News at Eleven" is sitting on the love seat.

I saw two visions.
One was an old lady and the other was a little boy. They came to me in the same day, and that night I checked myself into Edgewood. That's why I love the world, 'cause it talks to you all the time. "The Home Shopping Club," it's talking to me. The guy down the street with the kiddie porn. I bet you he's got something to say to me. They all do. If I just open myself up to it.

The other day when I was taking the bus to see the ocean, I saw this little boy. Jumping up and down and banging himself on the head, real hard. Like the Ayatollah's funeral. And he was laughing, like he enjoyed it. Down on Olympic I saw an old lady. A bag lady that looked like my Grandma Consuelo out at the dump in Tijuana. She was crying. One of those long, painful cries of death. And she was banging herself on the head. Really hard. And you know what I thought? I thought to myself, that's me all right. Not the old lady.
Not the little boy.
Something in between.
That's the nite I checked myself in.
That's the nite I made the Kraft Macaroni and Cheese.
I'm getting better all the time. I even have a daughter who's half nuts. Someone to talk to. She's gonna pull me over to the other side. And when she does I'm gonna put on one of those *quincinera* dresses with the hoop and the lace and I'm gonna have myself a coming out. I'm gonna go down and rent that dress from the bridal place with the mural on Broadway. It'll be my coming out. Just like the guys in the gay bars. I'm gonna call my mom and everybody on the block and say, "Hey, you guys, guess what? I'm back. Just like I was in 1969. I went to somewhere like hell, like Hollywood and Western, and I'm back."

I lived to tell.
I saw the El Pollo Locos and the 99 Cent stores and the girls who throw up their dinners to stay skinny.
I saw the T.V. evangelists and the kiddie porno rings.
The Winchell's beggars and the Bob's Big Boy massacre.
I saw it all.
I saw anger and loneliness.
Sadness.
Ooh, the sadness.
I saw desperation and isolation.
I saw America. I saw America all over the place.

I saw my cunt.
The power that is my cunt. I reached down there and I tasted a force of nature. And it opened itself up to a pain. Something bigger and more painful than my four kids who raced through me.

I saw my mother and my dead father. I saw the roof cave in at my wedding. People crushed under centerpieces, wedding cakes and big slabs of marble.

I saw an interview with the top ten serial killers on "Hard Copy."
I did.
They were celebrities and we were nobody.

I saw this poor house with its carved wood and drooping arches. This house with its rooms full of memories and that attic full of sadness. I looked in the den and I saw my first kiss. Holding hands on the porch. Walking in the backyard. I saw my husband fucking me in the kitchen. That beautiful round ass of his. His body on top of mine in the breakfast nook.

I saw my daughter and she was smiling. God, how long has that been?

I saw it alright. All of it.
I saw America.

Love Is
Thin Ice

DAVID VERNON

Rob and I are on our bed having sex. Outside there is nothing but bad air, rapping at the window with its thick knuckles to get in. As he is going down on me I start thinking about the Menendez brothers and their ongoing trial. Actually just about Erik, there is something smarmy, something smug about Lyle that I can't quite put my finger on.

"Kurt, mind if I come up for air?" Rob asks.

"Keep going," I say. "Just getting good."

And I imagine that it is Erik Menendez that I'm with. We are not surrounded by Rob's fine walnut-colored furniture. I am in Encino, at the Menendez estate. Erik and I have just finished a game of tennis. Jose is at work and Kitty's at the therapist, so the house is shadowy and empty. Erik has just taken a shower and emerges from the bathroom, smelling of too much Dial soap and wearing a pair of white pressed jockey shorts. It is unspoken that whoever loses the tennis match has to service the other. "Tough luck today," I remind him. He falls to his knees. We have exactly twenty minutes for this to happen and to clean up before his father gets home from work. "Pronto," I call out. He is on his knees—his face in my lap. Then there is a rattling at the window. The sound approaches. "Erik," I call out. I open my eyes and see Rob's well-polished furniture surrounding me. Rob stops and sits up. The sound of the breeze hitting the window is the only sound in the room. "Erik who?" Rob asks.

"Sorry," I say.

Rob gives me a confused stare.

It is at this very moment that I realize our relationship is in serious, serious trouble.

"Will this bus take me to the Van Nuys courthouse?" I ask the glassy-eyed bus driver.

"Close to it," he replies.

It is five in the morning and the darkness underscores what will probably be another unbearably hot, five-alarm smoggy, fucked up September afternoon. There are only four other people on the bus—even so, I take a seat in the back. My heart is beating like war drums. I know that I'm doing something wrong, something illicit—but there is a rush that I can't deny. Rob's alarm won't go off until 6:30. He won't question the note I stuck on the refrigerator saying that I went on a hike before class. There are two traits that I love about Rob; he could sleep through an earthquake, and he has an undiminishing amount of trust in me as well as mankind. That and the tiny glasses he wears that seem like spotlights searching for his eyes, eyes that are always moist with compassion.

I became interested in the Menendez case almost from the beginning. The whole city was so flattened by the L.A. riots that I think everyone needed something sensational to focus on. But I had a more personal connection to the case. I have things in common with Erik and Lyle. My parents, you see, were also killed in the family house. An intruder. But I was in San Francisco. I had nothing to do with it. We were all going to San Francisco on a Thursday about four years ago. Frank, my father, had business that came up. I was restless. I didn't want to wait. I left on that Thursday and they were supposed to join me the next day. Then there was this intruder on Thursday night. So you see, like Lyle and Erik, I am in a deficit parental position. The difference is that they are probably guilty and I am probably innocent.

Rob and I met a year after all of this, yet he still feels very protective with me about my parents' death. I tell him that I don't care—that I was finished with them anyway. Once I told Rob that every boy wishes that his parents were dead, I'm just the boy whose wish came true. When I say things like that, instead of acting shocked, Rob looks at me with his pity face; and if looks could caress, this one would have me padded down with baby oil and nestled to sleep. Rob tells me that I haven't come to terms with

the death of my parents. That I haven't mourned. I tell him that
it's something I *plan* on doing, perhaps after painting the living
room and refinishing our hardwood floors. The truth is that there
are no tools that will assist me in dealing with the grief I own. I tell
Rob that I keep it in storage, just pay the maintenance. There are
no tools.

I arrive at the courthouse and scope out the line: five people
in front of me. Daylight hasn't quite happened yet. The woman in
front turns to face me.

"Who do you like?"

She is a tall, commanding woman in her late forties with
shoulder-length black, wavy hair. She wears a visor to keep the
sun out of her face. One look at her and there is no doubt in my
mind that she is a pro at attending court cases. She wears Sergio
Valente jeans and a white sweatshirt that reads, "SAVE OUR BOYS."

"Pardon?"

"Which one do you like, Lyle or Erik?"

"Erik."

"Me too," she sighs. "Poor Lyle. Nobody likes him. I would
change if I could, I'm always rooting for the underdog, you know,
but I can't change, now can I?" She shoves out her hand. "I'm
Bettina. I used to work at Hearst Castle, selling knickknacks, that
kind of thing, but you know, you've got to move forward. What's
your name?"

"Kurt."

"First time?"

"I borrowed my roommate's car one day last week, but I came
way too late. All the slots were taken."

"Here, sign my book." She pulls out an autograph book with a
photograph of Hearst Castle on the cover. "I'm keeping a record
of everyone I meet." She fishes out a handful of pencils from her
pocketbook, all of them with either "San Simian" or "Hearst Castle" on the side. She tosses them back in her purse and comes up
with a pen for me to use. I start to write my name on one of the
pages, but she stops me. "Not here." She shuffles the pages of
the book, then stops on one particular page. "There."

By this time others have arrived in line.

"That's it," someone from the back of the line announces. Two
minutes later a woman wearing a green jogging suit steps in line.

"No space. Slots are all full," Bettina yells at the woman as if she were an umpire and this woman had tried to steal home base.

"We've gotta look after each other," she says.

I turn and for the first time see the man standing behind me; tall, blond, almost white hair and the palest, most translucent skin that I've ever seen. He is like white sand. I almost need sunglasses to look at him.

"Want one?" he asks. He is eating something. "Little Debbie cakes. This one is a Fudge Round-Round. They make over a hundred and fifty kinds, the most popular being Swiss Rolls, followed closely by Nutty Bars, Oatmeal Creme Dreams, Zebra Cakes, Star Crunches and Devil Squares. Some are regional, like Little Debbie Sweet Potato Pies, sold only in the southwest." He hands me one.

"No."

"No what?" he asks feyly, licking the cream off his fingers.

"God, no," I reply.

"You may not think you want one now, but they'll win you over. They will," he says, teasing.

I take out one of my philosophy textbooks to read so everyone will leave me alone, but I can't concentrate enough to get any studying done. I feel guilty that I am skipping classes and lying to Rob. After all, he pays for what my meager trust fund doesn't provide. I sneak a glance at Bettina in front of me. She's finally gotten the hint and is taking a book out of her expansive purse. It's a paperback, called *Felony Bride.*

I continue reading my textbook and it occurs to me that there are just too many theories—and they all seem to say the same thing: The line between good and evil is a delicate, tenuous line. Rob is all good. He is unbearably handsome, dark brown hair that hangs over his face, his boyish looks edging toward middle age. He works as a social worker. He's the person they call out to accompany the police when there have been reports of child abuse. Rob has many projects. I am one of them. Rob Baum says that I am someone to be loved—sends me notes of inspiration in the mail, even though we live together. Rob promises me that my life will work out. Still, I feel like a brooding Judas, a bad vine that threatens to uproot the rest of the garden with my bad, thorny heart.

A few hours later we are finally escorted into the courthouse. The first time I see the brothers my heart feels electric. The

Menendez brothers just a few feet away. Rob would never understand this—I barely understand this, yet it feels inevitable, being
here.

The day itself is uninvolving. At one point a mention was made
of what Jose and Kitty's bodies resembled after the gunfire. It occurred to me that I had never seen the bodies of my parents after
they were killed. I think someone asked me and I decided against
it. I wanted to picture them as I last saw them, involved in the
mundane aspects of life—defrosting meat, picking up the dry-
cleaning, absently kissing each other good-bye.

All day during the proceedings I keep hoping for a moment
for my eyes to lock with Erik's; a moment he would take me into
his life, perhaps even come to recognize me, miss me on days
when I'm not here. For the most part he keeps his gaze straight
ahead, once or twice passing a secret whisper with his brother.

As I am leaving a voice calls after me. It is the blond guy.

"I thought you'd wait."

I keep walking and he follows.

"Wanna do something?"

"I need to get back."

"Wanna come over and have some Little Debbie cakes? If you
tried them, I know you'd succumb to their charms."

"Another time."

"My name is Drew," he says. "As in, another time, Drew, or
thanks anyway, Drew." His tone verges on dangerous. He keeps
following me. "I love this city. Born and raised," he says.

As we're walking, someone hands us both a yellow flyer. It's for a
Homeowner's Financial Service. The bold print on top reads:
CAN'T WE ALL JUST GET A LOAN? A homeless man walks past us and
asks for change. Drew digs in his pocket and gives the man a dollar.

"Especially homeless people," Drew says. "They're angels, you
know."

We arrive at the bus stop.

"Until tomorrow," he says.

"I have classes," I tell him, praying for a bus, any bus. "If you
miss too many you get dropped."

A bus inches toward us.

"I'll see you," Drew says the way an adult talks to a naughty
child. "You're hooked. You know. This is your Woodstock. Your
most significant event, besides meeting me."

Once on the bus I am trembling with fear and exhilaration—too wired to sit down even though there are plenty of seats.

I get home and Rob is in the kitchen preparing dinner. He races around several steaming pots, checks out a chicken roasting in the oven, then returns to the counter top where he is creating a salad. It's always fun to watch him cook—he always has too many flames going at once, and everything is just threatening to boil over or burn.

Over dinner, Rob tells me about a case he was working on today. I try to listen attentively, even though I am bursting with the concealed excitement of attending the Menendez trial.

"You should have seen this kid today, Kurt. He was only seven. I asked him when he was going to be eight, and he just shrugged. He said that they don't get a birthday every year. God, it broke my heart. The mother's boyfriend has been hitting the kid. The mother said she didn't know anything about it, and I believe her. I told her that either the man was going to move out of the house or I had to take the son away. I took the boy to his grandparents' house until it gets sorted out. He'll be okay there. God, he was so cute, though. It just broke my heart."

"Sounds like you did the right thing."

"I hope." Rob eats his dinner vigorously, seeming to gain pleasure from each morsel. "How was your hike?" he asks.

I hesitate. I wonder if he is asking me this because he knows that I'm lying, wants to catch me further in a web of deceit.

"Hiking was good."

"Looks like you got some sun."

"Guess so."

"It looks good on you."

Then Rob asks me about my classes. I find that the very first lie out of my mouth stings, leaves a metallic taste. But every lie after that gets easier and easier, flows out with the elegance and grace of a fashion model on the runway. I pick at my salad and tell Rob all about my day at school.

The next day in court is relatively uninvolving. Much of the time is spent on arguments over whether or not to admit some of Dr. Orziel's audiotapes as evidence. I sit as far away from that Drew character as possible. He frightens me. I spend much of the morning staring at Erik. I am fascinated at how still he is. He doesn't squirm in his seat or scribble on the legal pad that sits in front of him on the desk. Again today, he never once looks my direction.

Bettina has invited me to lunch with a few of the other regulars, so when the court breaks I maneuver my way over to where the group is meeting. Drew grabs me by the elbow, looks like he's about to make his pitch, but before he can say a word I tell him that whatever it is, I have other plans.

The special of the day in the courthouse cafeteria is enchiladas. There are six of us at the table, and all of us have ordered these enchiladas that lie helplessly on the Styrofoam plate, pinned down by a pool of rust-brown enchilada sauce. Bettina introduces me to the table. There is Pearl, a housewife from Arcadia; Sean, a man in his early sixties who has just retired from being a postal worker; Dawn, a twenty-year-old waiflike thing with dyed black hair who claims to have an ongoing correspondence with Lyle Menendez; and lastly, Gail Ann, a woman who collects all the newspaper clippings about the trial. Gail Ann's scrapbook is so extensive she even sells packets to the press. I eat my enchilada and listen to the conversation rallying back and forth across the table.

"That *L.A. Times* article yesterday was the worst. They are so biased, it's unbelievable!"

"That dress that Leslie Abramson was wearing yesterday, I saw it in Loehman's. And it had been marked down for the third time."

"You'd think with all that money . . ."

"If they make a movie, I hope they get someone handsome to play Erik."

"Like Timothy Hutton."

"All those boys who played the Billionaire Boys Club were all so ugly."

"It looked like juror number two was falling asleep today."

"Someone's writing a story for *Vanity Fair.*"

"No jury would convict these two boys."

Bettina finishes every bit of her enchilada, wiping up the last bit of sauce with a biscuit. She shows the group a new T- shirt she bought from a street vendor that says, FREE LYLE'S HAIRPIECE.

"Isn't that awful?" Gale Ann says. "How much was it?"

"Twelve bucks," Bettina answers. "A person could make a bundle out there if they had a concession stand. That's the wave of the future, you know. Some people don't even go to the museums, they just go straight to the gift shops. There's a mint to be made in merchandising. When I worked at Hearst Castle, they sold enough pencils, T-shirts and stuff to make three or four castles."

Listening to all of this, I feel like I'm going to scream. These people are fraudulent, drifting from one sensational event to the next. They have nothing to learn from this trial. They are the crowds of people throughout history, the Romans at the Coliseum watching the Christians thrown to the lions. Indeed, if Bettina had lived in Biblical times, she would have been the person at Jesus' crucifixion with the concession stand. Beefy tees. Photo coffee mugs. She'd be the one with the large painted canvas of Jesus on the cross, a hole cut out where his head should be and a line of tourists waiting for the two-dollar Polaroid. I see Drew sitting at a corner table by himself. I regret not having lunch with him today. He makes me queasy, but whatever he is, he's the genuine article. I excuse myself from the table and go over to join Drew.

It is hard spending the night with Rob and keeping the day's events under my hat. Just like my parents, Rob has no ability to sense what's going on in my life. But still, in all my nightmares of falling from the sky, it is always Rob who catches me. I put much stock in the belief that one day, given the opportunity, Rob will save me. It's not much of a religion, but it's my religion.

A Lana Turner movie is on TV. Rob sits on the white Ikea couch and I sprawl out in his lap. In the movie, Lana plays Kit, a woman of a certain age who wears flowing Edith Head gowns that make her look like a butterfly from Palm Beach. Kit is married to a megamillionaire played by Cliff Robertson. She loves him and his money, but still she has a sweet tooth for underage beach-bum gigolos. One such gigolo has turned up drowned and a police inspector questions Kit, who claims never to have dallied with the young thing. But in the boy's pocket was a bracelet with the inscription, *Love Is Thin Ice. Kit.*

"What religion are you?" Drew asks, his stringy blond hair a foul kite in the valley breeze.

"Was Catholic." I say.

"Was, yeah, right," he says.

"I stopped," I tell him. "One day I told my parents that I didn't want to go anymore. That was it, they never made me go back. I wish I had something like that in my life now, you know, like a religion or an AA meeting or a gym membership. For the structure."

"That's important," Drew nods.

We're at a Denny's not far from the courthouse. I've been ditching my classes for the past two weeks and going to the trial. It is late October. I told Rob that I've joined the track team. He bought me a pair of Nikes. Drew and I have been hanging out, one day even ditching the trial completely at lunch to go to El Coyote, which, as Drew told me, was the restaurant that Sharon Tate went to the night before she died. I'm nauseous all the time around Drew. Yet I hand it to him, he notices everything, even things that aren't there.

"Do you want to come over and have dinner?" he asks. "I've got some Mrs. Friday's Fan-tailed Shrimp."

"I've got to get home," I say.

"Do you want to come over and have sex? Forget about the Fan-tailed shrimp?"

I look away, horrified. At another table, a waitress explains to a group of black teenagers about their policy to demand payment *before* being served.

"I've never cheated on my boyfriend," I say cautiously. "I don't think I should."

"I'll bet he's cheated on you," Drew sneers. "Dozens of times."

This makes me laugh, breaks through my nervous skin. "Rob? Never. You have to understand, Drew, this relationship is what holds me together. Once, though, I woke up in the middle of the night and he wasn't in the bed. I heard the TV on in the living room. I walked in and caught him masturbating. He was so horrified. I thought that he was watching some porn tape; turns out he was jerking off and watching the infomercial with Don Lapre, the guy who has those cassettes about how he made millions operating his own phone services."

"Where do you guys live?" Drew asks, eating a Little Debbie's Marshmallow Pie and drinking a swig of ginger ale.

"Not far. We're at the Northridge Meadow Apartments."

"I know the place. Which floor?" Drew asks.

"Bottom."

"Maybe I'll visit you sometimes," he says, smiling, revealing a mouth full of crooked teeth.

Once, months ago, in bed, I told Rob that I had killed my parents. He gave me a look that consisted of three parts sympathy, one part anger.

"Of course you didn't do it. You were in San Francisco that night, Kurt. I don't know why you tell me things like that."

"Sometimes I imagine doing it. I picture myself doing it."

"It's just guilt popping up," Rob said. "Guilt for not feeling grief yet."

And he was right. Since my parents were killed I felt many things but I've never felt grief. Not a sprinkle.

It's been three weeks since I've started attending the trial; three weeks of missing classes and lying to Rob and there have been no repercussions at all. Everyday I come home drunk with worry that there will be a message on the machine from a teacher or classmate—or one of Rob's friends might have seen me on Court TV, in the audience. Nothing.

Today in court a cousin of Lyle and Erik's told how even as kids they were always brats. During the break, Pearl, the housewife from Arcadia, tells me that the regulars are putting together a scrapbook of pictures and personal remembrances. The group has bonded. After the trial they're planning a trip to Tahoe. I admit, it feels good to be included. As Pearl is telling me this, Drew is in the bathroom.

"We'd love to include you. But not your friend. We, being the group, don't like him."

I lean over and whisper to her, "Well, we, being all the collective me's, don't especially like him either, but I'm hooked. He's sorta like a bad trial. I can't wait to see how it turns out."

Drew and I decide to skip the rest of the trial today and walk around the Northridge Fashion Mall. Drew says that this is the most beautiful mall on earth. Even prettier than the one that has live birds living in it. That one back east.

Outside, a homeless man asks for change. Again, Drew searches his pocket and gives him a dollar.

"They're angels, you know."

"So you've said."

"No, really. I know this. They're angels but they're trapped here on earth. Angels who have shown lapses in their judgment. They lead a tortuous life. Poverty, hunger, all the bad stuff. But when they die, it's like they've served their penance and they can go to heaven. But if they freeze to death, then they never get to heaven. They're on ice, they're stuck. So every winter I try to help out, do my share and liberate a few of them."

"Liberate?"

"Help them get to heaven before they freeze." Drew makes a motion of a knife being stabbed then twisted. "Only takes a moment, and boy, do they appreciate it. They can't commit suicide, you know. I'm just racking in those frequent flyer points to heaven," he says.

I move away from him, so nothing is touching. I want to block out what he has just told me. "Do you really do that?" I ask, my voice unsteady.

"Sure. Maybe you'll come with me. It'll be winter soon."

"It's only late October," I say. "And it's still warm."

"Just around the corner," Drew says.

I stay away from the courthouse for a few days to get my bearings. I tell Rob that I'm sick. That my equilibrium is fucked up. He buys me Welch's grape soda. It's what my parents used to bring home when I was sick.

Thursday I go back to court. I dress in a suit. I think it's a suit. The pants are pinstriped but the jacket is solid. Nothing seems to match. I've forgotten how to dress. I stay away from Drew in line. Wear a Walkman. Inside I sit next to Bettina and let her talk nonstop. Drew comes over, waves and says in a lover's voice, "Miss me?"

I say flatly, "I don't know what you're talking about."

During court, Erik talks about the sexual abuse he suffered from his father. There were four types of sex: "Knees," which was oral sex; "Nice," which was massages; "Rough Sex," which was when his father would stick needles and pins in him; and "Sex," which was actual fucking. Erik weeps. For a moment, I almost feel his pain, for a moment I almost feel something. Then Bettina leans over to me and points to Erik and says, "Liar, liar, pants on fire."

Outside after the session, the Van Nuys sky is shady, unforgiving. I'm walking to my bus stop when Drew catches up with me. He starts circling me. I don't know what he's doing until I realize that he is mocking the TV reporters that hoard and harass the court participants. He holds an imaginary microphone up to my face.

"Just one question, please, just one question."

I stop and look at him patiently.

"Are your clients guilty?"

"Of course they are," I say grandly, imitating Leslie Abramson.

"Do they have nightmares?"

"They sleep like pups," I reply.

"Do you have nightmares?" Drew asks. "Do you, Kurt? Do you have nightmares?"

I walk away. He follows me and keeps shoving his coned hand in my face.

"Did you kill your parents, Kurt?"

"No."

"You wanted them dead?"

"No."

"Did you kill them?"

"No."

"Do you even give a shit?"

"I don't know."

"Do you care about anything?"

"Fuck you."

"Is anything worth caring about?"

"Leave me alone."

"Do you want to come over to my house?"

"No!"

Drew grabs me by the shoulders. Holds me in place.

"I said, do you want to come over to my house?"

"Sure," I whisper finally.

Drew's apartment is dark. Most of the lightbulbs are out. My shoes peel away from the sticky floor each time I make a move.

"Water's out," he says.

The apartment smells like old cat litter. He instructs me to sit on his unmade bed while he goes into the rest room. The room feels hot, oppressive, like the heat is angling down, ready to pounce on me. Drew emerges from the bathroom naked. His entire body is white, hairless. He resembles one of those plucked Foster Farms chickens from the supermarket. Drew sits next to me. I'm shaking badly. "Cold in here," I try to say, but it comes out unintelligible. Drew strokes my hair for a few minutes then looks me in the eye and whispers, "Knees." It takes me a moment before

I know what he means. "Knees," Drew repeats. I move down on
my knees and put my lips around his cock. Drew has me get up
and take my clothes off. "Nice sex," he instructs, then lies facedown on the bed. I start massaging his bony back, kneading his
muscles. I look outside and see that it is getting darker. Drew instructs me to lie in his spot on the warm bed, facedown. He goes
into the next room. I hear him search through a drawer. When he
returns I peek over my shoulder and see him cupping a handful
of thumbtacks and a jar of Vaseline. He kisses my ear. "Rough," he
says, like a chant.

"Rough," I tell him back.

When I get home, it's after midnight. Rob is asleep. I come into
the room and apologize for being late. He says that he was worried; that I should have called, then he's asleep again.

On TV, the channels are bulging with stories of firestorms
torching all across southern California. Houses are being eaten
alive. People are running down the highways, fleeing the devasta-
tion. People are just running.

There is a panic, a quiet panic that is bubbling inside of me. I
need to talk to Rob. Some kind of dread is consuming me, gnaw-
ing at me from every angle. I feel the need to join those people, to
run out my door and flee down the highway. I need to talk to Rob.

I climb into bed with him, shake him. He opens his eyes.

"What is it?"

"I have no family," I tell him. "They're dead and I miss them so
much."

Rob moves me to his chest.

"I have no family. I have nothing I believe in. I feel like I'm
going to die." I pull closer to Rob's chest. I'm crying like a crazy
person. "It's true. I loved them. They're dead."

I look up at Rob—his hair mussed. I'm looking for the words
that will come out of his mouth that will embrace me.

"Have you been drinking?" he asks.

I shake my head no.

"Sleep. Just go to sleep. Okay? It'll all be different in the morning. You'll see. Sleep."

We spoon. In two minutes Rob is back asleep and his hands
wrapped around me feel rigid like a corpse. He snores. When I do
finally sleep, I'm awakened by a rapping at the window. I glare at
the clock. It's five-thirty in the morning. I get up and look at the

window and see Drew dressed in winter clothes. He motions for me to come outside.

I put on a robe and meet him out front. "What the fuck are you doing here? And dressed like that?"

"It's snowing," he says, like a little kid.

I take in the air and see that there are ashes flying everywhere. Parts of Santa Monica. Parts of Riverside. Thousand Oaks. Circling, commingling, parading around the air.

"It's winter," Drew says and smiles at me with a sixth-grade smile.

I go back inside and dress in my wool slacks and my thick pullover sweater that my mom bought me for our trip to San Francisco. I put on a scarf and return to Drew.

"Now come on," he tells me, waving his arms in the air, his black winter coat covered with white. "We've got work to do."

The Seizure

PETER CASHORALI

"Which way?" Mark asks. Mark and Ricardo are driving on Melrose and the traffic is sluggish, even this late on a weeknight. People window-shop, cruise, just enjoy being in the strip of open shops and activity. Mark stops as a trio of guys in painted leather jackets steps into the street at mid-block, one with his palm raised to halt the cars.

"We're not there yet," Ricardo says, checking out the guys as they pass in front of the headlights. "Keep going." It's not his usual rapt appraisal, just a distracted glance. One of the jackets has a Byzantine Virgin and Child on it, their faces almost black against gold leaf. Mark drives on. "I'm glad you wanted to come with me tonight," Ricardo says.

Mark grunts, not sure "wanted to come" quite catches his feelings about tonight, not sure what would. What do you call the territory between terrified and obsessed? Anxious probably.

"You're sure you're going to be all right there?" Ricardo asks, peering at him from a tapestry of cigarette smoke. His face, a handsome full moon, is wide open to catch information Mark may not be interested in sharing.

"I'll be fine," Mark says, hearing his own voice. It's calm, reserved, the voice of a man looking up from a day-old newspaper. An Anglo voice, coming out of a face from the Mediterranean. "How about you, pal? How are you doing?"

"Nervous," Ricardo admits, unusually candid. "But Randy made me promise a month ago I'd come and give him a cleansing tonight. More than a month ago," he adds, wistful.

Since Mark tested positive he's only seen Randy twice. Once was just a glimpse, at the Gay Pride parade. The second time was toward the end of summer. Mark was reading in the yard behind Ricardo's shop, the screams of the parrots and macaws turning the air to confetti. Randy's flower shop on the alley shared the backyard, and Randy, on his way to trade Ricardo a joint for a favor, stopped to say hi to Mark. Though Randy was just out of the hospital from another bout of pneumocystis, his body wasn't one of the sticks-and-string bundles that so many men became as they fought infection after infection. He was all wire, his face still tight with intent, if more thoughtful than Mark had seen it before, as if he had so many things on his mind he had to exercise a little care not to lose any. They talked about, what? Nothing important. That Randy hadn't seen Mark for a while and what was Mark reading, anything good? Mark hadn't mentioned he was positive, and feeling more fearful than he had since he was a little kid, Mark talked about his status to his friends, not the world at large, and Randy was just someone Ricardo knew.

But Mark looked into Randy's face and saw a message for himself there. It wasn't "I'm going to die" and it wasn't "Let's pretend nothing's going on," though Mark saw those messages often enough in other faces, his own included. Behind Randy's blond widow's peak and the crinkles just starting to dig in at the corners of his eyes, Randy said and never stopped saying, "I know, but I've got a business to run and friends to go out with and I need to get laid. And so do you." So tonight, Mark is accompanying Ricardo to Randy's house, uncomfortable or not, because he wants to look into Randy's face and see if that message is still there.

"Alright," Mark says as they cross La Cienega. "Which street is it? Are we close?"

"It's, let's see," Ricardo says, watching the corners pass as if he's going to pull the right street out of a hat. "That one."

"Shit," Mark says, not sure which one he means and hitting the brakes. "Which one?"

"Oops, no, I mean that next one." Ricardo refuses to notice the names of the streets, and early encounters with nuns—who interpreted the pen in his left hand as a spiritual state in need of correction—have given him a grudge against the distinction of left and right. He relies entirely on visual cues, which makes him a harrowing guide. Mark groans but it deepens into a growl.

Ricardo puts his hand on Mark's shoulder. "Let's not be mad at each other tonight."

"All right," Mark sighs, letting go of it. "Which way do I turn?"

"That way."

It turns out to be a left, and Mark finds himself on one of the narrow side streets that feed into Melrose. The neighborhoods here make him think of Holland, the houses small, old for West Hollywood, not crowded together so much as just extremely cozy. "That's it," Ricardo says, pointing. "The one with the queen palm in front."

"Great," Mark frets, anxiety dancing in his stomach. "Where are we supposed to park?"

"Just go down the block. There'll be something," Ricardo says, craning his head around as they pass a white house with a thick palm tree almost pushing it out of the way. "Baby's here already: there's his car."

Mark finally finds a tiny bit of space left over between a Volvo and a Rabbit. He backs into it, parallel parking even more of a trial than usual. He can't get close enough to the curb, his hands like blocks of wood on the wheel. Ricardo watches him swear and struggle for a few minutes, then says, "You don't have to talk with anyone if you don't want to. You can just be there with me." He strokes Mark's leg. "Come on, we're parked enough."

"All right," Mark concedes, giving the wheel a final twist. Randy's friends will be there. When Mark came out in the early seventies, he thought every gay man should be what Randy's friends are: independent and loyal to each other, canny, intrepid in following their pleasure to its source, like explorers tracking the Nile through the regions of the interior. It's a paradigm Mark's always kept, though not always lived up to. Now the men he once wanted more than anything to be like are either dying out or evolving in ways that couldn't have been predicted, like a species of dinosaur changing into either fossils or birds. Men who once wondered about the source of pleasure are now facing off against the federal government and its police, taking care of strangers, wondering where the spirit goes when it spreads its wings.

Ricardo gets his big canvas bag out of the backseat, checking for the hundredth time to make sure he's got everything he needs. He starts up the sidewalk wearing the white denim duster one of the *santeras* made for him, but spots a weed growing from a crack in someone's driveway. It turns out to be one of the thousand plants he has a use for, and he uproots it, taps it on the cement to remove the dirt, and drops it in his bag. Mark jams his hands into the pockets of his jeans and follows. Ricardo was earning his pocket money in the other world when they met during their first year at Los Angeles City College, reading tarot cards at The Sorcerer's Shop. Later he threw love spells for customers at his parrot shop ("I'll need his photograph. Without clothes: it makes the spell stronger"). But he doesn't joke about Santeria, and Mark's never really been sure why. Perhaps it's just that the times changed and the moment for dabbling and sampling passed. For whatever reason, Ricardo has gotten serious; Mark can hear it in the stories he tells when they're lying in bed at night, stories about the *orishas*, the deities of Santeria. They're becoming harder to follow, practically incoherent, and he understands Ricardo is telling the stories from the inside now.

Ricardo reaches the door first and rings the bell, then says, "Oh, before I forget. Here, put this in your pocket." He hands Mark a small green leaf.

"What's this?"

"*Siempre viva.* Just put it in your pocket."

"But what's it for?"

Ricardo looks at him as if Mark's retarded. "Protection."

The door opens and it's Baby. "Come on in," he says.

Ricardo does and Mark follows, his face losing all expression the way it does when he's uncomfortable. "Hello, dear," Ricardo says quietly. "How are you doing?" Baby shuts his eyes, tilts his head back and says, "Ohhh," as if bringing a bucket of ore up from the depths of a mine. Ricardo sets down his bag, hugs him, is hugged back, and as they embrace a burst of laughter—two? three people?—comes from the next room. An elegant white room screen is unfolded just inside the doorway. "Mark," Baby says, turning to him. "Thanks for coming."

"Sure," Mark says, and then, feeling like an elephant venturing into a narrow corridor, he says, "I'm sorry."

Baby smiles, a brief tug at the corners of his mouth. The lines in Baby's face take Mark by surprise; they look delicate and fresh, as if they've only just been cut. Baby started out a grade lower in high school than the other men in the group. This is the first time Mark's seen him when he wasn't wearing his mirror sunglasses and army fatigue cap. It's like meeting the actor who plays Baby, a man who is nothing like Baby and must be close to forty, with a name like Bill or Robert on his driver's license.

A panel of the screen folds back and Arthur comes out. "Jesus Christ, it's the witch doctor," he says, his voice tired and grainy. He pulled Ricardo to him for a hug. "I'm glad you're here," he says, kissing the top of Ricardo's head.

"Arthur Thompson," Ricardo murmurs. "I promised."

"Yes," Arthur says, patting his back. He turns to Mark. "Mark, it's nice to see you again." The dark clouds under his eyes contrast oddly with his tan face, wheat-sheaf hair.

"Hi, Arthur," Mark says.

"So," Arthur says briskly, then falls silent and stares down into the carpet, perhaps checking to see if anything there needs attending to. "Well," he says, looking up again, "are we all ready?"

"I brought everything. We just need to light the charcoal," Ricardo says.

"All right. Good." When Arthur raises his eyebrows his forehead breaks into ripples; he says, "Mark, I'm afraid we're going to have to ask you to entertain yourself for a while. I know that's rude, but . . ." He expresses how unfair things sometimes are with a lifted shoulder, an upturned palm.

"No, that's okay," Mark says. "The cleansing."

"Well, family, more than anything, I'm afraid. But we'll have champagne later on, and I hope you'll join us for that."

"Sure, Arthur," Mark says.

Ricardo says, "Okay," and picks up his bag. Arthur takes him into the next room. Someone inside greets him.

"Make yourself comfortable, if you like," Baby says, and Mark nods. Baby closes the screen after him. Mark looks around Randy's front room.

It's sparsely furnished. Shelves of art books, a CD player, and a couch make up one side. The other is a long walnut table, chairs, and an odd television set, its screen protruding from a tall black cabinet. It looks like the idea people had in the 1950s of what the Space Age was going to be like. Mark wanders over, pulls one of the heavy chairs away from the table and sits in front of the TV.

There's a documentary on, about a mountain, perhaps. Or perhaps not. It's hard to tell because the sound's turned down, and Mark doesn't see any controls. The mountain looks familiar, though, one of the worlds's landmarks, and he tries to decide which one it is. Fuji? But there's no vegetation on its slopes, and he's pretty sure Fuji is covered with cherry trees. Maybe Kilimanjaro. He can almost hear George Page's narration: "...the arid slopes of the mountain are actually home to a wide variety of wildlife." He looks more closely at the screen and realizes those tiny birds darting around the mountain are actually very small black fish, and this isn't a TV but an aquarium. The curve of the bowl magnifies a triangular sheet of rock inside. What's really strange is that he can still hear George Page talking about a mountain baking in the African sun. Randy did this, Mark thinks; he put this illusion together so well it keeps working even after its parts are identified. He leans his elbow on the table and stares at the documentary.

Ricardo met Randy at the baths back in the late seventies, in the days when the baths opened into the unconscious, not the cemetery. Ricardo had been standing in the hall, chatting with someone he knew; at some point in the conversation he referred to himself as a Mayan princess. It was a joke he discovered he could make in the United States, a reference to being from Honduras, and to having Indian blood, which in Honduras had been a mark against him. A guy was passing by. "Mayan princess?" he said, looking Ricardo over. "You want to be in on something?" "*Do* it," the friend urged. Later, describing his part in the "something" to Mark, he said, "I was one of the handmaidens." "I don't understand." "Well, there was this tall thin boy in a leg brace and he was being sacrificed by a stallion in front of two old men. It was supposed to be a god doing the sacrifice, but he wasn't very good, so Randy made him be a stallion. The handmaidens fanned the boy and held his hand while he was being mounted." This had been the only one of Randy's "somethings" that Ricardo had participated in—his tastes running more to wearing out the biggest cocks he could find. Also, he and Randy quickly went on to become friends, and Ricardo had scruples about having sex with friends, or even sex under the direction of friends. But, in late-night conversations over the phone, Ricardo would question Randy about what he did.

Randy staged dream-events at the baths. These were like the scenarios to a hundred porno movies, where a sailor is on shore leave or a biker kidnaps a college student or a plumber comes

over; Randy's scenes just came from further down in the unconscious. A horse-man might sacrifice a boy in front of a pair of ancient high priests. Pearl divers might defeat a great white shark
only to fall prey to a giant squid—played by three guys lying on
top of each other, using their legs in concert. Or a man's reflec-
tion might fall in love with him, or become resentful or envious
and come out of the mirror to have it out with him—the two men
wouldn't have to look anything alike. The story would depend on
who was at the baths that night, what they looked like to Randy
and if they were interested in "being in on something." Not everyone could have carried it off ("Excuse me, but we need a third for
Octopus; are you available?"). But Randy's no-nonsense, almost
grim expression as he hunted up and down the halls got the message across: this was going to be sex without any of the more senti-
mental trappings, almost without recognizable sex acts. Sex from
beyond.

Ricardo's incense had been building up in Mark's throat for
the last few minutes. Now the screen opens and Ricardo comes
out, smoke streaming from the iron pot he's carrying. The room
beyond is all white vapor and candles, like a cloud full of heat
lightning. "Stand up, baby," he says.

"What's happening in there?" Mark asks, getting to his feet.

"I gave him a cleansing. Then I had to clean everybody else,"
Ricardo says. "Spread your legs." Mark does, and Ricardo swings
the smoking pot between them, singing a little song in the African
language *santeros* speak. He taps Mark's leg and twirls one hand,
and Mark slowly turns in a circle.

"Can I go in after this?"

"Wait. Hold this." He hands the pot to Mark and takes a cake of
ground eggshell out of his shirt pocket, works his forefinger over
it. He puts a hand on Mark's shoulder to steady him and raises his
finger to Mark's forehead. Mark frowns and pulls his head away.
"No, hold still," Ricardo says.

"I don't like that on my face," Mark says. "The incense'll be
enough. And I've still got my leaf." He tries to hand the pot back
to Ricardo. The smoke has dwindled to nothing.

Ricardo pushes Mark's hand away. "You need some *cascarilla*,"
he coaxes, trying to appeal to reason. "I don't want you picking
anything up tonight."

"I don't want any," Mark says.

Ricardo, impatient, digs his fingers into Mark's shoulder to make him comply. Sometimes this works, and Mark just rolls his eyes and lets Ricardo have what he wants. This time Ricardo's thumb goes into the deltoid muscle and right against the bone. It's acutely unpleasant and he doesn't stop. Mark puts his hand to Ricardo's chest and tries to push him away. He's the stronger of the two, but Ricardo's less concerned about not hurting either Mark or himself; he grabs the back of Mark's neck and squeezes, trying to force Mark's face down. "I'm just trying to help you, asshole," he mutters angrily. "Fuck you," Mark grunts, and he arches his neck, trying to break Ricardo's grip. Now Ricardo gets both hands around Mark's neck and Mark, pot of glowing coals still in his hand, is at a disadvantage. "Hunhh," Ricardo says, and begins to pull Mark's head down with every bit of strength he has. Then someone comes out of the bedroom and Mark glances over—it's Tom, Randy's lover. Ricardo lets go of him and Mark flies backward, his footing gone. "Shit," he says. Before he can fall, Ricardo grabs hold of him and pulls him back on balance, saying "Ha!" as he does and making a cross on Mark's forehead.

Tom's watching them, smiling but distant, faint almost, as if he's being broadcast in on a weak signal. Ricardo once showed Mark Tom's photograph in a calendar—he was the image for August in loose drawstring pants, the shot taken from below so that the rack of his shoulders and his harsh, turned-away features seemed to be rising into the cloudless sky—and since then Tom's face has always looked a little incomplete to Mark without the shine of glossy paper. Tom has a cross in *cascarilla* drawn on his forehead. "We're ready for the champagne," he says. "How about one of you helping?"

"Mark will," Ricardo says, retrieving the pot from him. "I want to smoke the living room."

"Mark?" Tom says.

"Sure," Mark says, relieved to be able to do something. He follows Tom into the kitchen.

It's stainless steel and tiny. A microwave, a food processor and an Italian espresso machine are lined up like the crew of a space station waiting for assignments. There's a framed poster on the wall, a blown-up woodcut of an artichoke. Tom opens a cabinet. "How do you put up with him?" he asks.

Everyone who knows Ricardo seems to ask Mark the same question. Usually he just brushes it off with the first thing that comes to mind, but he doesn't think Tom is making idle chat. "Well, I don't 'put up with him,'" he says. Tom sets glasses out on the counter—champagne flutes, tall, so fragile they might shatter from a movement of the air. The artichoke listens over Tom's shoulder like someone in a medieval plague mask. "I like him," Mark continues, picking up the glasses, not sure how he can manage more than two. "I just like everything about him. Even the things that drive me crazy." He decides to carry them in the crook of his arm, like a bouquet of lilies.

"Yeah," Tom says, closing the cabinet. "That's it, isn't it? Liking the things that drive you crazy." He looks at Mark and smiles. The smile is gentle, a fond if distant uncle's, but the look passes through Mark effortlessly. Mark gets out of its way.

"Come on, we're ready," Baby says in the doorway. There's a cross on his forehead. "Do you need help with those?"

"Uh, no, I can handle them," Mark says, tightening his grip on the bundle of glasses. They squeak against each other, an alarming sound, and he has to make do with hunching over them protectively.

Tom takes a bottle of champagne out of the refrigerator and shows it to Baby. "Yeah, he got himself something good," Baby says. "Only the best." They leave the kitchen.

The screen's been moved out of the doorway to the other room but Mark, bearing his almost weightless burden, can't look up, afraid if he takes his eyes off them the flutes will escape his embrace and meet the floor. The incense is like gauze in here. He stops at the foot of the bed. Baby relieves him of two of the glasses, and while Tom opens the champagne, deftly, so the cork barely pops, Mark looks down at the bed.

Randy's been laid out in a light blue suit, something from a *GQ* cover, impeccable, perfectly pressed. A stuffed animal so old its specie has worn away is tucked under his arm. And Mark, who came here looking for a guide, instead finds himself face to face with the guard at a closed border. The set of Randy's features dismisses him completely, not for being Mark but for being alive. Randy looks heavy, brutal, brutish. It's not just Mark who's being sent back the way he came, it's everyone in the room, everything in the world. It makes his stomach whirl, as if between one step and another all the ground has fallen away and there's nowhere to put his foot. Ricardo's smoking a cigar; he puts the lit end in his mouth, leans over the bed and blows a cloud of smoke up and down Randy's body. Mark blinks and looks around at the other men in the room.

None of Randy's friends looks like this is the worst thing that could happen. Perhaps because Randy had been positive so long, into and home from the hospital so often? And everyone's grief has been burning a long time, so that the more obvious manifestations have all been consumed. It makes them seem like a band of tough old warriors, Vikings completely at home in a narrow boat out on the ocean—Tom, carefully filling the fragile glasses that Baby holds out for him; Arthur, sitting beside the bed, presiding over what is after all a social occasion. Everyone's already eaten this death and digested it. The only person who shows any misery is a good-looking boy Mark's never seen before, and even he doesn't appear grief-stricken so much as shocked, staring down on the bed at something that wasn't really supposed to happen.

Baby takes the last empty glass from Mark and hands him a full one. Mark brings it up to his chest, waiting for the toast, and when he glances over at Ricardo, Ricardo's watching him, his eyes like a safety net in case Mark falls. Mark smiles with one side of his mouth to show Ricardo everything's okay. I don't want to die, he thinks, or he doesn't think it, it just pops into the front of his head. With it comes the unlikely image of himself having an audience with God. God is twice Mark's height, and thin; his face is clean-shaven, androgynous, and for some reason his hair is like maple leaves in autumn—yellow, red, some nearly black, some still green. Mark is ticking off requirements on his fingers: I don't want to die, I don't want to get sick, I don't want to be afraid. God listens attentively, interested in what Mark has to say, interested in everything, but the expression on his face is unreadable. Ricardo returns Mark's half-smile. Then Arthur says something to him and Ricardo bends down to listen, his eyes still on Mark.

The boy starts crying, not sobs but a sudden contortion of his features, and Baby slips an arm around his shoulders. "It's okay," Baby says. This is not being offered as a blanket for the boy to tuck around his brain, it's an instruction—hard, harsh even, but not without a certain humor, an acknowledgment of what a difficult instruction this is to follow. "No, it's not," the boy says, his face twisted, but Baby won't be moved. "Yeah, it is. It's *okay*," he says, close to the boy's ear, and for a moment he's a father teaching his son how to ride a bike, holding it steady for him.

"Well," Arthur says, getting to his feet. "Tom? The toast?"

Tom shakes his head. "I don't know what to say. Somebody else make it."

"I will," Baby says, and holds his glass out over the bed, his arm still around his protégé's shoulders. "Good luck, Randy."

"Good luck," everyone agrees, and Ricardo adds, "*Aché*," the word for the spirit, power, grace. There's a brief confusion of crystal in the air above Randy as everyone taps glasses with everyone else. Arthur drinks and then says, "It's a good thing he's not here. He'd be bitching at everyone not to chip his glasses."

The laughter that greets this is light, relieved, as if people are just letting go of everything and rising into the air. Mark doesn't laugh; neither does Baby's protégé. But Ricardo does and Mark envies him. Maybe what makes him feel most separated from the others is that they've given up all hope and faced what terrifies them, lived with it awhile, but Mark still carries hope the way a bag lady totes shopping bags of old newspapers. Maybe everything will be okay, he thinks two, three, four times a day, and when he does the thought turns into an impossible narrow path he has to stay on, with fear and confusion spreading out on either side. Ricardo gives everything he can lay his hands on to Santeria and he's practically weightless, while Mark feels like a mammoth skirting the edge of a tar pit.

"He used to sweat every time we used his fucking crystal," Tom says.

"He was always really grabby about what was his," Baby says. "It was always 'That's mine, *give* it to me.'" He gives a growl to illustrate what he means and Tom nods, bearing witness.

"Well, you know, he never told me how he got his hair that color," Arthur confides. "He said if I knew, I'd show up at the funeral the same shade as him."

There's more laughter. This time Baby, who hasn't let go of his friend, gives him a squeeze, encouraging him, and the boy smiles tentatively and then laughs, a brief cough. He looks at Baby to see if this is what Baby means. It is.

Tom drains his glass and sets it on the nightstand next to the one standing there for Randy. "There's not time for all the little shit," he says. "There's just time to do what you really need."

"He got it all done," Baby says, dismissing any worries about Randy along this line.

Arthur sees something about the knot of Randy's tie that doesn't quite please him and sets his champagne aside, leans over the bed. He says, "He was never afraid. Mad, at first; just pissed as hell." When he gets the tie just the way he wants he looks at it critically a moment, then straightens back up.

"He was a fighter, dear," Ricardo agrees, then gasps and shakes his head. "The scandal he used to throw if somebody cancelled flowers they ordered from him!"

"Honey, I could tell you about scandals over tricks. With me," Arthur laughs.

"We picked up a hustler together one night," Baby begins.

"*One* night," Arthur crows.

"Fuck you. This one night we picked up a hustler. And we took him to my place."

Mark finishes his champagne and turns around to set his glass on the low bookcase behind him. There's a wall-hanging above it, a piece of fabric like heavy velvet or velour, with a picture dyed into it. Ricardo's mother has a Last Supper on similar fabric draped over the back of her couch. This isn't a Last Supper.

Most of it is an indifferent copy of a medieval tapestry, a forest scene, all chilly dark greens and grays. Two men in tunics and leggings walk in the left foreground, lost, or at least each of them points in a different direction and neither looks happy. Small wonder, since there's no sky to be seen and a variety of animals show between the trunks of the trees—leopards with beards and crowns, a black bear tiptoeing on its claws and, most fearsome to Mark, a stag with teeth and alert human eyes. But in the right foreground, all white, cream and yellow is Marilyn Monroe. Her skirts lift up like wings, her hands press down on her crotch as if to hold it in place and her head arches back in joy. Mark can't tell if the two men are meant to know she's there; he hopes so, but she's on a larger scale than anything else in the hanging and nothing has been done to integrate her into the scene. "And he hauls off and slaps him across the face as hard as he can and says, 'I *said* fuck me *hard*,'" Baby concludes, and everyone howls.

She reminds Mark of something; it stays just out of sight behind her, tugging a string. He tries to remember but then Ricardo's next to him, giving his arm the double squeeze. "Mm-hmm," Mark says, a little surprised Ricardo wants to leave so soon.

"That's *Ochún*," Ricardo explains for Mark's benefit, naming one of the main *orishas*. "See? Yellow. And that's how her *aché* is, flirtatious like that. Those boys are lost in the forest and she's making an apparition. She helps them get out."

"They see her?"

"They're just about to. *Ya lorde*," he says, saluting Marilyn Monroe. He links fingers with Mark. "Arthur Thompson, we're leaving. Mark gets up early in the morning."

"Jesus, so do I," Arthur groans, standing. "And we've got a case coming to trial this week. The office is a zoo." He takes Ricardo's hand and holds it. "I'll stop by the shop. He left money for a party, when we've done the funeral."

"You take care, dear," Ricardo says, and Arthur brushes it away. "Oh, always," he says. Ricardo hugs everybody while Mark waits to make a general good-bye. He looks at Randy again and the room gives a sudden slight shift, because Randy's almost gone. What's on the bed is a heavy body, the features of its face expressionless, a little collapsed as if they've been rained on. Ricardo puts his hand on a shoulder and says something under his breath, then gives it a sharp pat, like a dismissal. When he straightens up, Mark lifts his own hand and says, "Good night," nodding to everyone.

Baby walks them out. "I want to get a canary or something for Kevin. Can you get me one?" he asks in a low voice.

"I don't sell small birds," Ricardo advises him. "But I know a breeder who raises Columbus fancies. The big fat giant ones. Good singers. You give me a call this week to remind me and we'll go."

Baby opens the door for them. "How about if I just come by your shop. Wednesday?"

"Thursday, better. About three," Ricardo says. "I see you then."

"Okay," Baby says. He holds his hand out to shake with Mark. "Later," he says.

"Good night," Mark says, and Baby closes the door after them. He joins Ricardo on the sidewalk. "Are they going to stay there all night?" he asks.

"No," Ricardo says. "Just Tom is. He wants to spend the last night with Randy."

"Sit up with him?"

"Sleep beside him."

Mark doesn't say anything. Ricardo takes his arm, claiming him, and they walk like that, a little awkwardly because they don't keep step together. The night has gotten older and the air moist, heavy, pressed down by the plum-colored overcast so frequent to West Hollywood. They reach the car and Mark opens the door for Ricardo, giving him time to arrange the skirts of his duster, and as he watches Ricardo settle himself the image of Marilyn Monroe steps aside and there's the waitress. He gets in and pumps the gas a couple of times. "I meant to tell you," he says, turning the key in the ignition. "I saw this waitress last week."

He was eating lunch in a Century City deli, reading, when he came up from his book because someone was standing next to the table. It was a waitress, staring out the window, a load of dirty plates in her hand. Mark glanced up, thought she was smiling at someone she knew, and went back into his book. But she stayed there and so he looked up again, a little more sharply, and her face had opened up considerably. She's sure trying to put a lot into a look, he thought, but then it suddenly seemed obvious: she was seeing her lover, they'd had a fight the last time they were together and now the lover was outside the window, the two of them were trying to patch things up through a long conversation of looks. And he discreetly glanced out the window, curious whether the lover was another woman or a man. There was no one there. He turned back to the waitress and she was just beginning to turn from the waist, her eyes iced over, her expression still speaking of the last thing she had seen, and he understood that was something inside her. "She was having some kind of fit," he says to Ricardo.

"Really? Did she foam?" Ricardo asks.

"No, she . . ." Mark says, not sure how to describe it. "It was like she went out the back door. Her eyes were open, and you could look in and see she wasn't in there."

"Did anyone help her?"

Mark half-rose in his seat and took hold of her dishes, thinking she might drop them, but her grip was like cement. For some reason his chair wouldn't slide back, and as the waitress continued to turn Mark found himself being pulled across the table toward that point where he would either have to let go or fall into his lunch. In a minute the manager was out from behind the cash register and had his arm around her shoulders, arresting her movement.

"Laurie. Laurie," he called, as if he had a good idea where she was, and he pushed her hand and the plates down to the table. Mark sat back down. Laurie's face came back together and she blinked several times. "Did I go away again?" she asked, a little dazed.

Mark slows down for a yellow light, stops and says, "Yeah, the manager came over. She must have had them before, he knew what to do."

Ricardo nods, says, "She was taken to the other world. That happens sometimes."

"I don't know," Mark says, shaking his head. "It was like, well, like we're driving tonight and we see this car, and it's stopped like at a light or something, and the engine's running and the lights are on, but there's no one in the car. And there's no place for them to be. I mean, no stores, or houses, and you don't see them getting a newspaper out of a stand or running down the sidewalk. That was her body standing there, right? And I watched, Ricardo, I was looking right into her eyes. She was nowhere, and then she was back."

"If she was nowhere, she wouldn't have come back," Ricardo says, watching him. "The other world's not going to let you see it, baby."

"Christ, why not?" Mark groans, putting his head down on the steering wheel.

Ricardo's losing his patience. "Because it doesn't make any difference," he snaps.

"Not for you," Mark says, and suddenly his mouth tastes like he's been chewing aspirin. "You've got Santeria. I don't have anything and I'm not going to have time to find my way." And then his eyes are running over, though his face feels hard as stone.

Ricardo, dismayed to see Mark crying, reaches over and pulls him into his arms. "No," he says, soothing himself as much as Mark. "No." Mark lets himself be taken, just barely able to keep his foot on the brake. "This is what happens," Ricardo whispers fiercely into his temple, where the gray increases almost daily. "You get held like this. Like this," and he crushes Mark into him until the wire frames of Mark's glasses bend. And it lasts forever, or long enough for Mark to make the journey deep into Ricardo's embrace, and set down everything he's carrying, and forget it. And he thinks, If there's heaven, this is it; if there isn't, this is still it.

He's roused from this temporary shelter by a car horn sounding behind them. Straightening his glasses as well as he can, peering over the backseat, he sees a large dark car that's pulled up in back of them from nowhere, a Mafia car, wide, square, all business. Light from the street lamp reflects off the windshield so the driver can't be seen, but whoever it is has no patience and leans on the horn, a long blast and then several quick pumps. "Do you know him?" Ricardo asks, but Mark's never known anyone in a car like that, and shakes his head. Now the driver leans out the window—no, it's no one Mark's ever seen before—and delivers his message in a voice that could roll aside a boulder: "The light's green, asshole! *Let's go!*"

Wig

PATRICK GALE

Wanda would never have thought of buying such a thing, never have *planned* to do so. In this case, however, her thoughts and plans were immaterial. She was put upon, the object, quite literally, thrust upon her. The salesman pounced as she was waiting for a friend and as soon as she had felt the thing's slippery heaviness between her fingers, her fate was sealed.

Wanda had never mastered the art of evading the attentions of department store demonstrators and had gone through life being squirted with unwanted scents. Where other women could stride purposefully by, freezing all overtures with a glare or a scornful laugh, she would feel coerced into buying small gadgets for slicing eggs into perfect sections or recycling old bits of soap into garishly striped blocks. On the rare occasions when she heard him speak of her to his friends, she gathered that her husband's image of her was colored by this weakness.

"She loves gadgets," he would say. "If she thinks it saves her time, she'll buy it. When they invent a gadget to live your life for you, she'll be first in the queue and let herself be talked into buying six."

In her youth she had become a not terribly fervent Christian in the same way—sold the idea by a catchy sermon involving some crafty use of props—until her faith went the way of the spring-loaded cucumber dicer and the Bye Bye Blemish foundation cream, gathering to it a kind of dusty griminess that dulled her guilt at its under-use.

"Excuse me, madam." It was a less vigorous approach than usual, tired and mechanical. He was evidently too drained by a long day of false charm to be mindful of his commission. "Would you like to try a wig?"

A chip slicer she might have resisted. She had one of those already. And a vacuum attachment for grooming the cat (not a great success), but the very strangeness of that little monosyllable seemed to pluck at her elbow. She paused and half turned.

"I beg your pardon?"

He was a nondescript, sandy man; the kind of man one looked straight through. She did not imagine he could draw in much business and yet, now that he had caught her eye, she perceived something confidential in his very nothingness. She felt an immediate sense that, in talking to him, she became invisible too, temporarily shielded from critical view.

"A wig, madam," he repeated. "Would you like to try one?" He did not smile. His manner was earnest, even urgent.

"Should I be insulted?" she asked, touching her own hair instinctively. "Why me? Why didn't you ask someone else?"

"I did," he said, with a ghost of a smile. "I've sold several." He considered the small rack of the things ranged on polystyrene heads on the trolley at his side like the grim evidence of an executioner's zeal, and stretched one over the backs of his simian fingers. "I think *this* one for you," he said. "Not our most popular model, because it's rather expensive. To be quite frank with you, designs from the cheaper range tend to go to people looking for fancy dress or hoping to cover the short term effects of medical therapy. Try it on. I know you'll be surprised."

She took it gingerly, expecting the cheap sweatiness of nylon but it was pleasantly cool, sending a kind of shock through her fingertips. It put her in mind of being allowed to hold a schoolfriend's angora rabbit for the first time; now, as then, she was seized with an immoderate temptation to hold it to her cheek. It was blonde, of course. To that extent he *was* like any salesman. He had assumed, quite erroneously, that being a quiet-looking brunette

with a sensible cut she could brush behind her ears or tame with
an Alice band, she harbored a secret desire for Nordic bubble
curls. Obedient, resigned to humiliation, she pulled out her hair
slides then slid the wig over her tingling scalp. Feeling slightly
dizzy, she bent her head forward—she was slightly taller than the
salesman—and allowed him to tuck in any locks of her hair still
showing.

For all its mass, it felt no heavier than a straw hat. She could not
restrain a soft laugh; she knew she would not buy, but this was
amusement as harmless as raiding the dressing-up box and, smiling at her, he seemed to enter into her childish pleasure.

"Good," he said. "*Very* good."

"Quick," she said. "Let me see."

He was stooping below his little trolley for the mirror when she
saw her friend—one used the term loosely—returning from the
haberdashery department with the shoulder pads and French
chalk she had been seeking when they parted company. The
friend was a conventional woman with a tendency to spiteful
tale-bearing when she caught any of her acquaintances doing
anything eccentric or irrational. Wanda froze as the friend approached, suddenly aware that the salesman had frozen too, in
suggestive complicity. It was too late to pull the wig off without
hopelessly disordering her hair, yet she could think of no plausible explanation as to why she was standing there trying it on. The
friend's worst done, she would find herself receiving pitying looks
as one bravely keeping a struggle with cancer or alopecia to herself, or she would be scorned as the frivolous vulgarian they had
long suspected her of being. The latter would be almost welcome.
Her friends were merely neighborhood women who had taken
her under their wings; ambiguous controllers she would happily
avoid. She could easily hide solitary days from her husband.

The friend passed her by, however, without the slightest betrayal of
recognition, continuing to look querulously about for her missing
companion. Wanda looked after her retreating form in amazement. Had she a bolder appearance, she might have thought it
miraculous. The salesman had found the mirror and was holding
it out.

"See for yourself," he said. "Of course, it *is* beautifully styled, but the reason it's so much more expensive is that, apart from the basic skull cap, every fiber in it is human."

She did not look directly in the mirror but, in the second before she tugged the thing free of her head in a spasm of revulsion, she seemed to catch a reflected glimpse of an angry stranger.

"Horrible," she stammered. "I'm so sorry. My friend's waiting for me." And she hurried off for a reprimand from the friend and a dour, unfattening lunch.

When he first singled her out for his special attentions—fumbling trips to the cinema, long, circular drives in his car, hectoring sessions of golf tuition—her husband had praised her normality.

"The thing I really like about you," he would say, "Is you're so normal."

Delivered in lieu of anything more romantic, the praise warmed her heart and briefly convinced her that normality was indeed her special feature. Pressing through on his advantage, he wooed, wed and twice impregnated her. By some sleight of hand, he managed to do all three without once mentioning love. She did not love *him*—this had been one of the certainties that lent her courage in accepting his proposal—but she nonetheless hoped that he might love *her* and be holding something back out of manly reserve. This fond delusion evaporated shortly after the birth of their second child, when he passed on an infestation of pubic lice and blamed it, with neither apology nor embarrassment, on insufficient airplane hygiene. She had learned to live with the delusion's residue. She had a nice house, two clean, healthy children and a generous housekeeping allowance from which she could grant herself occasional treats without detection. Although she had only ever experienced orgasm by accident, her husband continued to grant her perfunctory sexual intercourse at least once a fortnight.

For most wives, that evening might have been a memorably bad one; for her it was much like any other. Their daughter, Jennifer, refused to eat supper, pleading incipient vegetarianism, and was sent to bed with no alternative. At several points during the meal, Mark, their son, imitated Wanda's way of talking, most unpleasantly, only to be rewarded with her husband's indulgent laughter. When she had seen the children off to bed, smuggling in an apple

and some cheese to Jennifer, he pointedly admired a Swedish actress's breasts throughout the thriller she had not wanted to
watch. After that, when she was ready to drop with exhaustion, he
made her sit up and play Scrabble. Scrabble, like her normality,
had been one of the things originally to bring them together. He
had made her play it the first time he took her to Godalming to
meet his mother.

An inveterate snob, he had learnt from his mother that most card
games apart from bridge were somehow common and bridge, he
swiftly learnt, lay beyond his impatient understanding. Scrabble,
however, appealed to him. He assured her it was a game "smart"
people played. When challenged, he would never say why, and she
suspected he was influenced by the game's appearance in a hack-
neyed advertisement for chocolate mint creams. His mother
claimed it was sophisticated because it came in a dark green box
and anyone knew that all the best things came in dark green—
waxed jackets, cars, wellington boots, folding tv dinner tables and
so forth. The problem was that Scrabble was one of the few pas-
times at which her husband seemed dim beside her. In front of his
friends he pretended to boast of her cleverness, her facility for
scoring forty-five with a four-letter word placed slyly across the
ends of two others, but in private she knew it maddened him. She
learned early on in their relationship to temper her glee at tri-
umphing over him. She avoided forming words like *gnomon* or
philtrum, which she knew he would vainly insist on challenging
and she tortured herself by passing up frequent opportunities to
score scrabbles. Try as she might, however, she could not let him
win. It was a game at which he could never excel. She hoped he
would abandon the challenge, dismiss the skill he lacked as being
feminine and therefore pointless, but it was as if he wished to
bludgeon the game into submission the way he did the television,
or the dog. He knew he could beat her effortlessly at golf, drive
faster and mow the lawn better than she ever would, but he would
not accept that in this one, insignificant area of their life, he had
no mastery and was her inferior.

As usual, tonight, she trounced him despite her best efforts to
help him win. She murmured soothingly that he had wretched
luck with the letters he picked up but she knew he was seething

from the way he splashed his whisky when he poured his night-cap, and the entirely unnecessary fuss he made over some small item of household expense for which she had failed to obtain a receipt during that day's shopping excursion. She was weary to her very soul and knew she would have to make an early start the next morning because it was her day to drive the school run, so she pointedly popped a sleeping tablet before pecking him a placid goodnight.

He ignored the hint, however. The cheap posturing of the film had left him restless and aroused and his humiliation at the Scrabble board had stirred in him a need for vengeance. She knew the warning signs of old. An unpleasant memory from when she was once laid low with gastric flu told her he would not be denied.

"You only have to lie there," he said when she demurred and, tugging aside the pyjama bottoms she suddenly remembered she had forgotten to include in that morning's wash, he thrust his erection into her face. It bumped her nose once then she obediently took it in her mouth, remembering to keep her teeth out of the way. She had once been ambushed by an article on oral sex while waiting in the dentist's waiting room for her son to receive some fillings. It had changed her life—at least, it had changed a small part of her life—with the advice to make a yawning motion so as to widen the entry to the throat and so avoid telltale, not to say unflattering, gagging. Tonight she found it difficult not to choke. As he pumped back and forth, his thighs weighty on her breasts, his grasp causing the headboard to bang against the wall, she fought back spasm upon nauseated spasm, diverting her thoughts onto undone tasks, recipe cards, the alpine perennials she had yet to plant on her rockery.

"I bet *she* never has to take this," he said, mentioning the actress, "I bet no one ever does this to *her*. She'd be on top. She'd call all the shots."

He spoke in so matter-of-fact a manner that she feared his mind was on rockeries too and the ordeal might be prolonged much further, but suddenly her cheeks were filling with his vile, familiar jelly. Never one for delicate gestures, he heaped insult on assault with a comment about helping to wash down her sleeping tablets. As he rolled off her and walked to the bathroom, she took a certain pleasure in spitting out his juices into the back pages of some golfing memoirs he had been reading.

Her children were enrolled in consecutive years of the same school, and she shared the school run with mothers of three of their friends. School runs were a far cry from the easy suburban slovenliness of dropping one's husband off at the station with an overcoat flung over one's nightdress. Other children were all too often hostile emissaries of their parents, spitefully observant as only children could be. Normally she presented them with as clean and careful a version of herself as she would offer her husband's colleagues at the Christmas party. This morning, however, she had dressed in a hurry, thrown into confusion by a bad night's sleep and the discovery that her son had unplugged the tumble drier so as to recharge some batteries, and so left in a sodden heap that day's blouse, which she had planned to iron before breakfast.

"You were wearing that dress yesterday," said her daughter's best friend in a tone of friendly astonishment.

"I don't think so," she said. "Hurry up and belt up or we'll be late."

"Yes you were," said the child. "I'm belted now, so you can drive on. Yes you were. I saw you when Mummy came to pick up Mark and Jennifer."

"Really?" Wanda replied, pretending to frown at some road works. "I really don't remember. Maybe I was. How funny. Now. What have you all got on your timetables today? Is it horrid maths?" Incredulously, she felt herself break out in a nervous sweat. The girl had turned away, oblivious to the bright conversational gambit. "Mummy changes at least twice a day," she told the others. "Three times if she's gardening or something. She says Daddy likes it."

Wanda amused herself briefly with the image of the woman in question actually effecting regular bodily changes—new hair, new teeth, new leg lengths—with the restlessness of a dissatisfied flower arranger. Then the unnervingly self-possessed Morag, the next child they picked up, physically recoiled as Wanda laughed her hello in her face, and she realized she had forgotten, in the rush, to brush her teeth. She was caught out in her hasty rootle through the glove compartment for a packet of peppermints and, forced therefore to pass them round, had to admit to her lapse if she was to justify taking the last mint and thereby depriving Jennifer of one. Any ground gained by doling out sweets was doubly lost by this tasteless revelation. The girls shifted slightly on their seats and giggled except for poor Jennifer, who pressed her nose to the window and stared with forlorn fury at the passing houses, condemned now for a mother not only slatternly but unhygienic.

After seeing the children safely into the playground, Wanda drove directly into town, while she was still fired with humiliation and rage. Only half-aware of why she was there at all, she found a parking space then half-strode, half-ran back to the department store. For a moment she froze, as it seemed that the salesman and his trolley had vanished, but then she saw with a start that he was only feet away, helping a woman peel a long, red creation off her own head of nondescript gray. Instinct and a kind of warning glance from him told her to stand back until the woman had made her purchase then, as she stepped forward, he greeted her with a blandly surprised, "Ah, madam," and asked if she wished to try on the same model again.

"No," she told him. "It's perfect. I know it is. I was just being silly before. About the hair being human, I mean. I don't know why. Perhaps it made me think of nuns. But now I . . ." She faltered, her mouth suddenly dry with nerves. His face briefly clouded by concern, he asked if she would like to wear it immediately.

"Oh no," she said, scandalized. "Wrap it up, please I . . . I'll try it on again once I get it home."

He wrapped it in tissue then shut it into a bag so discreet it might have contained a roll of curtain heading tape or a box of talcum powder.

Meeting the extravagant price with a handful of notes from the horde she had pared from her housekeeping budget, she experienced a dizziness that verged on the erotic and she had to hurry to the coffee bar to eat two slices of cake to recover her equilibrium. It was only as she sat there, terrible booty on the chair beside her, softly munching, reduced like the immobilized shoppers around her to a contented sugar-trance, that she noticed the bag was not one of the store's own but of a different provenance entirely. It was black with small gold lettering that boasted outlets in France, Luxembourg and Florida. *Silence*, the company appeared to be called, which put her in mind of libraries. Perhaps it was meant to be pronounced in a French accent to sound less an imperative, more a bewitching promise. In small curly letters beneath the title the bag whispered, *Your secret is Our pride.* She wondered if the store's management knew the salesman was there at all or whether he slyly played on the employees' ignorance of one another's purpose and throve in their scented midst like a parasite on a sleek but cumbersome host. As if to confirm her suspicion, he had moved his trolley again when she glanced around her from the downward escalator. He had shifted his favors from foundation garments and hosiery to between costume jewelry and winter hats.

At first she only wore the wig at home, when she was safely alone, honoring it with all the ritual befitting a complex pornographic pursuit. She would lock doors and draw curtains. She took off all her too familiar clothes, the better to focus on the wig's effects, and wrapped her body Grecian-style in a sheet or bath towel, much as she had done as a slyly preening child. Every time she stretched it anew across her knuckles and tucked it around her scalp she felt afresh the near-electric sensations that had first surprised her in the store. She was fascinated by what she saw, transfixed before the unfamiliar woman she conjured up in the mirrored doors of the bedroom cupboards. If the doorbell or the telephone rang during the hours of her observances, she ignored them, although, lent courage by curls, she made a few anonymous calls to people she disliked, words slipping from her lips that the unwigged her could never have uttered. Had her husband come home unexpectedly, he would have caught her in as much guilty confusion as if he had surprised her in some rank adulterous act.

And yet with each resumption of blondeship she grew less timid. The woman in the looking glass would not be ignored, it seemed, and her influence proved cumulative. Wanda grew bolder. She began to make short daytime excursions in the wig and did things she imagined a woman with such hair would do. She drove to smarter districts than her husband's, where she sat in pavement cafés and ordered a glass of red wine that brought a flush to her cheeks or a searingly bitter double espresso whose grounds she savored on her tongue. She bought expensive magazines, flicked through them with a knowing smile as though she recognized the people within, then, casually profligate, left them behind on restaurant tables without even bothering to retrieve the small sachets of free samples glued to certain advertisements.

She had a pedicure at an elegant chiropodist's, which left her feet dangerously soft in the new black shoes she had bought herself. Then, inspired by the pleasure of watching a woman crouch below her working at her feet with little blades and chafing devices, she paid to have her toe- and fingernails painted traffic light red. This last impulsive indulgence seemed a miscalculation at first, since it could not be shut away in her wardrobe like the wig and the shoes or easily washed off like the new, distinguished scent, but her husband seemed to like her with claws. Or at least he did not seem actively to *dislike* her with them. A few weeks ago she would have thought them entirely out of keeping with her rather homely character and what she thought of as her "look," but now they seemed no more than a newly exposed facet of her personality. Her fingers seemed longer and more tapering than they had before, her clothes less a necessity and more of a statement.

It was only a matter of time—two weeks, in fact—before she dared to leave the wig on when she picked the children up from school. As she waited by the gates, other mothers complimented her on her bold new style. She did not duck her head or offer bashful thanks and explanation as she might have done before but merely smiled and said, "You think so?" for their opinions were now entirely unimportant to her well-being. The children, especially the other girls on the school run, usually so slack in their compliments, touched her with their enthusiasm.

"It's amazing!" they cried ingenuously. "You look like a film star!"

She knew that children's ideas of glamour were hopelessly tawdry and overblown, that, in the undereducated estimation of little girls, anything forbidden them—lipstick, bosoms, cigarettes, false eyelashes—was of its very nature beautiful, so that mere prostitutes acquired a near-royal loveliness for them. She knew she should not take their effusions as a compliment. She knew she should play along for a moment or two then expose the wig for the fraud it was. After all, she would still have shown herself to be that rare thing among mothers—a good sport with a potential for sexiness. But then she saw how her daughter was sitting, squeezed into her usual corner of the backseat, mutely glowing at the praise her mother was receiving from these all-important peers. She even received a rare gesture of affection from her son; a warm, dry hand placed on her shoulder as he boasted of the points he had received for a geography test. She imagined the disappointment, disgust even, on their faces if she suddenly tugged the wig off. They might not praise her as a good sport; they might simply declare her mad. She was not yet so far from her own childhood as to have forgotten that madness in mothers was even less forgivable than bad hats.

So she drove on. Wigged. A game, laughing lie made flesh. She laid rapid plans. If she could make it through the night un-detected, she would cash in the rest of her rainy day fund, call at her usual salon the next day, throw caution to the winds and have her own hair dyed and styled to match the wig. At the thought that she would thereby become the woman in her looking glass, the stylish, effortless woman of her daylight excursions, she felt herself suffused with a warm glow that began in her scalp and ran down her neck and across her breasts and belly. She gazed at the suburban roads unfolding ahead of her and smiled in a way that might have scared the children had they been less absorbed in their own chatter by now. She dreaded her husband's return, how-ever. She dreaded his mockery or anger. Once supper was safely in the oven and the children were bathed, she locked herself in the bathroom to check with a mirror that no telltale label or lock of her own hair were showing. The look was perfect, however. She reapplied her new carmine lipstick, gave the back of her neck a squirt of scent then stood back to admire her full-length reflec-tion, stepping this way and that. He had a treat in store. He had a whole new wife.

Which were his own words exactly. At first he was perturbed. He wanted to know what had suddenly made her do it.

"You," she said lightly. "You said you wished I was blonde like that actress. So I am. I can always change back if you don't like it."

"No," he said, looking at her in an uncertain, sideways fashion as he mixed his gin and tonic and poured her a sweet sherry. "No. Don't do that. Was it very expensive?"

"Not very." He had no idea how much women's hair cost to fix. He naively thought it was maybe twice what he was charged by the barber in the station car park.

"Supper'll be about five minutes," she said, "as I'm running a bit late. And I don't want a sherry. I want a gin."

"But you like sherry. You always have sherry," he insisted.

"I'd rather have what you're having," she said. "If there's enough, that is."

"Sure. Of course there's enough. There's always enough." He tipped the sherry back into its sticky lipped bottle and poured her gin. "I dunno," he said. "I go to the office and when I come back I find a whole new wife."

She simply smiled.

"Plenty of tonic," she said girlishly. "Or it'll go to my head."

Over dinner he admired her nails too, apparently only noticing them for the first time now that she was blonde. He tried not to stare, but she felt him watching her whenever she walked over to the cooker or the fridge.

"What are you staring at?" she asked at last, amazed that he had made no comment on the unpleasantly chemical pudding she had made by whipping milk into the brown powdered contents of a convenient packet and tossing in a few biscuits soaked in cherry brandy.

"You've killed her," he joked. "Haven't you? You've gone and killed her and put her outside in the deep-freeze or something."

She paused at the dishwasher with her back to him and shuddered involuntarily.

"Don't be silly," she said as soon as she could. "You'll give me the creeps. Coffee?"

"Please."

"In here? Or are we playing Scrabble?"

"No games tonight," he said, affecting a yawn. "I thought perhaps an early night..."

She had always wondered how oral sex would feel when performed on her, but in all the years of their marriage he had never offered and she had never thought it entirely proper to ask. Tonight, emboldened by the unprecedented interest he was showing in her hands, her feet and her borrowed hair, she realized that she needed no words to ask him. While he was giving her breasts more attention than the usual cursory lick, she simply placed a hand on his head and pushed. He hesitated for a moment as though unable to believe what she was suggesting so she pushed again, quite firmly, so that her wishes should be unmistakable. The surprising pleasure he proceeded to give her had little to do with anything he was doing to her and everything to do with what she was doing to him. She had always supposed that sex was a matter of submission, patience even, but now it dawned on her that it was eight-tenths power.

She woke with a headache. She wondered if it had anything to do with the gin, then thought that perhaps the wig was too tight. Could her head have expanded? *Did* heads expand? Like hot feet? The headache intensified as she dressed. She scowled as she brushed her teeth and teased the wig back into shape on her scalp. Downstairs the pain broke out as sulkiness, when she complained about being expected to polish her husband's shoes, and naked temper when she shouted at her daughter—her beloved Jennifer—for complaining that there was no fat-free milk for her cereal. Where these displays would normally have been beaten down by louder ones from the offended parties, she was amazed to see her husband mutely take up the boot polish and her daughter reach for the gold top with something like terror. Landed with the school run again by some cooked-up excuse from another mother, she thought her head would burst with the added burden of the children's chatter. She paused at some traffic lights to rifle her bag for painkillers, which she gulped down without water, heedless of curious stares from behind her. Odious Morag— whose favor her children only cultivated because her parents had a swimming pool and threw vulgarly ostentatious birthday parties for her—had already riled her by insisting on sitting in the front like an adult because she said the back of the car "had a bad smell." She then began to tease Jennifer for having a crush on a teacher.

"That's enough," Wanda said, wincing at the pain her own voice caused, booming behind her eyes. "Stop being horrid."

"But it's true," Morag insisted. "She always tries to sit in the front row."

"I don't!" Jennifer protested.

"She *does*. And yesterday she stayed behind to ask him questions before break."

"I said that's *enough!*" Wanda said and found herself slapping Morag on her soft, pink thigh.

For a moment there was stunned silence as Morag looked from thigh to driver and back again. It had been a fierce little slap; Wanda's palm still stung seconds later.

"I'll tell," Morag said at last.

"Good," Wanda told her, giddy with the release of uttering words she had too long swallowed. "Then maybe you'll get another slap for being a telltale as well as an ill-bred little madam."

Morag made as if to cry at this but Wanda silenced her.

"Stop it," she hissed, astonished at the scorn in her tone. "You're too *big* to play the baby."

The euphoria of the others was palpable behind their silence as Morag stifled her petulant sniffles. Pulling up outside the school, Wanda defied the pain in her head. "Jennifer," she said, "I'm *glad* you're showing an interest in your lessons. I'm *proud* of you, darling."

Jennifer shone with pleasure even as Morag seemed to shrink in significance.

Wanda tore the wig off with a gasp as soon as she was clear of the area. Glancing in the mirror to flick her own hair back to a semblance of life, she saw a livid, purplish welt where the thing's netting had been grinding into her forehead. From time to time as she drove, she would rub hard at it with her fingertips. She had a tendency to raise her eyebrows when people were talking to her, especially when she had no interest in what they were telling her. Possibly this habitual action had made the wig's chafing worse, producing this shaming record of insincerity.

Back in her house, before she had even loaded the breakfast things into the dishwasher, she hurried to the telephone and called her hairdresser's. To her dismay, no one, not even a junior, could see her for anything more than a dry-it-yourself light trim for two days. She had a deep, almost pathological sense of consumer loyalty, never being lured by a bargain rate into forsaking the tradesmen she had always patronized without a commensurate sense of guilt which she felt obliged to own when she next entered her usual shop.

"I bought half a pound of these in that other place on the parade," she would confide in a confused salesperson. "I never normally shop anywhere but here but, well, you know how it is. I just saw the price and in I went."

Often as not she would add some placatory lie about the bargain goods having proved inferior to those from her usual stockist, as though the thought that her dereliction had been punished would comfort them over her momentary infidelity. It was with a heavy heart, therefore, that she reached for the Yellow Pages and looked up the numbers of rival salons. She would not tip, she told herself, however good they proved; that way the disloyalty would seem less wounding. But neither Bernice of Bromley, Shy Locks or Louis D'Alsace could fit her in. After a few more, similarly disappointing calls, she gave up, called back her usual salon, and made a morning appointment for the next day. It was only another twenty-four hours, she told herself. If she had fooled her small world so far, she could fool it a little further.

To soothe her nerves she left the wig on the hall table for swift snatching up should there be any surprise callers, then she threw herself into a satisfactory penance of housework. She scrubbed the bath, pulling a skein of matted hairs from the plughole, cleaned the nasty fluffy bit of carpet behind the loo, wiped the tops of the door surrounds and descaled the shower head with a powerful caustic she had recently heard of being used in a desperate suicide bid. Then, with no break for coffee, she set about taking every saucepan and labor-saving device from the kitchen cupboards, cleaning it, washing down its shelf, then putting it back again. She even wiped the sticky residue from jam and marmalade pots. The varnish on her new nails chipped off in places but she slaved on, taking a kind of delight in finding other unpalatable tasks to tackle. She skipped lunch, eating only aspirin because she still had the residue of her morning's headache, and forged on with polishing her husband's collection of silver-plate trophies and the fiddly cake stand with matching slice which his aunt had given them on their wedding day. (Wanda had kept it in the back of a cupboard, polishing it still more rarely than she used it because it had too many little nooks and crannies and something in her rebelled at using even a discarded toothbrush to clean it.)

Suddenly she saw it was time to be picking the children up again. Cursing clothes, time, duty, she ran to the hall, tossing aside her apron and snatching up the wig. The wig no longer fitted. She glared at her pink-cheeked reflection as she stuffed her hair back behind her ears and tried again. She even checked to see if the label were the right way round. She glanced at her watch and let out a whimper. She caught herself toying with the possibility of driving into school as she was, only with a headscarf on in the vain hope that the children would prove less sharp-eyed than usual. This was ridiculous! Wigs did not shrink. It was not in their nature. And heads, healthy adult heads, did not grow. Brooking no nonsense, she tried one more time.

Never had the saying that one must suffer to be beautiful been so rigorously brought home to her. She succeeded in donning the wig and styling it much as before, but it might have been made of cheesewire it dug so fiercely into her. The headache, which had never entirely left her all day, paled by comparison with such immediate pain. Driving to the school, she felt herself multiply martyred. She was not yet so vain as to have become irrational. She wondered if she were sick. Women such as she had become, women with scarlet nails and borrowed splendor, were never ill. They had everything organized, and disease was not part of their plan. They vomited with tidy aggression in other women's bathrooms then partied on, lips painted afresh. They scorned hospitals. Illness bored them and the surgeon's knife filled them with selfish fears. They died violently, she sensed, in a kind of anger at a world that had cheated them. Women who made love in blonde wigs and took pains to deceive their children died crushed beneath the wheels of trains or skewered by the steering columns of their lovers' cars. A trickle of warm moisture ran from under the wig across her temple. She glanced fearfully up at the mirror,

half expecting to see blood, but it was merely sweat and she
dabbed it away with a handkerchief.

She was one of the last of the parents to arrive but there was not a
breath of complaint from the children, and she remembered her
show of strength that morning. She noticed its effect almost immediately; a change had come over the pecking order in the
group. To her surprise she saw that it was her daughter who now
held sway, telling people where to sit, holding power of ultimate
disapproval or permission. And it was Morag, normally so haughty
and spiteful, who was now the po-faced wheedler and appeaser.

"Mrs. Spalding, I know it's very short notice," she began, with
such soft shyness that Wanda anticipated mockery, "but my parents are taking me to the cinema tonight and I wondered if you'd
let Mark and Jennifer come too. We've all done our homework already. We did most of it in break and we finished it in the last lesson because Mr. Dukes was off sick. Daddy would drop them off
afterward. So you wouldn't have to do anything."

Wanda aquiesced so easily they seemed quite startled. Jennifer
began to plead automatically before realizing her wish was already
granted. Wanda could think of nothing but the cruel way their
voices played upon the pain in her head. The possibility of empty-
ing the car that little bit sooner and facing an evening of relative
tranquillity was an unlooked-for blessing. Her immediate impulse
on swinging clear of Morag's parents' long drive was to snatch the
wig off, but she checked herself with the thought that she would
only have to pull it on again for her husband's benefit, possibly
with even greater difficulty and pain than before.

When she reached home, she walked swiftly round, drawing all the
curtains and turning on a few lights to create a pleasant, welcoming atmosphere, then she kicked off her shoes and lay in the middle of the drawing room carpet, breathing gently. The scents of
potpourri and cleaning products soothed her. The tang of carpet
freshening powder was a reminder that she had not rested all day.
She closed her eyes, concentrating on breathing slower and slower,
counting to herself as she drew in the fragrant air. The pain in her
head began to subside and, fancying she felt the wig loosen per-
ceptibly about her skull, she slipped into a sensuous doze.

She had given no thought all day to what they were to eat for supper. Normally it was something she did after the children had been taken from her after breakfast. She would load the dishwasher then allow herself a cup of coffee and a couple of the biscuits she kept hidden inside the drum of the electric potato peeler and she would pore over recipe books and a shopping list. Given though she might be to the blandishments of kitchen gadgets, she had never been one of those modern mothers (slatternly mothers, she thought of them, lucky, happy slatterns) who contented themselves with a hoard of frozen meals and a microwave oven. Apart from *Instant Whip*, the nearest she had ever allowed herself to fast food was a pressure cooker, and *that* she only used for steaming puddings and root vegetables. When she woke to find her husband standing over her asking if she were all right and what was for supper because he couldn't smell anything cooking, she stared up at him and felt panic in her very soul.

"I...I fell asleep," she stammered, climbing to her feet and padding, shoeless, into the supperless space across the hall. "Morag's parents have taken the children to the cinema. I had a headache when I got back and I lay down and I must have fallen asleep. Sorry." She looked about her. The lack of lights and steam, the lack of sizzle, formed a dreadful, silent accusation. She could not pretend that the automatic oven switch had failed to come on when there was palpably nothing in there waiting to be cooked. There was not even a piece of meat. She opened the fridge door then closed it again hurriedly as he came in behind her. There was nothing. No bacon. No chicken breasts. Not even some humbly reassuring mince.

"I work my guts out all day," he was saying, as to some invisible jury, "and it's been a bugger of a day too, and I come back to find you fast asleep, looking like nothing on earth, and the table not even laid." She darted a hand to her head and was relieved to find the wig still in place. "What's got into you?" he asked.

She decided to brazen it out.

"I forgot," she said.

"You *what*?!"

"I forgot. I've never done it before and I won't do it again. But I forgot. I spent the whole day cleaning and scrubbing and I completely forgot about supper. And I've had a terrible headache.

Why don't I fix us both a nice drink? Better still, why don't we live a little and go out. The children are safe with the Hewitsons until nine-forty. If we went now I'm sure we could get a table. I've had a bugger of a day too." From somewhere deep within her she found a reserve of flirtatious gaiety. "Come on," she said. "You mix us both a nice gin and put your feet up while I go and put on something pretty then we can pretend we're young and free again and you can take me out for dinner. Somewhere cozy. Somewhere French with candles!"

There was a pause, perhaps for only a second, in which she was intensely aware that the fridge had developed a louder buzz than usual, which she knew was the sign that it was reaching its point of built-in obsolesence, then he began to shout at her. He called her filthy things—filthier things than he ever did when they were having sexual intercourse. He implied she was a failure as a wife, a mother, a woman even, and then he slapped her. He had offered her many insults in his way and in his time but he had never, until this evening, touched her in violence. She fell back against the sink. Then, all at once, the shock of his big bony hand against her jaw seemed the ultimate denigration and she took a knife from the wooden block beside the bread bin and pushed it into his stomach. It was a big knife, her biggest, and the block was a particularly cunning one with a discreet mechanism which sharpened each blade as it released it for use.

She had often heard of the similarities between pork and human flesh, in particular their skin structure and the thickness of their fatty deposits. After the initial resistance, which might as well have been caused by the starched cotton of his shirt as by any strength of skin and muscle, the knife slid in with appalling ease and swiftness. The sensation was not unlike slicing into a rolled pork loin. Her husband gasped and staggered backward, then forward, then slumped to the floor. Never having taken a first aid exam, he did not know better than to pull the knife out. She had punctured his liver. By the time he was writhing and coughing on the linoleum, his suit was turning purple with his gore. She tried to stanch the flow with tea towels, but he was beyond her help. He seemed to spit in her face as he died, but perhaps he was only coughing.

She called for an ambulance and the police, telling them her husband had been stabbed but not by whom, then she looked up the relevant cinema in the local newspaper and telephoned to leave an urgent message for the Hewitsons that an emergency had arisen and they were to hang on to Mark and Jennifer until contacted by the authorities. Turning back, she saw the big red thing on the kitchen floor and was suddenly sick, just as she had imagined women with blonde wigs should be. She vomited nothing but acrid juices, having eaten nothing all day, but it ruined the parts of her clothes the blood had not already stained, and she determined to change into something cleaner before the emergency services arrived. Both hospital and police station were a good fifteen minutes' drive away. Skidding slightly, because her feet were wet, she hurried across the kitchen and up the stairs to the bathroom. She tugged her blouse over her head and stepped out of her skirt. She began to wash her bloodied hands in the sink then realized that there was so much of the stuff on her that a shower would do the job better.

Having been descaled only that afternoon, the jet was extra strong, and she welcomed its buffeting. It was only as she raised her hands to her face that she remembered she was still wearing the wig. Blinking the water from her eyes, heedless now of how badly she treated the thing, she took a handful of curls and tugged. She recoiled with a gasp. Crying out as though the water were scalding her, she flung back the shower curtain and struggled to see herself in the looking glass. The mirrored surface had steamed up and her flailing hand could not reach it so she tugged once more at the curls and felt once more the unmistakable agony of her own outraged scalp refusing to yield.

The Wedding Dress

JASON FRIEDMAN

One Saturday afternoon, as he was crossing Route 12 on his way to the station, Junior came upon a wedding dress in the middle of the road. It was zipped up in a see-through plastic bag and straddled the double yellow line as if it had been set there deliberately. Before he had time to wonder, he saw a red pickup rounding the curve toward him, so he threw the dress over his arm and darted across the road. He eased down the grassy embankment, jumped the ditch, then headed up the incline on the other side. He crossed the cement plaza between pumps numbers three and four and went inside the food mart part of the gas station. His mother was ringing up a customer, so she could not see him cross the store behind her and go into the back room, where he put the dress down on top of two stacked cases of cherry bombs.

Except for finding the dress, Junior's routine was no different than it had been every Saturday afternoon for the past year. On the day his father died, struck by a truck carrying chickens into town as he crossed Route 12 on his way to work one miasmic morning eight years before, Junior's mother had told her son, "You and I are going to build your daddy's business into something he can be proud of, wherever he may be." He was named John James Grumley, Jr., but from that day on his mother called him Junior and began taking him to the station with her or having him meet her there after school. For his fifteenth birthday present she gave him his very own shift, and the following Saturday he came in to relieve her at two and remained there until ten, when Eddie Hawkins came in for the night shift.

Junior did not mind working at the station. Even as a kid he ended up covering for his mother and Eddie so often that he knew he should be getting paid more than free candy bars and Cokes, though he never said anything about it. So it was only fair when he started to get paid, even if it was his mother signing the checks. The Saturday shift was all right. On Saturday nights the other kids from Thomaston High went to parties he did not know about or drove to secret clearings in the woods to drink, so he wouldn't have had anything to do anyway. At some point in the evening they came in to play the machines in the back or put gas in their cars or buy cigarettes or even rubbers. At first he was shy to wait on them, but he got used to it.

And when they were gone, when the store was silent except for the humming of the refrigerated case and the surge of the air conditioner, he walked over to the magazine rack. He stared at the covers as he listened for the sound of a car or truck turning off the road. On the covers there were usually girls with lots of curly blond hair, and his heart beat faster as he ran his hands along the plastic wrap covering their faces and breasts. Anyone could have walked in and caught him. Sometimes his heart beat so loudly and quickly that the beating was in his ears and he couldn't hear cars turning off the road. Sometimes when he was looking at the magazine covers kids on foot or bicycle came in to buy candy, and when that happened he fumbled at rearranging the display, then returned to the cash register.

It was a miracle his mother had never caught him. Although they lived in a two-bedroom block bungalow in the woods directly across from the station, his mother refused to cross the road on foot. Instead she drove their faded yellow seventy-nine Plymouth twenty yards down the old Cohoochee Highway, turned right onto Route 12 until she came to its intersection with Route 13, then made a U-turn at the crossroads and doubled back to the station. If she had walked in while he was looking at the magazines, his heart certainly would have exploded in his chest and in his ears and he would have dropped dead at the magazine rack.

Sometimes he took one of the magazines and put it on the shelf under the cash register. Back home in his room, he ripped off the plastic and turned the pages so quickly he could hardly see the blond girls, only smell the magazine's gluey chemical smell. He would turn and turn until he found a man with one or more of the girls, and then he would stare, feeling his heart now in his crotch as well. He would scrutinize the picture, imagining he was in it as well, but not a willing participant, forced. He did not even want to look at the picture, but he could not put it down, and in his confusion and mounting panic he sometimes tore at his hair and clawed at his cheeks, though he could not say why he did these things either. By the time his mother knocked at the door to remind him about supper, there were tears in his eyes, and he threw the magazine under the bed and said, "I'm coming, Mama," having first rehearsed quietly to monitor his voice for signs of weakness, of distress.

"That you?" she called out from the cash register.

"Yes, ma'am." He arranged the dress bag so that it hung evenly over both sides of the top crate of fireworks.

"What are you doing back there?"

"Nothing," he said, coming out front. He kissed her and said, "I just found something in the road."

"In the road? What were you doing looking down at the road? I told you to be careful crossing that road."

He stood opposite her with his palms on the counter as if he were a customer. "I am careful. I just couldn't help seeing it."

She squinted through glasses with square red frames. Her hair was newly curled. "What was it you found, then?"

"A dress," he said, looking down, as if the word itself shamed him.

"A dress! Why, how could there be a dress in the road? Who would have dropped a dress in the road?"

"I don't know. There just was."

"Well, what did you do with it?" she asked, winking. "I could use me a new dress."

"I'll go get it," he said.

When he came back out his mother was reaching up for a pack of cigarettes for a black woman in flip-flops. After the woman had left, he set down the dress bag and he and his mother stared at it in silence. Someone called from one of the fireworks aisles, and Junior went over to help him.

When he got back to the register his mother whispered, "Did you know this was a wedding dress?"

"I guess," he said. "I mean, not really."

"That's what it is. And an expensive one too. Where'd you say you found this?"

"Right out front in the road."

"Route twelve?"

He nodded.

"Over the last thirteen years I have seen more than my share of things in that road, but they usually run to the roadkill side of things." She ran her hand along the bag. "I'm going to take this home for you so it doesn't get all wrinkled."

"All right."

"I mean if that's all right with you. This dress is your responsibility now, and far be it for me to presume."

"Oh, Mama," he said, looking down.

"I mean it."

When he looked up, his mother was holding the dress, sprung from its transparent cocoon, in front of her. "It sure is nice," he remarked.

"I'm not completely washed up yet, am I?" she said, stealthily slipping the dress back into its bag. Then she took off her name tag and stuck it into the pocket of her sweatpants. "I mean, I know I'm no spring chicken."

Before Junior could respond, the young guy from the fireworks aisle made his way over to the counter and set down a box of Red Devils next to the wedding gown. "Somebody getting married?" he asked.

Junior could feel the hot blood in his face. His mother picked up the dress and said, "Not at this rate they ain't."

The following Wednesday, the main headline on the front page of the *Thomaston Town Crier*'s Round the Town section read, "Teenage Boy Finds Wedding Dress in Middle of Route 12." There was a picture of Junior sullenly contemplating the cover of *Bride's* magazine. His mother, who was standing off to the side at the photography shoot and urging Junior to smile, was responsible for the story. After telling Junior her plan, she had called Ed Sanders, the editor of the paper and a regular customer of the station, and told him the story while he jotted down notes. The bride, she explained, was advised to drop by Grumley's Amoco service station on Route 12. The gown's exact description was purposely kept obscure.

On the day the story came out, Junior's math teacher called him over after class and said, "I see you're a local hero now." Nobody else said a word. But the next day his homeroom class greeted him with a mixture of backhanded congratulations and sly taunts. "I see you found yourself a wedding dress," said Bobby Bryson, who had a pale scar over one eye and played basketball and had never before even looked at Junior. "Now all you need to do is find yourself a bride." Everybody but Junior laughed, and then the bell rang and Mr. Fowler walked in.

There were two kinds of women who responded to the newspaper story. It got to the point that whenever Junior was helping his mother out at the station or working his own shift, he could spot them as soon as they walked through the door.

The first group that Junior came to recognize were the down-on-their-lucks. These were the girls whose wedding gowns really had been lost or stolen. They usually tried to enter the food mart by pulling instead of pushing on the left door, then, thinking they had figured it out, decided to push, but on the right door, which opened by being pulled. And when they made it to the cash register they held out a ragged clipping of the newspaper story and said, without much hope, "You the people that found a wedding dress?" They told their stories flatly and succinctly, then surveyed the store from the counter as if they had come for something more mundane. When asked they would describe the dress to Junior's mother, their words trailing off before they had really begun. And when Junior's mother told them how sorry she was but that the dress she had wasn't theirs, they nodded, as if the verdict could not have been otherwise. They usually picked up a cold drink on the way out.

The other group were the lonelyhearts. These women had been unlucky in love—either jilted at the altar or some unspecified time before reaching it. Some of them came to talk, pouring out their troubles to Junior's mother as other customers looked on uneasily and the older woman passed across the counter miniature packets of Kleenex.

Those lonelyhearts who did not come to talk came for the specific purpose of meeting Junior. When they showed up during the week they asked for him, and when Junior's mother asked if they had come about the dress, they would reply that if she didn't mind, they'd rather just speak with Junior himself. Junior's mother soon confessed that if they weren't too trashy looking or too old, she told them when his shift was.

So they showed up Saturday nights. They were easy to spot. They didn't smile much. He watched them walk past the counter with their eyes down, circle the store until it had emptied out some, then stand in front of the cash register staring at the floor. They were as skittish looking as he probably was when he examined the magazines.

"Can I help you, ma'am?" he asked one of these girls one Saturday night. Bones jutted out from the top part of her chest, where her lacy white blouse was unbuttoned. Her lips were smeared with Vaseline or clear lip gloss.

She looked up and said, "Oh, am I next?"

When he said yes she replied, "I mean, you can go ahead and wait on somebody else first if you need to." Finally she said, "Were you the one that found a wedding dress in the middle of the road?"

"I did," he said, silently cursing his mother for sending her here tonight. She insisted on interviewing the girls herself, so there was no reason for him even to be talking to her.

"I saw your picture in the paper."

He smiled.

"You don't really look like that."

"Like what?"

"Like your picture in the paper."

He didn't know what to say. He wished he could be easy and charming like Bobby Bryson and most of the other kids at school, but he couldn't. He didn't know how. In the chill air-conditioned store he began to sweat, and he grabbed a napkin and wiped his forehead. He could end it here. All he had to do was ask if she'd come about the dress. He'd expose her in her folly, and she'd leave with her head hung low.

"You don't look worse or anything, you just look...different. Taller."

"Well." And then he resorted to something he'd read in the paper, in a column about manners. It was bad manners to ask someone what they did, but it was good manners to ask them where they were from. "Are you from around here?" he asked.

"No. I'm from Brookletville. Have you ever been there?"

"Naw."

A bearded man with a package of baloney, a loaf of white bread, and a jar of mustard was standing behind the girl and staring with his lips set at the ceiling. When Junior gestured for him to come forward, the girl moved aside. She stood perfectly still and stared at her feet.

When the bearded man had gone she came to life again. "There's nothing in Brookletville," she said. "There really isn't a damn thing there at all."

That night, at the end of his shift, he crossed the two-lane highway without looking both ways, without even listening. It would serve his mother right if he got hit. His family had never been religious, but he knew that thinking this way was a sin. He couldn't help it. He trudged through the underbrush as slowly as he could, choosing his path so that the porch light was hidden by the greatest number of trees.

Inside she leapt up off the couch and met him in the kitchen. "You'd think that by now I could hear you coming," she said. "I guess I must have the TV on too loud. Old ladies tend to be hard of hearing."

He kissed her brusquely, then went to his room.

"How was work tonight?" she called from the other side of the locked door.

He took off his pants and folded them across his chair.

"Nobody give you any problems, did they?"

"No, ma'am," he said, taking off his shirt. He removed his underpants and socks and stood before the full-length mirror on the door.

"Did bachelorette number one come by to claim the dress?"

"Uh-uh." He ran his fingers down his cheeks. He didn't think he looked so bad in the paper. That was what he looked like, at least in black and white. Longish light-colored hair, wide face, big eyes, a few soft hairs above his mouth, droopy lower lip. What did that girl really mean when she said he looked "different"?

His mother knocked four times and said, "Baby, what are you doing in there? Ain't you going to wash up for dinner?"

"I'm not hungry."

"You're not hung— You haven't been eating those nasty hot dogs again, have you?"

"Naw."

"Well then, I can't understand why you're not hungry." She knocked again. The knob turned one way, then the other. "Unless you're not feeling a hundred percent. Baby, are you feeling all right?"

"I'm fine." He ran his hand over his skinny white body, pressing his fingers into his ribs, his breastbone. "I'm just going to lie down for a second."

The TV boomed from the living room. "All right, but I fried you some fish, and it'll get too dried up if it sits in the oven too long. I put your plate in the oven to keep warm."

He examined the sparse brown hairs at the bottom of his chest, the soft trail of them leading down to his crotch. He did not want to lie down. He did not want to look at his magazines. His fingers slid along his what's-it, cupping the end of it, then sliding along it again. He thought of that girl who came in tonight. She was skinny like he was, and if she just smiled, she might be almost pretty. He imagined her taking off her white blouse and her bra too. Imagined himself cupping his hands over the little mounds of her breasts. He closed his eyes and rubbed himself so hard that his what's-it began to hurt. He imagined her taking off her jeans too, but now Bobby Bryson was in his head. It was Bobby Bryson taking off his jeans the way he did before PE, then snapping on his jockstrap. The hair on Bobby's legs was blond and thick.

Junior tried to picture the girl from the station again, but it was hopeless. When he opened his eyes the side of his what's-it was the color of a ripe tomato. He bent humbly to examine himself but almost cried out when his sweaty finger touched broken skin.

His mother's footsteps trailed away on the carpeting.

Because the gown was so expensive looking, it occurred to Junior's mother that it might belong to someone in Hilton Head or Savannah. The Amoco station was in the country exactly halfway between the two, and perhaps some wealthy Savannah family had been transporting the dress out to Hilton Head for the wedding. "I hear that's the in thing to do these days," she told Junior. "Getting married on a beach. That sounds awfully uncomfortable to me."

A month after Junior had found the dress, his mother told him she was going to phone the papers in Hilton Head and Savannah.

"Can't we just forget about it?" Junior asked. His mother looked up from the hot-dog broiler, which she was wiping with soda water, and said, "No, we can't just forget about it. Do you think that dress will just disappear?" "We could sell it," Junior offered, but his mother kept wiping and did not reply. When she had cleaned the broiler to her satisfaction, she stood back and appraised it and said, "In my heart I promised your father I'd show you the right path in this life, and until now I thought I'd set you on it."

The following week a story about the dress appeared in the Metro section of the *Savannah Morning News and Evening Press*. "Thomaston Teen Finds Wedding Dress in Route 12," read the headline. "Cinderella Search Is On." Because Junior had refused to be photographed, the Savannah paper used the same picture that had appeared in the *Town Crier*; the story was skimpy because he had refused to be interviewed. "My son's just modest," his mother had explained to the reporter.

One Saturday night in early June, Junior was straightening up the counter displays when a thin, good-looking man walked in and said hello. He had short brown curly hair and a moustache. Junior said hey and asked if he could help him. "Yes, I think you might be able to help me," the man said. He pulled out a card from his wallet and handed it across the counter. The card read "The Bridal Boutique/Savannah, Georgia/Richard Kersey, Bridal Consultant." By now Junior had thought he could spot just about anybody with any interest in or claim to the dress. In addition to the merely curious, the latest newspaper stories had attracted several crooks, whom Junior could identify chiefly because they seemed resentful rather than grateful he had found the dress. He felt he had gotten pretty good at hearing them out, then sending them away. But a man! How could he possibly figure out a man who came to claim a wedding dress? What would he say to him? He stared at the card until he had it memorized.

"Now don't go ripping my business card into shreds," the man said. He stuck out a hand and said, "Hi, my name's Rick Kersey."

Junior put down the card and shook the man's hand. His own hand was cold and damp.

"As you can see, I run a bridal shop over in Savannah, and I think you might have found my dress. Tell me, is it in good condition?"

"When I found it it was in a bag and it's still in it."

"Thank goodness. I try to take extra care when I'm delivering a dress to a client, but you know, you can't take every variable into account."

Junior nodded. The man's shirt was unbuttoned three buttons, and soft hair massed at his neck.

"Do you think I might have a look at the dress?"

"My mother has it," Junior replied. He wanted to keep standing here across from the man, but now there was not much more to say.

"Oh, yes. From the article. Where might I find her at?"

He looked down and said, "Well, she likes me to kind of ask people who come in a question or two, if you don't mind."

"Of course."

"Well," said Junior, slowly, searching for the right words. "Do you think, I mean, would you mind describing it to me?"

And without hesitation the man began talking about lacework and beaded trim and a hoop skirt. The dress, he said, was one of a kind; its color was ivory cream, he said, pronouncing *cream* as "crem."

For all Junior knew, this man might be the true owner of the dress. His description sounded good enough, and Junior just couldn't place him in a category as easily as he could the women. But what did Junior care? It was his mother who was so interested in the dress, in returning the dress—not him. That dress could have burned up in a big fire and he wouldn't have cared. He just wanted to stand here and talk to this man, not send him away. But it was no use. "We live just across the way," he said, pointing to the street lamp broken up by trees rising from the lowland.

"Thanks a lot, buddy," the man said, and Junior met his eyes and tried to smile. His heart beat in his throat. He stared at the man as he walked out the door.

Junior thought about the man for the rest of his shift, and he kept thinking about him as he crossed the highway and made his way through the woods and up to the house. He thought of the way the man had winked at him—so subtly that most people would not have been able to catch it. He thought of the way he walked— with determination but lightly, as if he were better suited to move through the air than most people were.

Junior let himself in and said hello to his mother in the living room. He could not remember when, but sometime recently he had stopped kissing her when he came in and she had stopped jumping up from the television. "Thank goodness you're home," she said. "Or am I not supposed to say that?"

Junior started for the bathroom.

His mother said, "Your friend came by tonight."

For a second he had the crazy idea she was talking about Bobby Bryson. But it must have seemed even crazier for his mother's voice to be saying the same thing that his mind's voice could not keep quiet about. He stopped, reached for the remote on the coffee table, and asked, "Can I turn this down?"

"Do what?"

He pressed the mute button and said, "I said can I turn this down."

"Well of course you can turn it down, but you don't have to turn it off. Now I missed that," she said, snatching up the remote and blaring the set again.

"So what happened?" Junior shouted at his mother. She looked different. She looked like she wasn't there.

"You can imagine how frightened I was at first, this strange man coming to my door in the middle of the night. Honestly, Junior, you really should know better."

Junior sat down before the television.

"Oh, now don't go worrying yourself over it. Your old mother can take care of herself, I guess. Especially around a man that's that way."

Junior turned back to his mother, who was holding up both hands limply at her chest, as if parodying an obedient dog. From somewhere he heard familiar laughter, then realized it was coming from himself.

"What are you laughing about?"

Then all at once the laughter stopped. Nothing seemed funny anymore. "Nothing."

"Nothing, huh." She stared at the television, then picked up the remote and turned it off. "You know, I'm trying my best, but I just don't think I can take much more of this."

Junior stared at the blank screen and listened to the air conditioner pulse.

"I mean," she went on, "every child goes through a rebellious phase, but that doesn't mean every mother has to play along. I always thought we had a different relationship."

"Different to what?" he asked, still staring at the screen.

"You know what I mean." She pulled out a clump of shredded yellow tissue and dabbed at her eyes. "Just different. Closer. I've tried to play along with you, I really have. When I saw you stopped wanting to kiss me it felt like a knife through my heart. But I kept all that to myself. Did you know I cry myself to sleep every night?"

He didn't reply.

"Well I do. And then to have you go and send a strange man over in the middle of the night to your father's house. I just don't know what you're trying to do to me anymore."

"Oh, Mama," he said, turning in her direction but not meeting her eyes. Lately, the house had become so tiny and close that sometimes he couldn't breathe. Now he took in breath after breath, then let them all out at once. "So did that dress belong to him?"

"What were you even doing having a conversation with a fellow like that?" she blurted. "He said he had such a nice 'chat' with you. He didn't try to do anything to you, did he?"

His ears burned with shame.

"Did he?"

"I don't know what you're talking about."

"Did he!" she said, her face reddening, the veins in her neck lying in relief against the loose skin.

He stood up and went to his room and locked the door. She pounded on it and said, "I wish your father was here. He'd know what to do about all this."

He leaned rigidly against the mirror and shut his eyes tight.

"I sure do wish he was."

The following week, area papers ran brief stories on the return of the wedding gown to its rightful owner. "Wedding Dress Saga Ends," announced the *Thomaston Town Crier*. The *Beaufort Bugle* ran a picture of Richard Kersey with the dress on a rack behind him. This time, Junior had not been the only one who refused to be interviewed. "There's nothing that I have to say on the matter," his mother told the reporters. "Case closed."

Overnight the dress seemed to disappear from the local imagination. No one came to the station to claim the dress or talk about it. The bungalow across from the station grew quiet. Now when Junior came home from work his mother let him take his supper out of the oven himself. Sometimes she got up from the couch and joined him, but she never said much, and when she did it was only about what she had been watching on TV. For Junior, it was a relief.

The wedding dress used to pop into his head at odd times—when he was crossing Route 1 2, for example, or swimming in the lake. Now it was the man who appeared in Junior's thoughts. He had clipped the man's picture and tucked it between the stiff pages of one of the magazines. In Junior's fantasy, the man walked in staring at Junior, as if he had not come for the dress at all. And behind Junior's closed bedroom door Junior set down the man's picture, closed his eyes, and stared at the hairy V below his neck. Afterward, he lay sweating on the bed, tracing cum around his navel. From the other room, television voices sounded evenly. For nearly an hour, he made no effort to rise from the sour-smelling bed. He lay there and waited.

One Saturday night toward the end of summer, the Bridal Boutique van pulled alongside the gas pumps and Richard Kersey got out and walked into the food mart. Junior had rehearsed this entrance so often in his head that at first he was neither surprised nor thrilled. Then Kersey met his eyes and seemed to be smiling—in the fantasy the man did not smile, only stared gravely—and at that moment Junior's heart began to thud in his chest and he felt a hollowness in his gut, as if he had been punched. "Hey there, buddy," Kersey said, removing a credit card from his wallet. "Remember me?"

Junior smiled shyly and said yes.

Kersey handed Junior the credit card and said, "I'll fill 'er up with silver on number three."

Did Junior imagine Kersey wink at him as he turned to go out? Could there have been any sense in what his mother was ranting about that night? Junior turned on the pump, and when Kersey was out of sight of the cash register Junior picked up an orange plastic–framed pocket mirror from a box on the counter and checked the cracks between his teeth for traces of hot dog. He put the mirror back and from another box withdrew a mint sprayer and sprayed.

Junior took care of two customers, and then Kersey was standing at the counter. Junior pressed the total button on the keyboard: $4.39. It was too low. No one filled up a van—or even a car—with a credit card and then put in only $4.39 worth of gas. Junior fumbled with the card and did not look up.

"I tell you," Kersey said as they were waiting for the receipt to print out, "I had no idea they'd be doing a write-up on me. I guess I should have expected it, but when the phone started ringing that kind of caught me off-guard."

"I bet," Junior said.

"Not that I mind it," Kersey said. His eyes were so pale blue they were almost white. "I am a businessman after all, and every little bit helps."

The receipt pushed out like a tongue and Junior handed it over.

Kersey removed a silver pen from his shirt pocket. "So how's your mother?"

"Oh, she's fine. The same."

"Good. That's good to hear. Because I think I gave her a little bit of a fright."

"Aw, she's all right," Junior said, then suddenly emboldened added, "She can be a little high strung."

Kersey laughed. "She can? I'm glad to hear you say that. I thought it was just me."

Their transaction was complete. Now Kersey held Junior's eyes with that grave look Junior had imagined as characteristic of him. Just then Bobby Bryson came in and pretended not to notice the man with the moustache stepping back from the counter. He threw five dollars on the counter and said, "Hey, Junior." Bobby Bryson's mouth curved up in a half-smile, a smirk. Junior took down a hard pack of Marlboros and handed them over. Now he had no choice but to go through with whatever Kersey had in mind, no choice but to make his humiliation complete—and worth something.

"You know," Kersey said after Bobby had left, "I really appreciate you finding my dress and keeping it so nice till I could come claim it."

"Well."

"No, really, I mean it. There's a lot of snakes out in the world these days. I'd like to give you a little reward."

"That isn't necessary."

"No, I insist upon it. Do you ever come into Savannah?"

Junior looked down. What could he be besides a disappointment to this man? "Not much."

"You don't?" Kersey did not look surprised. "It's so close and
all, I'd expect you to be out every night there with your girlfriends."

"I don't really have any girlfriends," Junior said, knowing full
well what he was saying, knowing his fate was sealed.

A week later, he drove the yellow Plymouth through the dark
countryside, past the trailer park, then the scrap metal factory,
and then a lone bungalow or two before the pine woods closed in
on both sides of the narrow road. Then the trees ended and he
was driving across the marsh. In the distance to his right, lights
from the paper mill twinkled and a fat coil of white smoke rose
into the unreal glare. Now he could see the bridge set like a great
jeweled bracelet against black velvet, and the low buildings of the
Savannah skyline beyond it. On one side of the road squatted a
pink-fronted trailer with a pair of big green neon dice in constant
tumble, and a single yellow street lamp shone over three cars in a
dirt lot. There was a similar establishment across the street. He
could remember when these were fruit stands, then firecracker
stands. He could remember when Grumley's Amoco service station had two pumps and no food mart and his daddy held him on
his lap.

Junior was meeting Richard Kersey at the Pirate's House, a famous old restaurant near the river where Junior had been once,
with the Cub Scouts. He remembered being taken on a tour of
the place, its tiny candlelit rooms and narrow passageways. In
one dim corner, he recalled, an iron gate blocked off a stone
stairway leading down to a tunnel, and a dummy pirate slumped
across the torch-lit landing began to speak: *Shanghaied. I was
shanghaied, ye mateys. Down to the river and onto a boat. Down to the
river and onto a boat.*

They have great desserts there, Kersey had said that night at
the station. You do like dessert, don't you? Isn't that how you got
to be so tall?

"Did you have any trouble getting here?" Kersey asked once
they were seated, at a table by a cold fireplace.

"Naw. I just told Mama I was going to a party."

They sat without speaking. Then Junior asked after the dress, and Kersey told him it had walked down the aisle the day before yesterday and was probably in an attic somewhere by now.

After they had ordered, Kersey grinned, revealing dimples, and said, "You look nervous."

"Naw," Junior replied. He stared at the fireplace. "I mean, I reckon I am."

Junior and Kersey had walked into the gay bar together, and Kersey had greeted the muscular man just inside the door by name, and as far as Junior could tell, no money had changed hands, though he had spotted a sign reading, "NON-MEMBER TEN-DOLLAR COVER CHARGE." Junior was six-foot-one, but surely no one believed he was old enough to be here. Rick Kersey seemed to know everyone, and Junior was sure he was talking about him with his friends as they stood near the bar and laughed into each other's ears and touched each other more than men usually did. Junior stood slightly apart from Kersey and his friends, smiling as brightly as he could. Kersey did not speak to him but brought him one beer and then another. When the two men walked out into the night a hot breeze blew over the river and Junior knew that he was not going to be home by midnight, as he had promised, and that he did not care.

Kersey lived in a townhouse on a square two blocks from the bar. Junior was led by the hand to the third floor and into a high-ceilinged apartment with tables draped in lace tablecloths and covered with white figurines. On the walls were old-fashioned pictures of rich looking people Junior knew Kersey had never met. By the bed was the top half of a sightless naked-woman manne-quin sprouted from a pole with a round base.

They sat on the bed and Kersey said, "You don't look so damn nervous anymore. I guess you must be used to me already."

"What?" Junior said, suddenly dizzy from sitting down. "Yeah, I'm all right."

"But you still have that distant look on your face."

"Well," Junior said, putting his hand over Kersey's. In the window of the bungalow he saw his mother's face, the lines on her forehead and the furrow between her eyes. "I was just thinking how weird my mother is."

Kersey withdrew his hand. "Now let's not bring her along on this ride."

Junior's laughter enlarged into a resounding burp. "Excuse me," he said and fell back laughing.

Kersey stood up and walked to the end of the bed. Then he removed his clothes, revealing his body in sections—first the milky chest with a nest of brown fuzz rising up from the center, then the muscular thighs and calves, and finally his dick, which emerged fully erect and with such momentousness that Junior could say only, "It's so big."

"Bigger than yours, I bet," Kersey said. He sat down next to Junior and placed his hand on his crotch.

Junior closed his eyes and the darkness turned and he remembered how he thought it would be. That was just a year ago, and in a sudden access of memory he remembered what he had not thought of since then, since he got started with the magazines. Surely, he had thought, his legs would rub against another man's and that would be it, the shame of it coming over him in Rick Kersey's bedroom as it had come over him in his own in those mad weeks when he had walked around and around his room with an erection and touched himself every now and then, hoping for something to happen. Then he had begun working in the station and discovered the magazines and his fantasies had grown more complicated. In his own way he had become experienced, he had become dirty, and he hoped Kersey could see that.

In bed, Kersey loomed over him like a statue, as beautiful as a god, and said, "I just want to fuck you a little. Your smooth white ass, I can tell it's tight."

It was all Junior had ever wanted. But suddenly he was in such pain that he cried out, and Kersey, inclined over him, clutched Junior's hair and whispered, "Your tight white ass. I bet you never had your ass fucked before." Then he drew back and spat on Junior's chest, whispering with a lover's tenderness, "Motherfucker. You goddamned motherfucker."

Junior, tapping a reserve of will he did not know he possessed, pushed Kersey backward. He had wanted to continue, he was simply in too much pain. "Hey, what the hell?" Kersey said, tottering on his knees to avoid falling onto the Oriental rug. Junior, to redeem himself, lunged forward and slipped his mouth around

Kersey's penis with its rubber dangling like a nightcap, sucking it with artless frenzy until Kersey pushed him away.

"I've never seen *that* before," Kersey said, and for a moment Junior thought he had proven himself. He thought he had done something good.

The Horses

DAVID WATMOUGH

At first I couldn't hear my uncle's voice over the din of the binder behind me and the three horses, as I sat perched high on the bony back of Duke. We had done nearly a further turn around the field of wheat we were harvesting before I looked back.

It was early August, high noon, and the Cornish sun was very hot. Duke sweated freely and my bare legs were chafed and sore in spite of the flour sack Uncle Jan had insisted I place beneath my bottom. The cart horse was too broad for a thirteen-year-old boy to properly straddle, and although the gunny bag minimally protected my thighs it quite failed to do service as saddle or prevent the horse's huge backbone jarring my spine and making my bum cheeks ache.

My turning around was as much a mute enquiry as to when we were to stop for lunch and relieve my sore back and stinging flesh, as it was to hear what Farmer Jan was shouting.

I was to be disappointed. "They'm slowing down, boy, 'cos they've forgotten you'm bloody well up there! Give 'em a tickle of that withy I cut and let all three buggers know it b'aint dinnertime yet. You aren't up there like Lady Godiva just to look pretty, you know! I could've used one of the village maids for that!"

I flushed, turned quickly away, and gave Tommy to my left a quick cut with the willow frond. He responded with a start and an angry shaking of the head. Good! He was the only one I hated among the three horses. Once he had tried to bite me as I put corn in his manger while he stood sullenly in the twilight of the stables.

Uncle Jan, who saw it happen, had given the horse a terrible thrashing. But although Tommy bellowed in pain and pranced so violently sparks flashed from his steel horseshoes on the granite floor, I knew he still hated me. His eyes had grown yellowish white in the enormity of his terror but that fear was reserved exclusively for my uncle.

I turned to the other side of me and gave Violet a similar thwack. She almost started to trot. Violet, mother of the steed on which I was somewhat precariously perched, wanted only happiness for everyone and was always the most eager to please. I was quite sure she regarded me as her lovable little master.

With somewhat more difficulty, I brought the withy branch down on the broad rump behind me—and felt Duke quiver as he, too, strained at pulling the noisy old binder more quickly around the half-mile oblong of still-standing wheat.

I was certain he hardly felt my puny slap, but I was never really convinced the coal-black gelding didn't resent obeying my youthful will. The biggest and strongest of my *troika* was the hardest to read.

I didn't want to turn more fully around to strike him harder because that would have risked catching my uncle's eye again.

I knew very well that the caustic "Lady Godiva" reference was generated by my taking off my shirt and placing it on the brass horn of Duke's huge collar. Wearing only brief khaki shorts and sandals on bare feet, I was now virtually naked in Uncle's Methodist eyes.

The sensation of exposed flesh and the honeyed tan a week of such harvesting had yielded made me feel good. I was also aware that working down there in the stubble, stacking the bound sheaves the binder threw out, was my sixteen-year-old cousin Jan, and that twice since I had divested myself of the shirt, he had glanced in my direction as I road proudly by.

I peered into the gently waving phalanx of uncut wheat, striving to see what beleaguered and now terrified wildlife crouched there. I prayed there were animals ready to flee when their cover was so consumed by the voracious binder there was no option but to run the gauntlet of men and dogs and seek the safety of the surrounding hedges. This, for me, was the supreme moment of harvesting.

I dared hope for a fox, even an improvident but swift-gliding weasel. The previous August, in Farmer Trebilcock's low-lying meadows when mounted on Duke, I had caught a tantalizing glimpse of an otter before it reached the safety of bulrushes screening the Amble River. I knew there would be plenty of rabbits—and so did the village dogs, which had already begun to assemble.

This thrill equalled the satisfaction of securing the attention of Cousin Jan and sustaining his interest when we lay together on the narrow bed that we routinely shared when I came from school for those wartime summer holidays.

As I dutifully touched their haunches as the horses endlessly encircled the field, buzzards glided so high above us their mews sounded as puny as those of kittens. My daydreams bounced between images of a lithe weasel gliding through stubble covered with scarlet pimpernel and the chest of swarthy Jan as I squeezed my smaller body into the S of his before drifting comfortably into sleep.

Such incongruous reveries ended abruptly when Jan's grouchy father on the binder-seat finally yelled a halt to the labors of all those scattered about the partially harvested field.

Men, women, and children streamed from a dozen directions to congregate in the shade of a clump of tall elms. In seconds a damask tablecloth was laid below the hedge bank, and wicker baskets crammed with either pasties or apples placed strategically along its length.

Grease-stained straw hats were discarded, work-worn hands run through damp and flattened hair. There was the chink of cider jugs against mugs as liquid refreshments were poured, raucous laughter from the village muscle that had been hired to help stack the sheaves into neat little pyramids.

The ubiquitous dogs barked and begged for food while growling at potential competitors. The girls from our village of St. Keverne retorted with pert quips to the lewd comments from the younger men.

I listened to the exchange of news, of death and dire accidents, learned in remote moorland village pubs, visited when working other cornfields for other farmers during this labor-hungry harvest season.

Then I turned away to tend the horses, tethering them to the stoutest branches, providing them with buckets of water, and seeing their halters enabled them to graze on the lush grass at their massive feet.

As I serviced my charges with food and drink, I lunged angrily at the evil-looking horseflies that zeroed in to the harness-chinking shade for their own sanguinary meal. I had a keen proprietary sense over my foot-stomping giants.

I was not a tall boy for thirteen and was rather slight. These factors gave impetus to my feelings of power and superiority over my three huge if obeisant animals. I was also aware of being eyed professionally by the cluster of sprawled helpers as they idly watched me work.

I protracted the activity as long as I could before the delicious aroma of stewing beef and potato insisted I turn to the rapidly diminishing piles of pasties that had not yet been stuffed into hungry mouths.

In distinction to these ravenous oafs, I selected one small enough for a refined taste—and then, just as importantly, sought a congenial spot to eat it. My heart quickened when I saw a space at the foot of an oak—a little removed from the elms and the main assembly of harvesters. There, in the cool shade, slumped the recumbent figure of Cousin Jan.

He was talking to Silas Jago, a toothless old man who had brought his dog for the rabbit chasing when the cutting was completed. His whippet's name was Sport, but everyone called it *Sportstha* behind his back because the retired roadworker for the parish lisped.

I waited patiently to get a word in but the old fool kept Jan's attention, persuading him to lay a bet on his stupid dog. And when that was over, instead of answering my questions about the village fete that was coming up, Jan turned his back on me and started to talk to Molly Pentreath, who everyone knew was both illegitimate and wanton.

I finished the pasty standing up. Without a word of good-bye from Jan (who was too busy making fatuous remarks to Gross Tits from Laneo Farm) I made my way disconsolately back to the horses.

I killed two horseflies on Violet and plucked a clump of succulent clover leaves for Duke to eat from the palm of my hand. I re-tied Tommy to a sapling ash at whose base the grass grew longer, and patted Duke's white muzzle and by blowing up his nostril made him sneeze and splutter as he always did in response.

Even that failed to lift my spirits. It seemed hours before Uncle yelled at everyone again, and it was time to put the horses back in the shafts and for me to remount Duke.

When Jan grinned at me just before the last patch fell to the chattering teeth of the binder's knife, and only humdrum rabbits scattered in all directions, I just scowled in return.

Back at Polengarrow I deliberately avoided him when it was time to wash up and sit down for supper. I had decided I would punish him until it was time to go to bed and only then, under the sheets and in the dark, would I whisper forgiveness.

I took my resolve to remain aloof further than ever before. After supper I volunteered to take the horses from the stable and let them loose in the field called Bullen. This was something Jan usually did each night.

Uncle gave me a funny look but said I could if I was careful to hang up their bridles on the proper pegs in the stable and lead them by rope halters up the steep hill to where they'd graze for the night. I was also to make sure the gate was closed after I'd set them free.

My aunt had the nerve to query whether I was big enough for the task, but as usual he squashed her with an oath and ordered her to stop spoiling me at the expense of his son, Jan. I sat there and smirked at my cousin.

Once outside, though, my attitude altered. It had grown dusk while we were at supper. There was also a mist rising about the various outbuildings.

Inside the stables I had to strain my eyes to fulfill Uncle Jan's instructions and by the time I emerged, pulling on the tethers of the three horses, stars pricked the night sky where bats piped shrilly. The scent of jasmine from the farmhouse porch hung heavy on the air.

As twelve hooves clattered and slithered noisily on the lane's granite hill past the well, I noticed something else. My daytime steeds had lost their distinguishing color.

There was no longer a fawn Tommy, a sorrel Violet, or an ebony Duke. Each great shape was now mysteriously dark. Only the white blaze on the head of each stood out ghostly in the feeble light. Their heads nodded in unison as they lumbered up the slope. Their eyes were fiery coals.

All three gave vent to loud snorts as we climbed the last few yards to the gate of Bullen field. Violet added a soft whinny. They were excited by what was about to happen. I knew a tremor of anxiety through my body, which now felt cold through the thinness of my summer shirt. I shivered.

Up to the moment I had carefully replaced the wreath of binder cord over the gatepost, even if my spirit did begin to fret, I could still find reassurance in familiar things. Inside Bullen, though, all that changed.

The mist swirled in grotesque wraiths up there. The hedge separating the two parts of the turf-clumped field had largely dissolved from the rabbits creating their underground warrens.

Someone had told me '*bullen*' was a corruption of a Celtic word meaning "harelipped man." As I led my progressively independent charges to where I intended to loose them, I thought I saw a face fashioned in the mist. It possessed an unsmiling mouth that sported an ugly fissure midway along its upper lip....

I realized I was not going to go farther. The horses were now too excited. Apart from even louder snorting and whinnying, the rope of the halters grew ever tauter. I was afraid one or another of my charges would tug theirs out of my hand.

I rushed quickly to Tommy and leaping up as he raised his head in alarm I managed to yank the halter over his ears and set him free. Violet was a shade more cooperative. Although still whinnying madly, she did fractionally lower her head. That allowed me two hands for the giant Duke.

When the rope fell away from him he did something that froze me in fear. I thought I would never breathe easily again. He rose on his back legs to an almost vertical position, came down with a smashing thud to the mound of the rabbit warren and then rolled over and over like a gigantic puppy-dog.

Then they all let out enormous farts. There was nothing humorous about it. Only an elemental defiance. The explosion of their cooped-up wind said GO AWAY!

By now the three monsters were all rearing up on their hind haunches to paw at the stars. Their stomachs rumbled like thunder and weird *un-equine* sounds arose from their throats.

They started to run in mad circles, stopping only to flop with an enormous thud to the ground and roll over and over in crazy glee before clambering noisily up once more and galloping faster than ever, as if chasing one another's cropped tails.

Then they were no longer horses. Gone was benign Violet, her secretive son Duke, and testy old Tommy who resented small boys. Instead, there were the three sacred centaurs from ancient Greece I had discovered last term at school: Philyra and Cronus and Philyra's son Chiron, whom Zeus had sent as a star to the sky.

I scanned the heavens for Centaurus, knowing I would not find it. How could I, when one or another of those looming shapes in the thickening mist was in fact the tutor of such Hellenistic heroes as Asclepius, Jason, and Achilles?

And then we were back from the Aegean to the Atlantic—to three transformed cart horses on a Cornish farm. From their thunderous dance of freedom they turned to gentle loving. Arched necks were rubbed by soft muzzles; chafe marks from human bondage were kissed away and the great feathered hooves drummed songs of mutual encouragement to vibrate through the earth.

I moved slowly back toward the lane. Not seeking safety. I was no longer frightened—only anxious to do their will and remove myself from the intimacy of their rites and games.

Cousin Jan was sitting up in bed reading by the light of our oil-lamp when I joined him. For once he initiated conversation, asking if the horses had been put up field and I had remembered to shut the gate.

I merely nodded as I undressed and put on my pajamas. Instead of striving to engage him in gossipy chat as I usually did when we got into bed, I gave him my back as he continued to read. And then I forgot him and slept—caught up in a sea of arcane dreams in which horses lived without the benefaction or even knowledge of the human race.

Guardian

SCOTT W. PETERSON

I came into Italy as if into a dream.

Yet I was wide awake in those Venetian hills, rock-strewn green and high trees; I knew that the sleeping years of my life were over. For evidence there was the presence of the old man riding beside me, and the young man at my other side. For proof there was the road leading downward, which our small train of mules and packs ate up by the hour. Soon we would be crossing the river Adige. I had never been so far from home.

My sense of dream came from new horizons, so long imagined and never seen. I had spent a boyhood in the alps of Kitzbühel; in those heights each valley is a world to itself, walled in, mountains and sky rising to build ice-blue fortresses on every distance. To judge it haven or prison, my father had said, one looks within. I had looked: my judgment was different than his, and he never blamed me for it. Instead he found me Doctor Cosgrave, and set me on my way. Now I looked around.

"*Jacta alea est*," said Gabrio, who was young like myself. I shook my head at the schoolroom Latin; I was new to this. He pulled his mule nearer and gave a grin. "'The die is cast.' You see, Fränz, I read your thoughts."

I allowed a slight nod. I was wary of Gabrio, who too often seemed to be smiling at me. And he was Italian; he was returning to his homeland, which could only make him more sure of himself. He seemed enough of that already. "You guess at them," I said. "A stone tossed in the dark will always land somewhere."

"Latin," admonished Doctor Cosgrave. The man had pulled
some paces ahead of us, but had good ears. Teachers are made so.

"I'm sorry, Doctor." I said. "I only forgot—"

"Latin," he called, not looking around.

Gabrio leaned closer and whispered to me.

"*Errare humanum est,*" I repeated aloud. Doctor Cosgrave's hat
nodded, and we rode on.

We stopped at Trento for the night. In the morning we would rent
boats; the journey was nearly done. This made the doctor cheerful, and he permitted us wine at dinner. The wine in turn made
Gabrio cheerful.

"At Caerella," he said when we retired to our room, "we will
begin to be paid. In real money. Have you ever had any money?"

I had not—none of my own, at any rate, though my family was
well placed—and I didn't yet know what I would do with some.
But it was a pleasant thought, nonetheless.

"We'll earn it," added Gabrio seriously. "The work can be very
hard. You'll grow to hate the shovel. One begins to think the Romans buried every potsherd and urn beneath a rock on purpose,
just to make us sweat."

"I will be happy if we only talk less Latin," I said. "Lessons cannot be so strict there, I think."

"Nothing is so strict there," he said with a smile. "Doctor
Cosgrave becomes a child with his toys, and the more we dig up
for him the less he will notice us." Gabrio stretched under our
blanket, bumping me with his long legs. "I've been with him three
seasons now. I've seen the pattern; when he takes a boy on he is
every bit the guardian, the great professor putting you under his
wing. But once your parents are many miles behind, and his purpose begins, you are only a mule with some education, and there
to serve him."

This news hardly troubled me. Parents and the Kitzbühel far behind suited me well enough. Already the world looked very large,
and I had seen only a week of it. I closed my eyes contentedly as
Gabrio blew out the candle.

In the dark he bumped me again. "We can do what we like," he
said. There was silence. I could hear his breath; he seemed to be
waiting.

"At Caerella," I responded uncertainly.

He sighed. "Yes. That's what I mean." He rolled over. In a while he sounded asleep, and soon I was too.

The river journey was uneventful. We had nothing to do but sit, and I finally began to make progress with my Latin. In the afternoons we were forbidden to speak anything else, causing the bargemen to look at us bemused. The mornings I liked better, when we sat on the deck and the doctor taught history.

"Hadrian," he said, scratching the name on a slate. "One hundred seventeen to when?"

"One-thirty-eight," I answered.

"Very good. Successor of?"

This one I did not have; he let Gabrio give it. "Trajan," said the Italian boy.

"Very good." The lesson continued: architecture, art, engineering. Cosgrave required assistants who knew what they sought and recognized what they found. Despite Gabrio's comments, the doctor took much pride in turning his boys into scholars.

As all this great past began falling in place I found an interest in it myself, and thought I understood how a man like Cosgrave could set his heart to it. He had not needed to; he was an Englishman of birth and money, with the leisure to do what he liked. This exploration of earth was what he liked, and the finding of all those lives in it. He revered the Romans, whom he thought had managed the world rather better than men did now.

He took out a valise of sketches and spread them before me. "On this spot," he pointed, "last year I uncovered the baths of Caerella. In the previous season my reward was to fix the location of the river bridge. This gives us the shape of the town and the direction of the *via*; what might we seek at the center of it?"

There were sketches of other sites alongside, and they gave me the answer. "The basilica," I volunteered.

"Just so. And when we consider this—" He held up a small pot, cracked and glued together. "—what period must we be in?"

"Hadrianic," said Gabrio, his eyes bright.

"Allow Fränz to respond, if you please," said Doctor Cosgrave. "He has no experience, and must learn."

For a while Gabrio stayed quiet while I learned. But his mind seemed very busy. On the oiled planks of the deck, between his feet, he traced and retraced the plan of the town. The odd thought came to me that Gabrio awaited Caerella with the anticipation of one who plans to meet a friend. Well, he had been there before; three seasons. Something of it must have stuck with him.

Cosgrave called my attention back. "The Emperor Hadrian was distinguished by what endeavor, unusual to a ruler?"

I thought hard. "He was a poet?"

"And a philosopher. Dio Cassius wrote of him—"

Gabrio interrupted, his eyes still alight:

> *Little soul gentle and drifting,*
> *guest and companion of my body,*
> *now you will dwell below in pallid places*
> *stark and bare,*
> *where you will abandon your play of yore.*

Doctor Cosgrave raised his brows. "Your recollection impresses, Gabrio. But I did not request a recital. I was speaking of the Senator Cassius—"

Gabrio turned to me. "The lines are Hadrian's. Aren't they terribly sad?"

"Attend me," the doctor said sharply. "Do you want to hear the lesson or give it?"

"I've heard it before, and you leave off the best parts," said Gabrio. "Perhaps Fränz is a poet too."

I was startled at this insolence, and conscious of Cosgrave's frown. "I would only like to know what the Senator Cassius said," I replied nervously.

Gabrio shrugged and looked away; for an instant I felt strangely disloyal. But a few moments later, when the doctor was wound up in his lecture and not watching us, I noticed that Gabrio was smiling again; and when he saw me looking he winked.

That evening we put up on the riverside, not far from a camp of Gypsies. These strange spirits were as new to me as everything else; the echoing sound of their music made the night exotic. But Gypsies are said to be great thieves, and Doctor Cosgrave spent much of his time minding our equipment. Gabrio and I were left alone to talk.

We shared dinner by the campfire, sitting on a hollow log. "What did you think of the lines I gave?" he asked.

"I thought them out of place," I said, "since the lesson was to another point."

Gabrio waived his hand. "Our doctor is full of facts. The emperor was a poet, it's a fact so we must learn it. But the poet was a man, and it was the man who wrote. Isn't it important what, and why?"

"I suppose so." To be honest the verses had lingered in my mind. "They *were* very sad. A feeling like—I don't know. Autumn, or the end of a life."

"You're young to speak of that. But the emperor knew it well."

"No doubt. He was a soldier."

"The poem was not for his legions." Gabrio lowered his voice. "Doctor Cosgrave will tell you that Hadrian wrote of his own soul. It isn't true."

"No?"

"It was Antinous he mourned," Gabrio said. "His favorite, a beautiful boy from Bythia."

I was unsure what to say. My innocence was considerable, but I knew what Gabrio meant. Such things were seldom spoken of in my upbringing; Doctor Cosgrave's lessons had not touched them either. I picked up a stick and pretended to be busy stirring the fire.

"He drowned—Antinous did—in Egypt. No one knows why. But legend has it that a prophecy had promised Hadrian long life only if he lost the thing dearest to him. Antinous meant to fulfill it, for love of him."

"Maybe he couldn't swim," I said.

I felt Gabrio's impatience beside me. "You resist the romance in your soul, Fränz."

"That's not true," I denied. "Or I don't think it is. I haven't given much thought to my soul, not at my age. Nor to romance, for that matter."

Gabrio took my stick away. "Antinous," he said, "was your age." It seemed that he had moved closer to me; perhaps it was a trick of the firelight. "And mine."

"Then he had time to learn to swim," I said defensively.

Gabrio laughed aloud. "I told you," he said, "no romance!" Behind us we heard steps, and turned to see Doctor Cosgrave emerging from the brush. Gabrio tossed the stick into the fire and sprawled out lazily on the ground.

"Is all well?" I asked as the doctor came up.

"It is. But one cannot be too careful. We will be in Caerella in four days, it would hardly do to arrive without our tools." He sat down across from us and removed his top hat. It was badly scratched; only an Englishman, I thought, would wear such a thing in the woods. Gabrio caught my thought and my eye, and the face he pulled gave me some work to keep from laughing.

"Well, then," said the doctor. "Have you passed the time in idle chatter, or thought of your studies?"

"We think of nothing else," Gabrio declared. "Dedication on top of devotion."

Cosgrave lit his pipe and chose not to respond.

"The subject was the Emperor Hadrian's poems," I offered. Gabrio could afford his impertinence, perhaps; I felt less secure.

"A curious man," said the doctor. "His villa at Tivoli was a museum of the world. Birds and flowers from the corners of the empire, sculpture of every style. He was a ruler of wisdom and erudition. Everything around him had to be the most beautiful."

"Everything," echoed Gabrio, nudging my heel.

I felt a sudden anger with him; he seemed to want to stir me all the time, to confuse me. "Gabrio has some tale," I said to the doctor defiantly, "that the emperor was in love—"

Gabrio kicked me again harder. I looked at him and found his smile gone. His eyes were intense and urgent; they enlisted me even as my mouth sat open.

"—with art," I finished lamely.

"Perhaps so," said Cosgrave, puffing his tobacco. "He was a creator. He lacked the passion for ruling that drove other emperors, and put it all into building. In Rome his mark is everywhere; in Britain, of course, there is the Wall. When I was in Naples five years ago we uncovered a masterful arch. It was seventy feet to the side...." The doctor talked on of excavations and measurements, stones and inscriptions. The fire crackled lower, shooting sparks, tracing our faces red and orange. Gabrio lay on his side by the coals and watched me. His dark hair fell down over his face, turned to bronze in the flickering light.

In the shadows along the ground, hidden, his foot returned to touch mine, brushing it, not once but again, and then again like a caress. I felt my cheeks grow hot. I could have moved away, but I didn't. I had left my home to discover the things of life; Gabrio was too much alive to ignore, and he fascinated and frightened me. My foot began to tremble. At this he rested his against it, and kept it there.

I was glad of the doctor's voice, which filled the little clearing and kept me from thinking. It left me free to listen to the noise inside of me. But I could not decipher the tune.

For some days I kept a shield about me, and spoke to Gabrio only at need. In the light of day it seemed that our sin was very great, though we'd done nothing. I remembered a scatter of talk in my village, when I was quite young, about some boys in the choir; one of them had been my cousin, and I remembered my aunt in tears. I had not understood it then. I understood little better now.

We finished the river passage and returned to the road. The doctor, true to Gabrio's prediction, seemed to have less and less thought for us as we neared Caerella. He constantly reviewed his maps and sketches, even balancing them on the mule's neck as he rode. Now and then he pulled a steel pen from his pocket and made marks. He announced that we would begin at the center of the site and cut shallow trenches east and west. He reminded me again and again of the way one must dig: cautiously, angling the blade against the earth, lest one should break something hidden below.

I did my best to think only of Romans, and to help it I made myself think in Latin. Gabrio rode a little away from me, keeping his mind to himself. Despite my intentions I could not help glancing at him now and then; when he saw me he returned a gaze gentle as rain. I would have found his guilt easier to deal with, or even anger. But his face held pure affection, which confounded me more. It was my good fortune to have been loved all my life, by father and mother and sisters; I was unprepared for tenderness to be so unsettling.

Through the rest of our journey he never touched me. This ought to have been a relief, but I could only think of him about to do it. At night I lay beside him awake, wondering how I should stop him if he tried. Wondering how he might try.

Wondering it, I found, even after he was long asleep.

Then, abruptly, we were at Caerella and a different world. From being a boy and a student I found myself overnight a worker and a professional. Doctor Cosgrave had hired ahead for thirty peasants, who awaited us at the site with barrows and carts. It was part of my job to direct their movements, and I quickly had to discover authority in my voice. Gabrio was a help in this; many of them knew him from before, and he backed me up when needed. Before long we had gotten the trenches started from the *via*. As the sod was broken and the topsoil carried away we separated, each with our tools, and began the careful excavations east and west.

Cosgrave hovered over us, flitting from one to the other, anxious as a hen. He was not kept long in suspense. We were at work only three days when Gabrio had the first news. "Hello!" he called. "Over here!" The doctor had been watching me, still afraid I was too free with my spade; he ran to the other trench, where Gabrio was brushing dirt from the tip of some shaped stone. "I see writing," Gabrio said excitedly.

"Yes? There, brush there. Yes!" Cosgrave knelt down with his line and began making measurements. "Exactly, just where I'd supposed. Come, Fränz, everyone! Over here." I left off my work and gathered the peasants. The doctor pointed and ordered, shovels here, barrows there. We busied ourselves around the spot like a colony of digging ants. In an hour the stone was free; we scooped under it, propping with boards to make way for the harness. Then the strongest of the peasants worked the pulley and lifted our find onto a cart.

It was a granite tablet, tall as I was and two feet across. The inscription at the top was mostly worn thin, but enough remained to put Cosgrave in elation. "'I, Hadrian and emperor,'" he read aloud, "'built and consecrated this place.' Remarkable!"

"There is more," urged Gabrio.

"I can see that." Doctor Cosgrave was busy writing. "Transcribe, one must always transcribe." The pen finished scratching and he returned to the letters. "'...consecrated this place before the eyes of gods and men, to the beloved one...'" He frowned at the faded letters. "I cannot make out the rest now. I must have it in my tent, with my tools and washes. Fränz, see it there safely. I will be along in a bit."

I left him at the trench with Gabrio, who had climbed down into the hole and was sifting earth. With a dozen of the men I moved the cart to the doctor's pavilion. There we set up the pulley again, and I held my breath while the men placed the stone over trestles. When they had unhooked the ropes, I sent them back; I closed the flaps and stood by myself under the cool shadow of the tent.

In the dim, filtered light the stone seemed to lie like a dead thing. I lit an oil lamp and hung it from the pole. The cast of the flame changed everything; the dusty granite glowed alive, the inscription leapt out as though newly written. The emperor's name was larger then the rest, in strong, precise letters, bold and heroic. It seemed the name of a man who had taken pride in all that he was, and in all that was his. *To the beloved one,* the doctor had read. Even with my little training I could recognize the chiseled words, and I trailed my finger across them. I never wondered who was meant; in my mind a voice like Gabrio's had said it already. I stood there in silence.

Before the eyes of gods and men, the voice added in a whisper. Unaccountably, I began to hurt, as though a sharp wind blew through my heart. I was back at the campfire, with Gabrio's eyes on me; I was back in the schoolyard with my rough, shouting friends, back in the lonely nights of the Kitzbühel watching the moon disappear beyond the peaks and thinking my soul would break. A great store of feelings, as long hidden and suddenly excavated as the stone, emerged from me to turn on a single truth. Once a man had carved such truth onto granite and left it for the world to see.

"Very well for Hadrian," I burst out angrily. "No doubt to be an emperor means one is never afraid." I turned my back on the tablet and strode out of the tent. Soon I was back in my trench, and worked so hard through the afternoon that my sweat poured like a river.

"I will own to you," I said to Gabrio a few evenings later, "that if I haven't come to hate the shovel, it has surely taken a foul dislike to me." This comment was made with a wince as I smeared Cosgrave's salve on my blisters.

Gabrio offered a rueful expression for my hands. But his eyes were happy. There was cause for this; it was the first I'd spoken to him in friendship since the night in the woods. He had taken my cool manners without reproach all the while, and only waited for me to change. Finally it seemed we had both waited long enough.

"The doctor is very pleased with your stone," I added. "He was with it all day, and hardly comes up to breathe."

"It makes him correct," said Gabrio. He shifted to look at me from his cot, which sat across from mine in our sleeping shed. "For years he has claimed that Caerella was founded by Hadrian as a dedication. He said the writings of Hieron proved it. But not all his colleagues agreed, and he hadn't a stick to show it by. With these men every difference of opinion becomes a war of pride; they blow a good deal of hot air at one another between diggings."

His turn of phrase made me smile. "You're a puzzle, Gabrio. You care for Latin only to joke with; you annoy the doctor at every chance, you poke fun at his profession. Yet you love this place; I see it. Why? What is there, season after season?"

"A season's pay, season after season," he answered. He didn't expect me to believe it.

"Come on. Tell more."

He looked at me again. "Do you really want that? That I should tell you more?"

"If you would," I said quietly, "I might like that you tell me several things."

He lay back and stared at the crude boards of the ceiling. "I should begin with you," he said after a moment. "Since that's what you most need to know of." He waited, I suppose for me to object. But he was right and I said nothing.

"A mountain boy of the Kitzbühel," Gabrio said then. "Of good family. A loving father and a fair position to aspire to. But restless. He looks about him and sees only walls. He cannot abide his life, or the thought of no change coming to it. An archaeologist passing through the Tyrol makes known his need of an assistant; the loving father hears of it and puts forth the restless son."

"This much you know easily," I said, "since you were there."

"True enough. So the mountain boy comes to meet the Italian Gabrio. He stands off; he extends only a little of himself, like a trader short on goods. Still, sometimes he laughs; he can't help it. Sometimes their eyes meet. Sometimes more is given than is known. And Gabrio...has waited a long time for such a gift."

His words left the room hushed. We had come to it quickly. I swallowed hard and said, "Then came a night at the campfire, when Gabrio talked of love."

"I talked of an emperor."

"And of his friend, who was my age and yours."

"Yes." Gabrio turned to the pillow, so that his voice was muffled. "And at this the mountain boy took fright. Because he saw that of all the walls he had run from, the strongest he had brought along. And then he found them pushed at." He lifted his head and looked at me clearly. "And then he wanted them opened."

Only the fear to stop toppled my fear to continue. "But how did you see so much, so quickly? Even I didn't know."

"Because I've seen your eyes before. Twice, I have."

"I don't understand."

"Here." He sat up and touched a finger to his face. "Once here."

I looked and saw it was true. "The other?"

He rose from the cot and put on this cloak, and tossed me mine. "You'll want it," he said. He went to the door and opened it, glancing around the site and at the doctor's lodging. The trenches and carts were silent, lit by stars; no one was stirring.

"Come, Fränz," he said. "The other I will show you."

The site of Caerella huddled in a small valley, shouldered on three sides by wooded hills, with a narrow river flowing alongside. We walked for three quarters of an hour in darkness and only lit the lamp when we had begun to climb up through the trees. Gabrio moved swiftly, as if his own purpose was begun now; he seemed almost impatient to wait when I lagged behind.

"Careful, there. The branch. Now this way, yes. Hurry." He gave these short commands; the light swayed ahead of me. I scrambled through scrub and rock, following without questions. He would know the way, I thought, as he had known me.

It seemed we walked half the night. But the sky was still black when we halted. Gabrio stopped before I knew it and I ran into him; he put out a hand to steady me. We stood on a steep incline, before a mass of tangled branches on which the lamp shone eerily. I strained my eyes to see what we had found.

"Doctor Cosgrave," Gabrio said, "will tell you that Hadrian wrote of his own soul. It isn't true." He stepped forward. We climbed down some stones into a narrow gully, which led below the tangle and into it. Gabrio put out the light; we moved by touch. I felt a drift of cold air ahead and pulled back.

"What is it?" I breathed.

"Come." He led me onward. The branches gave way to rock; it brushed my head and I ducked down. "Lower here," he whispered. "We must crawl a bit." We did, on knees and arms. We climbed into the earth like a secret. It was perhaps a dozen feet; I had just begun to feel fear when the rock lifted again. The air above was dry and chill. Gabrio took my hand and pulled me up.

"We are here, Fränz. We have come to Caerella." He lit the lamp and raised it above his head. "The Doctor was guessing all along," he said. "But I knew."

Only cold air in my lungs and his fingers gripping mine told me it was not a dream; all else demanded it. The lantern blazed, washing the walls of the cave in pale gold. Cobwebs flared and tiny night creatures fluttered madly from the corners. In front of us the space rose like a cathedral, arched in ribs of stone.

At the center of it stood Antinous.

"It was the first summer," Gabrio said. "I was like you—I mean no offense—but I knew nothing. Not of Romans. Not of myself. I only knew I was going mad. Like the Kitzbühel, my village is mountain country; not so high as your alps, but high enough. I came with Cosgrave as you did, to find anything beyond. I found nothing. The other assistants were clods, the peasants worse than home. The work..." He shrugged. "It was all of a piece with farming, so far as I could see. Grub in the dirt and hope a prize will come up."

We sat with our backs to the hard wall, our hands still together. I listened but could not take my eyes from the statue. "It seems that one did," I said.

"Not from down there. From within me, more like. I came here...by accident, you can say; what else? Many days I wandered off on my own. I knew Cosgrave was going to drop me anyway; I lacked interest. He only kept me because the summer was half gone. But then—"

The light wavered. We would run out of oil soon. Gabrio turned the flue to a slit, putting us in shadows. The statue, one arm raised to heaven, the other beckoning, glowed luminescent before us.

"Then I found him," he ended simply.

"And you told no one? You could have been—what, a hero. Famous." I only said this because it was obvious. I already knew.

Gabrio shook his head. "No. Doctor Cosgrave? He would have been delighted, he would have given me a reward. He would have written a paper and annoyed his doubters. Then men would come here with a crate and an oxcart. No."

I stood up, letting his hand untwine from mine. He gave me the lantern and I walked slowly to Antinous.

He stood just over life-size, tilted a little back on the rough floor. The marble was almost undamaged, only a patch roughened here and there, and one knee chipped. The stone was white as milk, save the eyes, which were olive shaped and had been polychromed in chestnut. The mouth was slightly open, lips strong and smiling. Finely chiseled hair came down in ringlets around his face.

Gabrio was beside me. "It was the eyes, mostly," he said. "You see?"

"Yes." The brows of Antinous slanted down, but not in anger. In longing, it seemed; or passion. And the rest of him spoke of that: We had no need to.

"Here I learned my secret," Gabrio said, "even before I knew who he was. In time I found out, of course; though with difficulty to the truth, since not all books will speak plainly of it. Cosgrave puffs furiously and changes the subject. But Antinous and Hadrian—theirs was not a love to be hidden. When I knew, it seemed more certain than ever that he was here only for me."

"Only for you?" I said with difficulty. "I think not."

"I said," Gabrio told me, "I knew two pairs of eyes. These and mine. Now yours. Now we are all together."

At that moment the light gave out, a last breath of flame that touched a glow on each of us; the cave went pitch black. Yet I thought, almost, that I could see Antinous still. I could feel his presence and his desire. For an instant it came like madness, that a block of marble could reach out to touch me in the dark.

But then it was not cold stone that I felt. It was Gabrio. And from that point the dark proved not to be a hindrance.

After a week of study Doctor Cosgrave pronounced the remainder of the writing a loss. "It's impossible," he said. "Too much time has eaten at it." We were at dinner, and he looked regretfully at his plate.

"There'll be more," I said encouragingly. "Surely such a discovery right away is promising."

"Sometimes, sometimes not. We are teased this way. What's first offered up may be best, and may be all one will find. I've seen it happen."

"At least it gives what you wanted," said Gabrio. "Proof of Hadrian's hand on Caerella. That much is clear."

"I fear not. We have a tablet with words on it. But words mislead. The inscription is formula, it might have been used anywhere under his rule. Proof of the emperor's hand requires more. It needs his mark, something truly and only his."

"Then tomorrow I shall dig up his pocket-watch," said Gabrio with a flourish. "I promise it to you." As was usual with Cosgrave the humor was wasted; as had also become usual, Gabrio and I shared a quick smile on it anyway. The doctor was oblivious.

There was in fact much that was new about his assistants, and that he failed to see: how our conversations had changed to become closer, and how in the sleeping shed our cots had moved closer as well. His disregard was entirely to our satisfaction, and we made the most of it. Even now, as we ate and he talked, Doctor Cosgrave would not have imagined that below the table four feet nestled together as one.

"Yet the key is still the tablet," he declared. "A dedication to the beloved one. Determine whom and we have it all. Most possibilities can be discarded out of hand. Sabia his wife, for example; the emperor was not overfond of her. Then there is Lucius Commodus, who was a great friend, and whom Hadrian later made praetor. But Commodus was a political favorite and an aristocrat. The inscription speaks of consecration, not policy." Cosgrave jabbed at the air with his spoon. "So we come to the necessary answer. It can only be Antinous."

Gabrio never blinked. I was less used to conspiracy and glanced up quickly. Cosgrave noticed.

"Ah, Fränz. I forget that you've had little chance to remember all these names. I speak of the Bythian youth whom the emperor adopted. The boy died young, most tragically. Afterward, Hadrian raised his memory almost to deity. Not almost, I should say; he demanded that Antinous be a god, that he live forever as a patron to men."

"He must have been dearly loved," I said.

"He was. However..." Cosgrave cleared his throat. "Mind what you hear of this. Some people take the worst examples of Roman life and claim them common. There are those who would ascribe to the relationship a taint of immorality. But I can assure you this explanation is quite discredited; respectable scholars today agree that Antinous was loved only as a son. It's possible, in fact, that he *was* a son—illegitimate, of course. I tend to that view myself; it would certainly justify the emperor's grief, where nothing else could."

I took Gabrio's cue and only nodded.

"At any rate." The doctor wiped his hands on his napkin and dropped the matter. "It is the Bythian we seek. The dedications to him were raised by Hadrian personally, across the empire. When we find Antinous, we truly find Caerella."

Gabrio raised his glass in a toast, his eyes with mine. "To the season, then," he said. "And to our good doctor discovering all he deserves."

The work ran twelve weeks more. In that time we uncovered the outline of the basilica, and beyond it the walls of a shrine that seemed to have been the focus of the place. We spent a month to clear this and the doctor sketched from every angle. But though he was sure it had been raised to Antinous, no artifact could be found to prove it.

"We can thank the barbarians," Cosgrave grumbled. "During the last years of the empire they poured across the borders and swept these places clean. What Goths and Huns failed to steal the Romans themselves fled with, or hid; the countryside is filled with caches of treasure. But one could never know where to look...." He gazed wistfully at the hills around us. Then he turned back to the pit, where I was filtering dirt through a sieve. I came upon a small brass ring and held it out to him.

"Piecework," he shrugged, examining it. "But thank you, Fränz. You do very well."

Indeed it seemed, as the end of our time neared, that I had made the grade as an assistant. Doctor Cosgrave was generous with compliments, and hinted that I would be welcome again. "Not all young men have the touch for it, or the understanding. But a few do, and a few more learn it as they go along. Gabrio, now—what a lout he was to begin with! I had no hope of him. But in time, he came around." The doctor seemed to congratulate himself on this. "Today I would not part with him. He has a feeling in his soul for Rome, and nothing is more valuable to me than that. I begin to see that you have it too."

I thanked him for his confidence and gave credit to his tutelage; it was easy enough to do and made him content. For me, contentment was to know that I could come back, and that Gabrio would too. The end of the season would now weigh less heavily.

"I will miss you every day and twice the nights," I told Gabrio in the darkness of the cave. We were making our final visit, the last of many. In the morning he would be returning to his Italian village; we would not meet again until spring. As lovers do we had found our little habits, and one of them was to lie with our heads at Antinous's feet while we talked. He stood over us like a protector; now I looked up at him. "You will keep us together always, won't you?" The marble was silent, which I took for assent.

Gabrio laughed softly. It amused him that I had become the more romantic of us; but to say he was amused is not to say he was displeased. He stroked my hair. "He says he will, and will be grief-stricken if ever we are untrue."

"I heard him."

"I know you did."

We lay awhile quietly. I began to think of what the doctor had said about hidden treasures in the countryside. "Gabrio. One day he'll be found. Won't he?"

"Perhaps. Cosgrave may widen his search and send groups of peasants into the hills. With his coins dangled before them, they will look closer than they are used to doing."

"It's a shame. You were right: He would be delighted and he would write a paper. He would sketch and measure and conjure his theories, or refute someone else's. But he would never understand. He would never know *why* such a thing is made."

"Men don't understand what they don't feel. You and I may find a difficult life ahead because of it, but that's the way of things. We can take comfort in knowing that what we do feel, *we* understand. And sometimes that will have to be enough."

"It's enough now." The lantern was between our feet, turned low. We always remembered to fill it with oil, after the first time; we didn't always need it. "Thank you, Gabrio," I said, remembering the darkness. "Thank you for everything."

A fortnight later in the mountains of Kitzbühel my father shared cigars and brandy with Doctor Cosgrave and praised what he saw of my journey. "I've no doubt Fränz has gained by it. A summer away, working like a man; it's what he needed. He has a brighter look about him already."

"Fränz is a bright young man," said the doctor. "He knows when he's found a thing to suit him. Happily, he found so this summer. Happily for me as well; I shall want him again if you're willing."

"We'll see," said my father. "If he chooses, I have no objection. He could have had no better guardian than yourself."

"Very good." The doctor rose. "I must be on my way. I'm going back to England, you know. Much to do, much to write up."

"Fränz tells me your theory of Caerella is nearly proved."

Cosgrave looked sad. "As nearly as it will be. I had been certain, this season...but there it is. One cannot spend a lifetime on a single question. There is wisdom in knowing when to quit."

I had sat politely through these pleasantries; now I looked up. "Do you mean, Doctor," I asked, "that you will not return to Caerella?"

He shook his head. "The site only interested me to prove Hadrian there. I did all I could. Next year we begin with the Vercelli ruins; they have much potential. But no; though it's a great disappointment, I'm convinced there is nothing more for me at Caerella."

I agreed solemnly, as Gabrio had well taught me to do. "I'm sure you're right, sir."

My father shook the doctor's hand, and the doctor shook mine, and we walked him to the door. He promised to write when the plans for Vercelli were set; then he waved and rode off. All things considered, he had been kind to me. But as I watched him disappear at the end of our village lane, I felt no pang at sending him away with a lie. If I had grown up, it had been more my work than his. And as it happened, I too had become a guardian.

Going
to Japan

PAUL ATTINELLO

I've never been to Japan before. On a crowded street corner, breathing the acid tang of the gray air, I look at the little hand-drawn map and try to figure out where north is. The oval, blank faces flow past as though they ride on swift, efficient engines, though occasionally one glances at me: *gaijin*, foreigner. I turn and walk through a great wooden temple, silent rows of shaved heads visible through a cloud of incense, and enter a tiny storefront bar. A karaoke machine sprays music across the narrow space; but as I dig for a red thousand-yen note for the waitress, voices come abruptly from the speakers: *He's not doing well; he hasn't recognized me for two days, and hardly opens his eyes any more.* I tune them out; it must be some American soap opera. The chef lines up sushi on a black enameled tray; the maguro is like butter, it's so perfect. I even eat the octopus, so his feelings won't be hurt. I leave by a different door and turn left, crossing through a quiet formal garden to the foot of the mountain, and climb to a gold and red shrine. A party of nobles has arrived just before me, and a young samurai, tattooed and carrying a vast sword, condescends to explain that they are going to view the iris fields. Idling outside in the afternoon sun, listening to the monotone chanting, I notice an intricately carved sedan chair draped with pale green silks. A delicate hand pushes the curtain aside slightly; it holds a Sony Walkman, from which come tinny voices: *I can tell you, he's not in any pain; the drugs take care of that. But there's not much we can do at this stage.* Annoyed, I turn and cross behind the shrine, push apart the great wooden doors, and take the long steel escalator down to the sub-way station. The crowds are dense around the car doors, but the tiny stores are nearly empty; a bookstall looks interesting, and I glance through a collection of haiku, feeling the roaring trains through the floor. A flood of uniformed children rushes past, running to get to school on time; two little girls break away from the group to stop and gaze at me. I'm surprised and can't remember the proper address for children, but as I stand tongue-tied the smallest dashes up and pushes a tiny, carefully wrapped package into my hand, and they run away, giggling like mad. I slip the package into my pocket, smiling to myself, and turn to ask the book-seller how much for the book, but he is gone. Shrugging, I put the book on the counter and turn to the door behind the stall; as I go through it, I hear voices booming over the public address system: *He didn't want to be revived. I know it's difficult, but you're going to have to make a decision.* Outside, the road outlines a chessboard of wet, green rice fields on the south, out to the horizon; to the north, there is a small wooden pavilion up the hill, open to the spring air. The path wanders through a patch of tiny white flowers; I pick one, sticking it in my buttonhole as I climb. Three men in the pavilion are talking quietly; they rise and bow at my entrance. We exchange many polite phrases, but finally relax and prepare to write a *renga*, a chain of poems. The oldest fusses, handing me paper, brush and ink while the others wrinkle their foreheads in concentration over their scrolls. *Can you hear me? We're going to turn off your respirator; forgive us, please; try to show if you can understand*—I turn and close the door behind me to shut out the noise. Sitting, I arrange things before me, ink on the left, scroll unrolled to the first panel. As the old man begins to snore, open-mouthed, under the enameled bowl of the sky, I chew on the end of my brush. I count syllables in my head, trying to work out the first line: something about, what it's like, to come to Japan.

The Option
of the Coat

FRANK DIPALERMO

I was not supposed to drink coffee. Juices (other than citrus), water, soft drinks without caffeine were all encouraged, but diuretics were discouraged. In fact, on the wall in front of me was a framed list with "Things to Avoid" printed in a cheerful, rolling script across the top. The first item on the list was coffee.

I took a deep, satisfying swallow from the oily, dark roast I had brought in a thermos from home. The other person in the waiting room looked at me in disapproval. I turned to face him and sipped again. Loudly. He sniffed and turned away. He must have been new at this. Only a new Reactor could be so officious.

A door on the other end of the mauve and pale blue room (all D & E waiting rooms were mauve and pale blue) opened, and Gladys stuck her gum-popping head out. "We're ready for ya, Jimmie. We got your usual place all set up." I wordlessly followed her lascivious, limping gait to the back corner cot, the only one by a window. I rolled up both my sleeves and stretched out.

"Happy birthday, hon," Gladys chattered as she slapped my right forearm to raise a vein. It required a thick layer of makeup to hide the pockmarks around her hairline. Her upper lip looked as if the left corner had been removed (probably melanoma) then clumsily reconstructed. She compensated for this with copious amounts of fire-engine-red lipstick.

I was transfixed, as always, watching her fingers with permanently swollen and twisted joints, as they slid the needle in. Her pile of platinum hair, sprayed with glitter and heaped on top of her head, bobbed as she connected the tube to the needle and checked to make sure there were no kinks. Immediately my blood filled the plastic conduit that ran from my arm into the machine on the table by the cot. The machine was a small black thing. On top of a stationary base, it rocked back and forth as it drew my blood out and (I'm guessing here) ran it through a preliminary set of filters before sending it on to another tube that disappeared into the wall. "Looks like we'll only be seeing you for six more months, ain't that right, hon?" Gladys said as she stroked my arm. Gladys is one of those women who could make the most innocuous gesture into something overtly sexual. "Damn shame," she murmured as she lowered her eyes to the IV. "You've got such great," she paused a moment, "veins." She leaned forward and kissed me with those heavily painted lips. I could feel the smudge she left sitting like a weight on my face. "What'sa matter, hon?" she cooed as she wiped it off with a Kleenex she wet on her tongue. "Cat got your tongue?" I didn't answer. "I know," she said. "It's rough. Do you have any plans for when you're through here? Anyone to take care of you?" I still didn't answer. "Ya know, there's a Reactor in England they say has made it to fifty with no auto symptoms. I read about it in the *National Enquirer.* The locals have started to worship him and attribute a few miracles to his grace. Who knows? Maybe there are exceptions. You still have a year, or even more. Maybe the Bigheads will come up with some new technique, some new drug...." I remained silent.

The machine by the cot buzzed. A red light flashed on its top. They were very efficient. They withdrew close to a quart of blood in less than five minutes. "My, that was fast. I guess time flies when you're having fun." She slipped the needle out and pressed an alcohol pad to the puncture. Gladys cultivated a look that made her appear as if she could do only one thing well. Despite this, she was very good at her job. When the bleeding stopped, she taped adhesive over a small wad of gauze pressed to the hole. She clutched my hand and whispered close to my ear, "Maybe you could come live with me. I would be glad to take care of you. I've done it before, ya know. Taken care of Reactors right through the whole thing." She smiled in a way that was not quite pleasant as she stroked my cheek and murmured, "Ah, such smooth skin. Not a scar on it. Not a one. You don't know how rare that is." Then she was off to the next cot.

I felt Henry slapping my left forearm to raise a vein and saying,
"Happy birthday, hon." He wore almost as much makeup as
Gladys, although it was somewhat more tastefully applied, but no
amount could hide the deep, cratered pits that marred the entire
surface of his face. "Looks like we'll only be seeing you for six
more months," as he slipped the needle into my arm and started
the IV that would hydrate and expose me to massive amounts of a
deadly virus, bacteria or mutated microbe that was posing a threat
somewhere on the planet. The infusion took much longer than
the extraction. I would have to lie there for at least two hours. "Do
you want a magazine, hon?" Henry asked as he stroked my forearm. I didn't answer. "It's gonna be a real shame to lose you," he
said. "You've got such great," he paused a breathless moment,
"veins." Then he was off.

When it was over, I slipped on my yellow trench coat with the
red hexagon emblazoned across the back and numbers stitched
in blue below that. It was getting ratty, dirty. Stains were bunched
around the sleeves and buttons. There was a time when I would
never have allowed my coat to get in such a state. I would have
stormed into a cleaners and demanded the service accorded one
of my rank. If the stains were bad enough, I would have entered a
tailor shop and merely tossed my coat at him, knowing he would
put all other work aside and furiously set about making me a new
one while I waited. On just such an occasion a tailor once made
the mistake of handing me a bill for services rendered. This
would be a considerable offense to any Reactor. But I am not just
a Reactor. I am a *Universal* Reactor. I promptly slapped the tailor
across the face, grabbed my new coat, and stormed indignantly
out the door.

I can no longer be bothered with such grandiose gestures. I can
no longer be bothered keeping the coat clean. What's the point?
In six months I will be forced to give it up. I found out yesterday
they plan to retire my number, the blue 77023 stitched below the
red hexagon. "It's in honor of exemplary service," the head of the
Department of Immunological Dispersion told me. There was a
time when I thought such nonsense meant something.

You know, the coats are truly effective. We are definitely visible.
From where I stood on the porch of the Deposit-and-Expose that
served the greater San Francisco area, I could see a yellow coat
like mine weaving uncertainly through the crowd. They must have

left the D & E just ahead of me. It looked like they were headed for the same Muni station I was.

The tram was pulling into the packed station just as I arrived. I walked to the head of the jostling lines and boarded first, as is my right.

On seeing me, everyone who had been sitting leapt to their feet so that I could have the seat of my choice. In front of me a woman I recognized struggled to stand. I felt an observational kind of intimacy with her. I had been seeing her on one tram or another almost every day for years. I had watched her diseases progress. She was having a bad time today. Her knees were extraordinarily swollen and painful looking. Her ears ran with a yellow liquid and she wheezed thickly as she pulled herself up. I was about to take her seat when I noticed through the double glass doors that separated the cars a flurry of activity and a flash of yellow in the car ahead of mine. The other Reactor was there. I headed through the doors into the next car. I don't know why I did this. I no longer feel any sort of comradeship with other Reactors. I find their company largely boorish and overbearing. Perhaps it was my cruel streak getting the best of me. I must admit I could not resist smirking when the crowd of people, who were obviously just resettling themselves, lurched to their feet as soon as the door slid closed behind me.

This custom of allowing Reactors precedence in all things (no Reactor ever has to wait in line, remain standing, suffer any avoidable delays, or pay for services) has taken on a religious flavor of reverence and fear. This is something that suits most Reactors quite well. But its roots are practical. After a Reactor has been exposed to, say, a combination of mutated infectious hepatitis and mutated yellow fever, it will take his body about a month to develop sufficient antibodies to be useful in Passive Immuno Therapy. While the Reactor will not actually develop the disease (or else he would not be a Reactor) he may, during the course of the month, feel quite ill, with symptoms ranging from fluish achiness to convulsions. Considering the invaluable service we are providing society, the least society can do in return is provide us with a seat on the tram.

You don't know me well enough to know how sarcastic I am being.

She was almost hidden by the people standing around her. She sat slumped low in her seat, swimming in her yellow coat. I walked over to her. Everyone scrambled to regain their seats except the people standing on either side. They looked most uncomfortable, uncertain as to whether it was appropriate to sit or not. Custom demanded they make their seats available to me without my request. However, I had chosen to stand. Custom did not demand that I inform them of my choice.

I stood between them. The one on the left had a coughing fit.

The numbers that are stitched across the back of our coats are also stitched on our right sleeves. Hers was a five-digit number beginning with three. She was a bacterial Reactor. Her apartment would be much smaller than mine and she would have to pay for some of her luxury items. Still, it would not be a bad life.

Bacterial Reactor. That explained the twisted look of her shoulders, as well as the evenly dispersed spray of scars on her hands. She had been sick, very sick, in the past. But it had been viral.

Her face was damp, her skin quite pale. She licked at her lips and breathed deeply, like someone who is feeling nauseous.

"Your first time?" I asked. I shifted my weight, which brought my hip and thigh against the person standing to my left. This made him most uncomfortable. He wheezed and gasped in a gurgling way.

She looked up, startled. When her eyes had focused on me she whispered, "Second," between deeply drawn breaths.

"It's harder in the beginning," I said. "After the first six or seven times you will start to wonder if they exposed you to anything at all."

"So they say." She was then swept over by a wave of intense nausea. I took a step backward to protect my shoes, but the nausea passed without event.

"Weren't you just exposed?" I asked. "Didn't I see you walking away from the D & E just now?" In answer to my question, she listlessly pushed up a sleeve to show me the adhesive tape stretched over the wad of gauze on the inside of her elbow. "Well, you shouldn't be manifesting this intensely already."

"I don't think I was done manifesting from the last time," she mumbled.

"Yes. Well. Sometimes it's like that." I leaned imperceptibly further into the person on my left and dropped my hand in such a way that it touched his own pockmarked hand. This was too much contact for the poor soul, who had another coughing fit and scurried in an embarrassed wheezing manner into another car. I took his seat.

"Did it happen like this for you in the beginning?" she asked.

"No. Never. The worst reaction, the only reaction I have ever had, was when I was three and a series of nasty boils sprang up around the infusion site. That's it. But then I'm a Universal. I think it makes a difference." She absently reached over to finger the numbers on my sleeve, noticing for the first time the seven stitched there. She did not seem impressed, merely curious in a distracted sort of way.

"Oh," she said.

It began in ninety-nine. Actually it began long before then, but that was the year it was admitted. It was proved conclusively that there was a definite relationship between the thinning ozone layer and the bizarre and deadly epidemics that were sweeping the planet. The first organisms mutated by the increasing radiation and cosmic rays in our atmosphere were microbes, viruses, and bacteria. It is estimated that over one third of the world's population died from one mutated disease or another between the years of 1999 and 2010. I understand there was a planetary stench from the corpses.

By 2010, mutations in all organisms were quite common. In humans the mutation most often reported has come to be known as a Lizard Baby. This is a baby whose brain has been stunted permanently during the first trimester of pregnancy. They have no mental capacity beyond that of your average goldfish. Less, perhaps. They also have the curious habit of continually darting their dexterous tongues in and out of their mouths and hissing. Hence the name. In a particularly cruel stroke, fate endowed them with a life expectancy exactly equal to that of the general populace. This has given rise to interesting debate in both religious and legal circles. The dilemma: should it be permissible to kill a Lizard Baby at birth if both parents consent? It is an allowable medical practice in three states already, but debate continues. There is a growing contingent that holds it should not only be illegal to kill a Lizard Baby, but goldfish as well.

We live in strange times.

In another, less common mutation, babies are born with hyper-active immune systems. In their bloodstreams are found quite ex-traordinary cells that operate with uncanny intelligence and speed identifying and destroying toxins and invading bodies.

There are degrees of this mutation. Some of these babies are born with immune systems only adept at identifying and destroy-ing bacteria, others viruses, still others toxins. A few quite rare ba-bies are born with immune systems adept at destroying all foreign bodies. All of these babies are called Reactors. The last class of Reactors is known as Universal. Me.

Universals are identified by the fact that they don't get sick. Infants who survive their first two years have usually had to over-come devastating illnesses, which leave unpleasant marks on the skin, twist the spine, or some such thing. Any baby that makes two years without suffering a major illness is required (by the govern-ment) to undergo testing to determine its Reactor status.

Universal Reactors are the only people on the planet who will never know infectious disease. But our lives are not unscathed by fate. Our immune systems will grow in power all of our natural lives. At some point our immune systems will begin to attack our own bodies, creating diseases that may not be infectious, but are easily as hideous as anything yet produced by a mutated invader.

It usually begins with crippling arthritis, coupled with a disease known as Vacillating Diaspora. This is a skin condition in which le-sions erupt over large portions of the body. They turn an ashen gray. The gray skin begins to flake off in large, thick chunks, often leaving muscle, nerves and bone exposed. This process generally begins when the Universal turns thirty. Universals are retired from service by the time they are twenty-nine and a half years old so they can wrap up their lives without distraction. By the way, today is my twenty-ninth birthday.

But I digress.

There is a third mutation that is the rarest of all. These babies are instantly identifiable in that they often emerge from the womb speaking in short sentences, or singing tunes the mother hummed during pregnancy. There is a rumor about one such baby telling its birthing doctor a knock-knock joke not fifteen sec-onds after the doctor had delivered him. It seems that for such ba-bies, in utero exposure to cosmic rays, rather than *inhibiting* the development of brain cells as had been expected, incites a growth *spurt.* Their brains begin to grow at an almost immeasurable rate. They are usually delivered by cesarean section as their heads are far too big to be passed in the conventional manner. They are known, unimaginatively, as Bigheads.

They are removed from their parents at birth and attend special schools beginning in their second week of life. They are mankind's last great hope. If anyone can find a way out of the mess the race now finds itself in, it is the Bigheads. At least that is the official line.

Fate also threw Bigheads a rather interesting curve. They are born with very weak immune systems. Almost no immune system at all. Is it surprising that one of the first advances made by the Bigheads was to develop a method of exposing Reactors to various microbes, giving them a chance to develop antibodies, then extracting said antibodies for use in others?

Because of their weakened immune systems, Bigheads live in quarantine. They have several underground cities scattered across the globe. The cities are in constant communication with each other but have no physical contact. In these cities, the Bigheads are working twenty-four hours a day to solve the myriad scientific problems mankind now confronts. Again, this is the official line.

I find it intriguing that the Bigheads' official mandate is to discover a way for mankind to recover its environment, to make the earth safe again, yet they haven't. They just haven't. Perhaps they can't.

It is true that the Passive Immuno Therapy system has saved millions of lives. But it is also true the Bigheads have not found a way to prevent the continuing mutation of microbes. When a new and deadly mutation occurs, there is always tremendous suffering and death in the area of the outbreak until sufficient stores of Immuno Therapy have been built up to stem the new disease. Suffering and death that never extends itself below the surface of the earth, never touches the Bighead cities.

Oh, yes. There is another advance the Bigheads have made. They have developed quite a line of protective clothing. This clothing minimizes the risk of infection posed by daily life. Such clothing has become quite fashionable. That is something, I suppose.

"How old are you?" I asked.

"Eighteen," she responded.

That is late for a Reactor to begin service. I guessed that it took eighteen years for her physicians to realize all of the diseases she suffered from were viral, or more importantly, that they weren't bacterial.

"Do you ever wonder..." she began, but then fell back, succumbing to a sudden weakness.

"Take it easy," I said. I had never seen anyone manifest quite this badly. After a few deep breaths she seemed to feel better.

"Do you ever wonder if it's doing any good?" Now there was a thought.

"Since the institution of Passive Immuno Therapy statistics have consistently shown..." I began persuasively.

"You sound like the head of the Department of Immunological Dispersion," she said.

"Yes, I suppose I do. But people are living longer."

"How do you know?" she asked.

"Like I said, the statistics..."

"Statistics can lie," she said. "Look around you. Even if people are living longer, are they living better?"

I glanced around the tram. I was surrounded by people with scarred faces and mottled skin. Everyone wheezed, coughed, and brought up phlegm. Every voice was hoarse and raspy except for mine, except for hers. People who did not look too thin had puffy, swollen, irritated faces and joints.

In other words, they were not sick. These days if you are well enough to move at all, if you are not dying, then you are well.

"The system of Immunological Dispersion is severely taxed," my voice surprised me with its strident false confidence, its patronizing tone. "It has been taxed since its inception. There has been no time to battle diseases that are not quickly fatal. No time to fight diseases that only disfigure, cripple, or cause pain."

"No time," she continued, "to stem the flow of mutated microbes that grind most people into ugly, scarred shapes and early graves. I have heard it before. Not enough time. How much time do they want? The population gets smaller every year. Have you considered that maybe the Bigheads just don't care? Maybe they aren't interested?" There was an audible gasp from someone behind me. She was speaking sacrilege and she was speaking it loudly. "But," she whispered close to my ear, "I have a few guesses as to what *does* interest them."

"What are you saying?" I asked, but her speech had cost her. She leaned her head back, closed her eyes, and panted. "What are you saying?" I demanded.

"This is my stop," she muttered and tried to stand.

"But wait a minute..."

"I'm afraid if you want to continue talking to me you will have to walk me home," she said and tried to stand again. This time I helped her.

She hobbled off the tram, with me supporting her elbow. I could feel the weight of the stares on our backs. They were the murderous stares reserved for subversives.

As we walked slowly along, she would begin a sentence, "There is evidence of chemical imbalances as well as physical mutation... Bighead cerebral cortex..." or, "Because of their separation, Bigheads...superiority...paranoia...unstable psyche..." but she was too ill to complete her thoughts and resorted to a series of vague gestures that communicated nothing. Occasionally she rested against a dead tree or trash can. Her eyes were glazed as she swayed on the perilous edge of consciousness.

I wondered what I was doing. I barely knew this woman. In fact, I did not know her name. And yet there I was walking her home, allowing her to hang weakly on my arm and try my patience with constant pauses, terrify me with ominous phrases.

She was becoming delirious. The farther we walked the less aware she seemed of my presence. Her phrases became disjointed and solitary, as if spoken in a vacuum. "Preventable suffering..." she droned. "Religious subjugation..." "Global domination..." Then she was reduced to single words. "Loss," she said. "Deprivation. Anguish. Death," and finally, "Grief."

Her apartment was just outside the park in a refurbished Victorian. I had to steady her hand while she let herself in.

There was a small foyer. The left wall was ornamented by an artfully placed group of picture frames. They were arranged the way people arrange photos of family members. All were empty.

My companion put on some music, classical, then collapsed on the couch still wearing her coat. She passed out.

It was suddenly urgent that I know her name. It seemed obscene that she had shared her delirium, words from the bottom of her brain, and I did not know her name. She did not know mine.

"Hello," I called out. She didn't respond. "Hello!" I yelled. "Wake up!" She tossed her head from one side to the other and pulled some long blonde hair out of her mouth, but did not open her eyes. I crossed over to her, sat next to her on the couch. I gently slapped her face.

"Hello!" I shouted.

She opened her eyes, but they did not focus. "Water," she said. He eyes fluttered closed.

I slapped her face again, this time a little less gently. "Wake up!" I commanded her. "Come on, WAKE UP!" Her eyes opened and I gave her one more sharp pat on the cheek.

"Water," she said to me.

"What is your name?" I asked her.

"I'm thirsty. I need water," she said.

I gave her face another slap. "What is your name? I want to know your name."

"I'm so thirsty. . . ."

"I know that!" I yelled. "That has been clearly established! What has not been established is YOUR NAME!!"

She looked at me and her vision cleared. For a moment aware-ness grew bright behind her eyes. A small smile graced her lips. She lifted her head slightly and replied, "Daisy. My name is Daisy Withers."

"Daisy Withers," I said. "Nice name."

"And your name is James Sebasta," she said. "I've been wanting to meet you for quite some time. Thank you for walking me home." She extended her hand.

I took it in mine. It was only then that I noticed my own hand, which was shaking. A sense of dread settled over me. Of having been manipulated.

"I will have to impose on your kindness a bit more, James Sebasta. I am dying of thirst and I need water. Go into the kitchen and get me a glass?"

"How did you know my name?" I asked, embarrassed at the tremor in my voice. She just smiled at me. It was a cold, hard smile, tinged with fanaticism. "What else do you know about me?"

"I will be glad to answer any questions you have," she said. "But first I need a glass of water. Would you go into the kitchen and get me one?" Though it was a question, it had the tone of an order. Or perhaps a test. A tiny examination, expertly administered.

I looked at her face, almost pretty on the pillow. "No, Daisy Withers, I'm afraid I can't do that." We looked at each other, both shocked at my unqualified failure. "I can't do anything for you, or for anyone else."

I got up quickly. I put on my coat, buttoned it tightly, and folded my arms over it. I looked back at her face, the clouds of delirium already beginning to move across it. I left her apartment, walked onto the street. The wind tore at my coat, tried to pull it away from me. Before I knew what I was doing, I turned on the wind, arms flailing as if at an invisible assailant.

I spent the rest of the day wandering aimlessly about the city. Always feeling like I was being pursued. Always feeling a large and ominous presence just outside my range of vision. Several times I spun around, expecting to see a threatening shape, but there was nothing.

Finally, exhausted, I went back to my house. But it followed me. The threatening presence came into my home. Lingering in the shadows, it stalked me.

I searched my home, looking for a distraction; a drug, a knife, anything. Finding only a half empty bottle of wine, I turned on all the lights, pulled off my clothes, wrapped myself in my coat, crouched in the living room, and waited.

The next morning I woke up feeling hung over. My eyes were hot and bleary, my stomach uncertain, and my head pounded like a piledriver. The night before was shrouded in gray haze, occupying a strange place between dream and reality in my brain. I vaguely remembered a few hasty gulps of red wine, slugged down as I lurched through the foreign landscape of conflicting emotions, but surely not enough to make me feel so miserable. As I got up, my body complained bitterly. Joints ached and my neck felt stiff and creaky. So this is how it begins, I thought with a strange calm. First achy joints, then gouty swelling, then the twisting deformations of bone. I headed slowly to the bathroom. On my thighs were three bluish marks. Vacillating Diaspora, I thought. Yes, that's what it is. This is it, the beginning of a hideous end.

I was urinating when the terror hit. It struck me from behind like a wall of water. I pitched forward, my head hit the wall in back of the toilet. The piledriver pounded louder and harder. Cold sweat stood out on my forehead and ran down my nose.

When I was able, I turned slowly, shakily, and sat on the toilet. I looked closely at the marks on my thigh. Bruises. They could be bruises. I had spent much of the last day and night lurching about the city and my apartment. A bump, a minor collision could have caused these marks. And perhaps that is why I was so sore, my joints so painful. I had probably walked twelve or more miles. Reason for anyone to be sore. Plausible. Plausible.

I walked into the kitchen where the coffee maker was already finished. The aroma hung rich and heavy in the air and did much to clear my head, restore sensible thought.

As I sipped the mug of black fragrant coffee I realized I was chanting. Over and over I said the same two words. I must have been doing it since I left the bathroom, but I didn't have the slightest awareness of it. Over and over, the same two words brought me solitary comfort. Only bruises...only bruises...only bruises...only bruises, I said.

Only bruises (knock knock) only bruises (knock knock) only bruises (knock knock) only bruises (knock knock). It was impossible to say how long the person had been knocking before I became aware of it. The sound meshed perfectly with my internal rhythm. Whoever they were, they seemed eternally patient. I answered the door as I was. Nude. I had done this before. I always told myself the reason was because the caller was intruding at an ungodly hour (ungodly being any time before 10:30) and I was not about to make any concessions to such rudeness. That is a lie. The truth is I sometimes enjoy being cruel, need to be cruel. The people on the other side of the door always gasped, but not at my nudity. They gasped at the sight of so much unscarred flesh, a skeleton held straight, erect, joints that operated smoothly and gracefully, genitals untroubled by boils and eruptions. Most of them had never seen anything like it, would never see anything like it again. I could see astonishment, shock, joy, fascination travel across their features. More than a few reached forward to stroke the skin on my chest, my hips. As I dodged the touch their faces would resolve into a mask of resentment and jealousy. I took great satisfaction from that.

On this particular day I needed as much satisfaction as I could get. I opened the door, placed myself prominently in the doorway.

"Mr. Sebasta?" the creature before me inquired. It was completely unruffled. It leveled me in its photographic gaze, was perhaps already broadcasting my naked image back to its home base. "Mr. Sebasta?" it asked again in precisely the same tones it had used before. "May I come in?" Without waiting for an answer, it walked into the living room. It brushed past me, actually touched me, and I could hear a faint mechanical hum as it did. My jaw was dropped and my heart pounded as I stood stupid in the doorway. Now the thing was behind me, photographing me from the back as well. "I think it would be wise to close the door, Mr. Sebasta," it suggested.

I closed the door and turned to face it. "I-I-I," I stammered. I had never felt more vulnerable in my life. "I need to put on some clothing."

"Excellent idea," it responded. I walked into the bedroom backward, feeling less vulnerable facing the thing.

I had never seen one before but I knew immediately what it was. There is not a person alive who would not know the gleaming white humanoid form, the red reflective photographic eyes of a Eunuch, android servants and bodyguards of the Bigheads. They ran all Bighead errands on the surface of the planet, and were designed to be sterilized on return. This one must have come from Compudown, the Bighead city under what used to be Concord.

I put on some pants and a shirt and took a few moments to compose myself. The thing (and whoever sent it) had gotten the best of me. I was determined to regain the upper hand.

"Yes, er...what are you called?" I asked as I entered the room.

"I am called Cyclone."

"Well, then, Cyclone, what can I do for you?"

"I have come to take you to Compudown."

"Excuse me?"

"The Executive Scientific Counsel would like to talk to you."

"Excuse me?"

"Am I being unclear?"

"No, no, Cyclone. You are perfectly clear. I just did not know that Bighe...uh, the Executive Scientific Counsel actually met with people from the surface."

"The last such meeting took place on July 10, 2020."

"Thirty years ago?"

"Since then all communication with the surface has been via fiber optics or through the use of Eunuchs like myself. A special

room has been set up for your visit, to allow full visual and audi-
tory contact while minimizing the risk of infectious transmission."

"That is quite a lot of preparation."

"What is to be discussed is important."

I considered refusing. How could I? There was something completely resolute, utterly determined about the thing in my living
room. I felt an illusion sliding away, the illusion that I had control
over my life. I grasped at that illusion, seized a corner of it, held
tightly. "I cannot go until I get my coat cleaned," I insisted.

"As you wish," Cyclone replied.

We left my home.

As we walked I told myself the attention we attracted was the
normal amount generated by my bright yellow coat. In the cleaners I adopted an air of disdain, nonchalance, as if I often walked
escorted by a Eunuch, as if it were my servant.

In my stomach terror sat like a lump of frigid lead.

BART, that stands for Bay Area Rapid Transit, was once a com-
muter train—when the population was large enough to support
it. I have seen pictures of the cavernous platforms filled with
throngs of people hurrying from the suburbs to the city or back.
It's very hard to imagine.

Now the platforms stand hollow and silent as cathedrals. Completely deserted but for the times Eunuchs use them to shuttle
supplies, Immuno Therapy, or, in this case, me, to or from Compudown.

I followed Cyclone through the entrance and down the stairs.
A train manned by another Eunuch stood idling. On the floor of
the platform was a thick layer of dust, disturbed only by the precise footprints Cyclone had made when it arrived. We boarded
the train.

The train pulled out of the station. Cyclone was silent but for a
discreet mechanical hum.

I tried to think pleasant thoughts but I didn't really think
much at all. Just a kaleidoscope of almost-thoughts, semi-images
careened through my brain as we passed one deserted suburb
after another.

The train pulled to a stop in the Concord station. I was led to a
waiting ground car. Cyclone drove us a short distance through the
deserted streets, past the crumbling buildings, to a concrete bun-

ker. It had a large folding metal door. I could hear a series of metallic clicks and whirs from Cyclone's head as it broadcast something. The door began slowly, evenly, efficiently, to lift. We drove through.

White tile. Everywhere was gleaming white tile. Cyclone parked just inside the door, which was already beginning to close behind us. It got out of the car and motioned for me to follow. It led me to a thick white metal door with no knob, no visible locking mechanism. Printed in red chipped paint were the words "Now Entering Stage One Quarantine Area. When Depressurization Begins Exhale All Air or Embolism And Immediate Death Will Result." Cyclone emitted another series of clicks and whirs. There was a slight hiss as the heavy door swung hydraulically back. Cyclone entered and stood in the center of a small white chamber. It beckoned me to follow. I hesitated, as if considering my options, before joining it. The door hissed closed.

There were two seconds of silence followed by the sound of my ears popping as a portion of the air in the chamber was slowly sucked away. I began exhaling and continued exhaling until my ears popped again and I realized the air pressure was being brought back up. Now the air had a distinctly medicinal taste and smell. It burned slightly on my eyes and at the back of my throat. Some sort of aerosol antibiotic, I guessed.

"We will remain here for five minutes. Please breathe deeply," Cyclone said. Was it programmed to sound contemptuous?

The five minutes passed very slowly.

A door in the opposite wall swung open. Cyclone led me out into a corridor. We entered the third door on the right.

The room was ten feet long and about as wide. Down the center of the room ran a solid panel of fire glass that went from wall to wall, floor to ceiling. A long table was pushed up against the other side of the glass. Around it three large high-backed chairs were arranged. They were turned away from me so the occupants could watch a monitor mounted on the facing wall. All I could see of the people in the chairs were the very tops of their heads, flesh colored half-moons that swayed back and forth as they whispered among themselves, or bounced in place as they giggled like nasty children.

On the sides of the chairs odd constructions rose up to shoulder height. They looked like padded armrests except they were concave. There was another such construction protruding out of the table in front of each chair.

"Run it again. Run it again from the beginning," one of them said between malicious giggles.

I turned my attention to the monitor. It was difficult to make out the image due to the angle of the monitor and the reflection in the fire glass. Eventually I understood. They were watching a tape of me, shot through Cyclone's eyes. There I was, opening the door in the nude. There was the dumbfounded expression as I realized who my caller was. This brought a fresh round of guffaws. I began to blush.

"Fast forward. Fast forward! I want to see him back out of the room again!" cried a woman's voice. I guessed she was the one seated on the left because some of the sparse and patchy hair on that half moon of flesh was caught up in a dirty pink bow.

"No way, Gretta. No way!" the one in the middle commanded. I could tell he was speaking by the way his head bobbed. "I want to see the shot of his butt. He has a wonderfully fuzzy ass."

Finally Cyclone spoke. "Scientific Counsel, your guest has arrived." They turned their chairs to face me.

Bigheads. The word was horribly inadequate. Their faces were normal. If anything, they tended to be smaller than average, but their foreheads rose straight up three feet above their brows, flaring outward to a width of eighteen inches, before cresting in bulbous crowns. Their hair grew in clumps with large bald patches between, as if their scalps were stretched too thin in places to support any follicles. The bald spots were a tight, angry pink.

They looked at me in silence, then burst into raucous laughter, no doubt imagining me in the nude. Their laughter resolved itself into a series of seductive moans and lewd giggles as their imaginations took them a step further. The Bighead seated in the middle leered at me with heavy-lidded eyes. A small ball of saliva glistened at the corner of his mouth, then traveled in a silver string down to his shoulder.

"Drooling!" yelled the Bighead on the right. "Alfonse, you are actually drooling!" He pointed to the corner of Alfonse's mouth and laughed. When he brought his hand back to the table it, quite independently, picked up a pen and began to scribble numbers across a piece of paper.

Alfonse, without taking his gaze off me, reached his tongue to the corner of his mouth and licked at the saliva. He smiled slowly and then blew me a kiss. Again, they started laughing.

Their heads were supported by skinny, fragile looking necks. As I watched, Alfonse's neck began to tremble. Still laughing and drooling, his head fell forward, but was caught comfortably by the thing protruding out of the table. Then Gretta's neck began to tremble. Her head fell to one side and landed safely in what I now realized were enormous headrests. Bigheadrests, if you will.

The third one's head fell backward and was supported by the back of the chair.

Alfonse broke through the laughter and tried to placate me with, "Please excuse us. We don't mean to offend. We just find you so amusing. Make yourself comfortable. Take a seat." I looked around. There were no chairs on my side of the room.

The ceaseless stream of numbers continued to pour from the pen of the Bighead man. By now it filled an entire page. Unthinkingly, his hand flipped the paper over and began anew.

As if on cue all the Bigheads placed their foreheads in the rests on the table and examined the manila folders below their faces. Almost as one they opened them and began to read.

"You are James Sebasta," Gretta announced. "Your hair is black, eyes dark brown. Six feet tall. You wear a forty-two long. Your home is in the Marina. You have lived there for five years. You live alone. Yesterday was your twenty-ninth birthday. Continue, Alfonse."

"You are a Universal Reactor and have been in service for twenty-seven years," he picked up. "You have not missed a single month's service in all that time. Isn't that impressive."

"You're hung like a horse, and are definitely not Jewish. Isn't *that* impressive," hissed the other Bighead man (who continued to scribble numbers).

They giggled. They all closed their folders and struggled their heads to the backs of their chairs so they could look at me. Gretta needed to be assisted by a Eunuch who was hidden in a discreet niche in the wall. "My, my," said Alfonse.

My attention was trapped by the numbers running, running, and running from the Bighead man's left hand. Alfonse followed my gaze and said to his companion, "Burt, you're doing it again."

Burt said, "What's that?" Then he looked down at his left hand.

"Oh! Oh, yes of course." He crumpled the paper, threw it to the floor and placed his hand in his lap. "So sorry," he mumbled. "Pi. Nervous habit. Completely unaware that I'm doing it."

"Excuse me?" I said.

"Burt has a nervous habit," Gretta informed me. "He figures out pi continuously. It gets most tiresome."

"So sorry," Burt said, but already his hand was back on the table and moving across a fresh sheet of paper, leaving a trail of numbers behind.

Alfonse saw this, rolled his eyes, and sighed deeply. After a moment he announced, "You are going to die soon, James Sebasta."

"It will be a horrible death," Gretta agreed. "Your joints rigid, swollen, and deformed..."

"Your skin falling away in great chunks," Burt chimed in, "leaving bones, tendons, and raw nerves exposed."

"Eventually your immune system will attack your internal organs, giving you heart disease, jaundice, excruciating gastrointestinal ailments. The process will probably begin before your next birthday. But you know all this," Alfonse concluded.

"You are telling me nothing new," I said through a dry mouth. "Surely I am not here so you may lecture me on what is common knowledge."

"No, that is not why you are here. You are here so we may make you an offer," Alfonse replied.

"How would you like to escape this hideous end and live out a normal life span?" Gretta inquired. My jaw dropped.

"We have developed certain drugs," Burt remarked as he scribbled, "that will suppress your immune system..."

"Entirely," Alfonse stated flatly.

"Entirely!" I retorted. "Is that the only option? Is there no way to *reduce* my immune system?"

"No. I'm afraid with your immune system being as powerful as it is, it will be an all-or-nothing situation," Alfonse said.

"That wouldn't extend my life! I wouldn't last a week with no immune system."

"What if you lived here," Gretta asked, "with us?" The question was trapped in the space between us.

"But...but...but..." it seemed my vocabulary had escaped me. I grasped at the first word I could find. Fortunately, it was appropriate. "Why?"

"Oh, we'll think of something for you to do," Alfonse leered.

"We're starting a breeding program," Burt informed me.

"What?" My vocabulary was slowly returning.

"A breeding program," said Gretta. "It makes perfect sense, doesn't it? With your superior immune system and our superior minds we will create a new race. Superhumans."

"It's the next evolutionary step," Burt put in.

"Yes, think of it," Alfonse whispered conspiratorially. "For the first time in millennia, the human race has the opportunity to evolve, perhaps into a new dynamic species! Only this time the evolution will be under our control! It's really quite remarkable." He paused a minute. "Of course, you will be required to provide other . . ."

"Services," Burt lisped. They began another round of laughter. "Eventually, we will need a larger gene pool than just yourself. But we wanted you to be the first."

"Why?" I asked.

"Because of the four Universals your age in the San Francisco area . . ." Alfonse started.

"You're the cutest," Gretta cooed. Again laughter. The sound petered slowly away. The Bigheads stared at me in silence for some time, appraising. Then they came to a collective, silent decision.

"You know," Alfonse said, "the poor fools on the surface are doomed."

"It's true," Gretta murmured. "If more than a few mutated plagues show up at the same time . . . something that's bound to happen sooner or later . . ."

"Perhaps sooner," Burt insinuated.

"Well, there just wouldn't be much anyone could do," Alfonse put in.

"But the system of Immunological Dispersion . . ." I said.

"Is woefully inadequate in such a circumstance . . . for the people on the surface," Gretta said.

"Then work on improving it!"

There was a considered pause. Then Alfonse coolly replied, "That is not in our best interest. Nor in the best interest of the race we hope to create."

It felt like ice water was running down my spine. "What are you saying?" I asked.

"We are saying," he continued, "the people on the surface are doomed without our help and we are unwilling to help them. In fact we have plans to hasten the next series of plagues along, so to speak."

"There are some things we want to put in order first," Gretta explained. "It will take time. But we have time. Plenty of time."

The illusion slipped out of my hands, fluttered away on the wind. No control. No one had any control. "How can you do this?" I asked.

"It's survival of the fittest," Burt answered.

My knees, my hands were trembling. "Why are you telling me?"

"Because no one would believe you if you repeated it," said Gretta.

"In fact you might be killed if you did," Burt said. "If the populace considers you royalty, they consider us gods. And in a way the description is apt." Gretta and Alfonse nodded in agreement.

"Why don't you go home and think about our offer?" Gretta advised. "You have a week to decide."

I had been dismissed and fell completely out of their attention. Cyclone led me silently out of the room. Before the door closed behind me, I heard the Bigheads laugh as they ran the tape again.

I don't remember much about the ride home.

As I left the station and began to walk, I realized two things. The first was that the strange, yawning emptiness I felt in my chest was a desperate need for companionship and compassion. The second was that there was absolutely no one for me to turn to. I laughed to myself as I walked. I tried to find the absurd construction of my life amusing, but my laugh had the bitter, metallic taste of hysteria.

I found myself knocking at a door, one I almost didn't recognize till Daisy answered.

She was feeling better. That much was obvious. "James," she said. "You're back."

"Yes," I said.

"Well, come in. I'm feeling much better today. Maybe I could offer you some tea?" she suggested.

"Coffee, if you have it," I said.

"It will have to be instant."

"Yes. Well," I resigned myself with a shrug.

She ushered me into the living room while she went into the

kitchen. I noticed her coat, thrown in a heap on the floor. I took off my own coat, folded it neatly. I sat with it in my lap, running my fingers over the lapel again and again.

"I had some awfully strange fever-dreams last night," she called from the kitchen.

"I can imagine," I said.

"I don't think you can."

She came out of the kitchen with two mugs and some cookies on a tray. She sat next to me on the sofa. "Here, have an Oreo."

"Why do you have picture frames arranged in your hallway?" I asked.

"What? Oh." She paused a moment. "They are a reminder."

"Excuse me?"

"A reminder of the people whose pictures used to fill them."

"Why not just leave the photographs?"

"Too static."

"Excuse me?"

"People change too fast for photographs to capture anything. January, four years back, my mother was a clerk in a grocery with a pretty smile and blonde hair. Three months later she was a bald quadriplegic with no teeth, and all of her skin covered with shingles."

"Oh," I said.

"Three months after that, she was dead."

"Oh."

"How can I put up a photograph of my mother, smiling and happy, when there are so many images of her in my brain that make the photo a lie?"

"I, ah..." For the second time that day, my vocabulary abandoned me.

"I leave a frame as a perimeter. Every day I look at the frame and see a different image. They were all her." She paused and looked at me while she sipped her tea. "I don't expect that makes any sense to you, seeing as you've never lost anyone." There was a subtle note of condescension in her voice.

"How do you know so much about me?"

"We made it our business to know." She took another sip of tea then announced, "You are the reason I became a Reactor."

I stared at her in blank shock.

"I discovered my Reactor status when my mother died. I should have caught the disease that killed her. I kept my status hidden. Not hard to do. Government bureaucracies have never been known for their efficiency. I didn't want to support a system that was exploitative." Again there was condescension in her voice. Strange thing, to *be* condescended *to*. "When we realized the Big-heads were interested in you I became a Reactor. You never speak to people that aren't Reactors and we needed to make contact with you before they did. But they moved too quickly and I was manifesting so badly I couldn't do more than give you hints. We hadn't counted on that."

"What are you saying? Who are 'we'?"

She smiled the way she would to a slow child she was trying to toilet train. "You could call us the resistance."

I bent forward and pressed my face into my coat. How could this have happened? How could I find myself at the center of a swirling vortex?

"We know you met with them this morning," she said. "Tell me what they spoke of."

I considered pretending I didn't know what she was talking about or falling obstinately silent, but there was something completely resolute, utterly determined about her. Numbly, with my face still pressed into my coat, I recounted the morning's experiences. I shuddered with revulsion as I told her they wanted me to become part of their breeding program. When I finished, I looked up from the coat. I expected to see shock or outrage moving her features. I was wrong. She was very calm.

"You must accept," she ordered.

"I...I must what?"

"Accept!" she commanded again. "It is the perfect opportunity for us! We have been trying to get an agent inside Compudown for years. They have played right into our hands."

"But I...They want me for a breeding program."

"Irrelevant," she said. "The important thing is you will be inside. Communication won't be easy, but something will be worked out."

"Do you understand what they will expect of me?" I protested.

She smiled that slow-child smile. "And you must fulfill those expectations perfectly. Look at it this way: All your life you have been making a living off the fluids your body produces. Nothing has really changed except the type of fluid and its manner of extraction."

I pressed my face back into my coat.

"But won't it be dangerous?"

"Of course it will be dangerous," she responded. "We have to get organized. You say they have given you a week? I hope that will be enough time. My friend," she said as she rose and took my cup, "the time for indulgence is over. You must be trained. I will send someone for you early tomorrow morning. Don't keep them waiting." She led me to the door. "This is really a remarkable opportunity, for us, for you, for all humanity. You must rise to the occasion. You had better rise to the occasion."

I felt a small trickle of sweat run into my left eye. Was I being threatened? I felt threatened.

She closed the door behind me.

Walking in the city. It was unsafe. I held tightly to my coat because it always made me feel okay, reminded me that I was protected, different from everybody else, invulnerable.

Was I being watched? Probably. But by whom? And was anyone watching the watchers? Strange sensation, being watched; not knowing if the watcher panted and masturbated, took copious notes on my activities, or held me locked in the cross hairs of a rifle's sight. Or perhaps all of the above?

Not safe. Danger, the unknown, perhaps death was everywhere around me, waiting, patient. If I weren't a Reactor this is how I would feel; knowing disease was present but not knowing where, powerless to avoid it.

When I got home I locked everything. I drew all the shades and hung sheets over the French doors that led onto the balcony. I doubt my actions did any good, but they gave me an outlet for my anxiety.

The day wound slowly into night. The night seeped into my apartment, oozing through cracks under windows and doors. I sat on the floor in the middle of the living room, still wearing my coat, fondling it. I was unable to stand or move. I lacked the will.

Images swept through my brain, knocking off my equilibrium, making me feel dizzy and nauseous. I saw the skin flaking off my arm in thick gray chunks, exposing muscle and bone. I saw Gretta, Alfonse, and Burt, all in high states of arousal, doing unspeakable things to me and forcing me to do unspeakable things to them. And then there was Daisy. I saw her staggering, looking weak and helpless, into her apartment, but not helpless, not at all. Instead it is I. I who am helpless. What a fool, what an arrogant clown I have been.

How long had I been sitting there? Had I dozed? I could have been there three minutes, I could have been there half my life. There was light creeping in through the window. That helped, gave me a point of reference by which to orient myself. Morning. This was morning.

I got up. I made coffee, my black, jittery savior. I sat at the table. I took several sips before I noticed the knocking at the door.

I took several more sips. The knocking was persistent, but irregular. It wasn't a Eunuch. I stood, removed my clothing, and carefully folded it. I have always felt there is something to be said for consistency. I went to the door. I opened it.

"Oh hon, you're even more scarless than I thought. Guess your parents weren't Jewish," she prattled as she popped her gum.

It was Gladys.

"I hate to be the one to say it, hon, but you'd better put something on. You'll catch your death. Course, in this day and age you'll probably catch your death anyway, but you're a Reactor, so what am I saying? Oh hon, cover that thing up will ya, just the sight of it has me all shit and falshimmeld." She ran her tongue over her damaged upper lip. "For God's sake, let me in and close the damn door." She walked into the apartment, trailing a hand over my chest, and I closed the door behind her. "Now put on some clothes and then let's talk."

I went to my pile of clothes and dressed in front of her. She stared with a blatant combination of jealous resentment and sexual desire. She was almost drooling. It didn't bother me. I suppose I was getting used to it.

I did not speak until I was fully clothed. "I'm ready to go when you are," I said.

"Fine, hon. Where are we goin'?"

"I assumed we were going to Daisy's," I said.

"Great. Is that a coffee shop or something? I could do with some breakfast. Your treat, ha-ha."

"You don't know Daisy?"

"Well I don't live in this part of town. Too rich for my blood. Ha! Ain't that fittin'? The reason you can afford this place is cause of your blood. Whereas I have to work for a living." It is possible the contempt in her tone was not conscious.

"Daisy isn't a place. She's a person. You don't know her?"

"Should I?"

"She's a Reactor. A new one. Just infused for the second time."

"Hon, I'll be honest with ya. I don't pay a lot of attention to the female Reactors. With them I just do my job and then get away from their bony asses. Too uppity, too prissy."

"So then why are you here?"

"I got your address off the files at the D & E. I just came by to talk about... you know."

"No, I don't know. Talk about what?"

"Taking care of you after, you know, *it* starts." There was her unpleasant smile.

"So you know nothing about Daisy?" Gladys shook her head.

There was another knock at the door. For a moment I considered disrobing and inviting the person in. Then a second thought occurred to me. "Gladys, the gardens in back of this house are lovely and we are only a short distance from the Golden Gate Bridge. Let's take a stroll."

"But hon, there's someone at the door."

"Yes, but there is no way..." I paused for a moment. Flattery is something new to me and it doesn't come naturally. "There is no way they are as interesting and lovely as you. Let's make a quick exit out the back door."

"Oh, the things you say!" Gladys responded. "I never realized you were such a romantic. Grab your coat and let's go."

We snuck around the back and onto the sidewalk with my coat bundled under my arm. The person at the door never saw us. We were no more than fifty feet away when Gladys began to insist that I put the coat on. "Hon, you'll catch a cold," she pleaded. I didn't point out that it would be impossible for me to catch a cold. "Please, doll, put on the coat. It would make me feel so much better." That was obvious. I put on the coat.

Gladys immediately lit up. She placed her hand under my arm. Her gestures became extravagant, her voice loud and cluttered with forced laughter. She looked with royal disdain at the few people we passed on the way to the bridge. She was enjoying herself except for the three times she was overcome by a sudden weakness and we had to stop and rest.

Once on the bridge, which was as vacant as always, her talk turned to matters more practical. "You could come live at my place," she said. "There's been one or two who have moved in with me. But your place is so much nicer, it'd probably be better that I come live with you." She patted my hand and gave me a patronizing smirk.

"I know just what to do. There's this poultice I make out of baking soda and eggs. It really seems to cut the pain of the lesions. It even helps a little with the arthritis. When you can't move around anymore, I'll wear your coat." She stroked the sleeve affectionately. "That way I can still get all those lovely free goods and services you've grown accustomed to. Plus with the coat I can walk into the pharmacy and get all kinds of pain killers that I wouldn't otherwise be able to get. And believe me, you're gonna need 'em. Course we should hold off on those as long as possible." We were at about the middle of the bridge. I turned to look back at the city. "I know. I know," Gladys continued, "I don't look like a Universal what with my scars and these twisted knuckles," she extended her deformed hands before her and sighed. "Ya know, as a little girl I had such pretty hands. Almost as pretty as yours." She smiled her ugly smile and ran a stubby finger over the back of my hand. "But soon your hands won't look nearly so pretty, will they? Poor baby. Poor, poor baby." She leaned over and kissed me. "Anyhow I can get away with being a viral or a bacterial. Most people don't even know what the numbers mean except government types. I'm pretty good with a needle and thread. If worst comes to worst I can always change that seven to a three." She wadded her gum between thumb and forefinger and tossed it over the side of the bridge.

"Toward the end it's better to go with the opiates," she continued. "They're the only thing that will work. You know, hon, morphine. They'll let me have it with that coat. It'll keep you in a quite pleasant buzz right up to the end. Plus, if I can get a little extra, I can always sell it. Oh I know, it's not strictly legal, but people are in such need of pain killers these days, and if you're not a Bighead or a Reactor, just try and get anything more effective than aspirin. Besides, what's wrong with Aunt Gladys making a little cash off her investment, so to speak?" She laughed in a way that begged me to join in. I didn't.

"Maybe you could let me try the coat on? Just for size?" she suggested. I leaned out over the guard rail, saw the water rushing hundreds of feet below me. The first strands of fog were beginning to roll in. "What do you say, hon? I just wanna wear it for a minute. Just so I can know what alterations I'll need to make.

These coats always fit you all so well." She extended her gouty hand. It was grasping like a talon at thin air.

I looked at her. I smiled. I nodded. I slid the coat off. Her hand grasped faster and her ugly lips puckered and unpuckered with a smacking sound. I held the coat out to her. She smiled and sighed, then took a step forward, moving her hips luxuriantly. Just as she was about to reach the coat, without realizing I was going to do it, I flung the coat out, over the side of the bridge. The wind took it, inflating it. For a moment it hung suspended like a yellow invisible man. Only six feet away from us it gestured wildly with its left arm: "Come on in. The water's fine." Then it crumpled and tore away, being carried off like a yellow comet that was finally extinguished in the bay.

Gladys had grabbed uselessly at it and was extended precariously over the bridge. She recovered and turned to face me. She was horrified, shocked, angry. "What the hell did you do that for?" she demanded.

"It was wrinkled," I said.

"It wasn't that wrinkled! You just didn't want me to try it on. That's it, isn't it? You just didn't want common, non-Reactor me to touch it. Isn't that right?"

"No," I said.

"The hell it isn't. I know your kind. So damn uppity. Well, we'll see how long you hang on to that attitude. When you're sick and dying, covered with open sores and unable to extend your little finger without howling in pain, we'll just see how uppity you are. We'll just see if you don't beg Aunt Gladys—BEG, do you hear me?—to put on your coat and run down to the pharmacy to get something for the pain. Oh, you'll be glad enough to have me wear it then.

"I'm leaving. Maybe I'll be back. Maybe pity will move my Christian heart and I'll be back to check on you." There was no doubt, she would be back. "I just hope you come to your senses before then and get another coat made. You'd better, or else no matter how much I want to help there's not a damn thing I can do for you." She turned on her high heels and lurched away, disappearing into the gathering mist.

I looked out to sea. I wondered where the coat was now. I leaned out over the guardrail and grasped one of the orange rusted cables. It felt cold and serious in my hands. I thought I could see, on just the other side of a finger of fog, a tiny fleck of yellow. I stepped over the guardrail and hoisted myself up a few feet to view it better. Then a few feet more. The twined metal of the cable bit into my cooling hands, slid grittily between my legs, rasped on the inside of my shoes. Yes, there it was, racing small but definite on an ocean current. I climbed a few feet higher. I could feel the wind on the tense cable, making it sing, sending vibrations echoing down my arms and across my shoulders. I laid my face against the cable, saw the speck of yellow disappear behind another advancing cloud and snuff out of my vision forever. Like a tiny flame.

I continued climbing. Slowly. Hand over hand. The cable had begun to splinter with age. Occasionally my hands would be punctured by a stray, rusty wire that sprung like an unruly hair. There was strange comfort in the pain.

Options. My life was so full of options. The Bigheads, Daisy, or Gladys. They all involved a giving up, a laying down of my will and surrendering to someone else's agenda. There is something to be said for that.

I stopped climbing. I looked down. The fog was getting thick. In a few minutes the platform of the bridge would not be visible.

I was surprised at how high I had come and yet it was not high enough. I was trying to find a vantage point. Some place from which I could view all my options clearly and then make a choice. But I felt strangely incomplete, as if I were overlooking something. Something that would provide a necessary symmetry. Something only for me. My option. Not the Daisy option. Not the Bighead option. Not the Gladys option. My option was missing. Perhaps if I climbed a few feet higher I would see it. Perhaps a few feet more and it would reveal itself to me. I started climbing again.

The fog was thick now. The cable and my face were glistening with cold moisture. I looked down and there was nothing but a blanket of undulating white into which the cable disappeared. Painted against that white I saw, like a movie replayed, my coat suspended, gesturing wildly, "Come on in. The water's fine," then crumpling and being torn away on the wind.

I realized that was it. I too could hang suspended a moment. I too could be torn away on the wind and extinguished in the bay. It was my other option. The option of the coat. Just its presence made me feel better, more balanced.

I was high enough now. I could stop climbing. I was completely separate, suspended there above the bridge, enveloped in white. It was a kind of aerial sanctuary, the one place where I could be completely alone with my options. And that was important because for the first time in my life, I had a decision to make.

Notes
on the
Contributors

Luis Alfaro

Luis Alfaro is a performance artist who writes poetry, plays, essays and short stories. "My desire is memory and yet I know it's not enough to just remember. I am learning that writing is the only way to pray." He is currently the co-managing director of the Latino Theatre Workshop at the Mark Taper Forum in Los Angeles.

Paul Attinello

I am a native of Washington, D.C., who fled to San Francisco in 1979 to pursue a career as a singer, composer, and writer on music. I moved to Los Angeles in 1984 to begin a doctorate in musicology at UCLA. After I tested positive in 1987, Terry Wolverton's HIV writing workshop goaded me to begin writing experimental prose and poetry. I owe my existence as a writer to Terry, as well as to her protective code of regulations about writing and being, which has enabled me to survive in the world of my own mind.

Much of my writing is about AIDS, as its various aspects of fear, loss, and wisdom sum up all the important things I have known. In addition to prose, poetry, and reviews in various journals and anthologies, I am co-author of the long running *AIDS Show,* of which I was an original cast member in 1984. As a "radical musicologist," I have published papers, edited newsletters, and lectured about philosophical and cultural aspects of postmodernism and the avant-garde, and on gay musicians. I live in San Francisco, where I am working on a dissertation on "chaotic" vocal music of the 1960s, and on my first novel, *The Voyage to Europe*. I hope to live to complete both, but if I do not, I know that I have recreated my personal universe to my own satisfaction in the miniature "Going to Japan," and that is, strange to say, enough.

Peter Cashorali

Peter Cashorali lives in Los Angeles, where his time is multiplied with Caesar Bonilla, his lover of twenty-two years, and his dear friend Rick Sandford. Like you, he understands this life isn't forever, and observes how the understanding enriches the life, sometimes unbearably. Whoever you are reading this, good luck to you and yours. The best of luck.

Bernard Cooper

Bernard Cooper is the author of *Maps to Anywhere* and *A Year of Rhymes* (both from Penguin). He has received the 1991 PEN/USA Ernest Hemingway Award, and a 1995 O. Henry Prize. "Arson" is from *Truth Serum*, a collection of memoirs forthcoming from Viking.

"I often begin a narrative in order to get to an image that haunts me. In the case of 'Arson,' the fiery bits of men's bodies floating through the air of my parents' garage. I had to learn again and again that my desire for men could not be diminished or burned away. Setting fire to pornography was only one instance in a lifetime of sexual reckonings.

"In some respects, 'coming out,' is a sorry term. It suggests that one makes a decision, leaps through an emotional hoop, and lands on two feet. To grasp one's nature is arduous and ongoing; there are many comings out, vivid and incomplete glimpses of what it means to be human and homosexual. This memoir, I hope, is one of those glimpses."

Gil Cuadros

Gil Cuadros is a poet, fiction writer, and PWA. He is the author of *City of God* published by City Lights Books. His work has been anthologized in *High Risk 2, Indivisible,* and *Grand Passion: The Poets of Los Angeles and Beyond.* Cuadros is a recipient of a PEN/USA West grant for writers with HIV/AIDS and a Brody Literature fellowship.

He writes of "Heroes," "As much as I try to disguise it, most of my work is autobiographical. I wonder, for myself, if a PWA can truly fall in love with another PWA? Do they cling together because of the fears they share? Are they heroic in their act of loving one another in this AIDS-phobic/homophobic world? How or do they accept that one of them will eventually die first? Do they assume who will die first?"

Frank DiPalermo

Bios lay out events in chronological order as if people *were* the events of their lives. Born in New York. Moved to San Francisco. Studied theater. Began to write. Moved to L.A. Started writing performance material. Moved farther south. Kept on writing. Writing now.

This does not express the evolution of a closeted individual (spiritually, emotionally, and sexually) into one enjoying tremendous freedom. Clearly, events in a life are half the story. The wondrous and mundane stuff happening in between is what *really* makes a life. How do you fit that into a hundred words or less?

Jason Friedman

I was born in 1963 and grew up in Savannah, Georgia. I got the hell out as soon as I could, and now my creative life is devoted to getting back. "The Wedding Dress" grew out of a newspaper article I read in the *Savannah Morning News* recently at my parents' house. In a Savannah suburb a boy—I recall he was an Eagle Scout, though I could very well have made that up—found a wedding dress and was trying to find its rightful owner. Luckily, the article was very short and my folks threw out the paper before I could clip it. As a result, "the truth" inspired me but had no chance to hold me in its sway. I recognized the described events as story material, a modern-day Cinderella tale. What will happen, I asked myself, when the dress's owner shows up to claim it? What happens when your desire shows up on your doorstep? Will you be able to recognize it? And what if you're a young gay man and your desire looks like nothing you've seen before? I still probably haven't come up with an answer, judging from the half-dozen endings "The Wedding Dress" has had. I thank my partner, Tim Dean, for advising me to scrap the first one. I thank my editor, Robert Drake, for helping me settle on the final one.

I teach creative writing at the University of Washington, in Seattle. I've published stories in *The South Carolina Review, Asylum,* Baltimore's *City Paper,* and the anthology *A Natural Beauty.* I also write scary books for children: *Haunted Houses* (Dell, 1992), a nonfiction book on the subject; and the forthcoming *Phantom Trucker* (Random House). My grown-up novel, *The Creek Is Gone,* was the finalist in the Associated Writing Programs Award Series in the Novel. My essay "Southern Gothic Style" is forthcoming in the volume *Goth Style,* edited by Lauren Goodlad.

Patrick Gale

Patrick Gale was born on the Isle of Wight in 1962 and now divides his time between wild northern Cornwall and the more sedate reaches of Kensington. His seventh novel, a family romance about AIDS and the Holocaust called *The Facts of Life,* will be published this year, as will his short stories, *Dangerous Pleasures.* Born so far out that he was nineteen before he even noticed the closet existed, he prefers to be thought of as a writer lucky enough to be gay than as a "gay writer," since he abhors any kind of marginalization. He believes that a gay or lesbian sensibility lends a writer unique insights into the deviant behavior of heterosexuals that lie beyond the grasp of the poor, benighted heterosexuals themselves. Unlike his novels, his stories tend to spring from real incidents. In the case of "Wig," this was catching a mousy housewife trying on an outrageously unsuitable hairpiece in a department store.

David Kelly

"The Road to Mary's Place" is David Kelly's first published work since penning editorials for his college newspaper at the University of Georgia in the mid-1980s. A native of South Carolina, David's writing is heavily influenced by such Southern themes as family, home, personal sacrifice, the meaning of tradition, and, of course, race, combined with the element of sexual orientation. David lives in Los Angeles with his spouse, Wade, and their two cats, Misha and Butch.

Tim Miller

Hi, everybody!!! I am a performance artist, activist, teacher, and troublemaker. I was born in Los Angeles (the apparent love-child of Maria von Trapp and Gustav von Aschenbach), and a lot of my work deals with exploring my life as a Big Fag in my stomping grounds of Southern California. This piece, "Tar Pit Heart," comes from a full-evening performance work called *My Queer Body*. I began this work when I wrote a fairy tale to my dick. This launched me on a journey to discover the stories my body has to tell. If you listen carefully, your lips remember your first kiss... and your first loss. Queer places have their history in flesh and blood and breath and spirit. Thanks.

Scott W. Peterson

Scott W. Peterson is a writer and student of history living in the Pacific Northwest. His work is anthologized in *Indivisible* (Plume, 1991) and *Shadows of Love* (Alyson Publications, 1989), and has appeared in the *James White Review, Seattle Gay News,* and *Wiggansnatch Literary Magazine.* He doesn't much like writing about himself.

Robert Rodi

I was born in Chicago in 1956 and am still here. In the meantime, I've written four comic novels, all dealing with aspects of gay identity and all published by Dutton/Plume: *Fag Hag, Closet Case, What They Did to Princess Paragon,* and (coming in November '95) *Drag Queen.*

"Affairs of the Day" was written to serve a specific purpose: to be read aloud on the many occasions when I'm asked to get in front of a microphone and be wonderful and witty and gone in ten minutes.

As for the story's origin: Even though I have been living with a truly incredible man, Jeffrey Smith, for seven years, I remain intrigued by the possibilities of the Road Not Taken. But not guiltily so; as my late grandmother, Edith St. Onge, once said, "Doesn't matter where you get your appetite, as long as you eat at home."

Rick Sandford

I am a Gentile man who is currently working on the third part of what I like to think of as my Jewish trilogy. The first part, "Förster and Rosenthal Re-evaluated: An Investigative Report," was published in *Indivisible,* and a story from the second part, "Purim," was published in *Blood Whispers: L.A. Writers on AIDS, Volume 2.* The story included here, "Levi," is also from this project.

As a person with AIDS, I believe that this affliction is a symptom, a sore of the Judaic/Christian disease that permeates our society. Luckily enough for me, I live across the street from an Orthodox Jewish boys' school. Being Orthodox, they believe that the Torah (the first five books of the Bible), are the actual words of God and not just something written by possibly fallible men. Ever since I first spoke to some of the boys during Chanukah of 1989/5750, I realized that, as a writer, I had a great opportunity to explore, in human terms, what I perceive to be the very essence of homophobia in Western civilization: "If a man also lie with mankind, as he lieth with a woman, both of them have committed an abomination: they shall surely be put to death; their blood shall be upon them" (Leviticus 20:13).

To the boys of Yeshiva Ohr Elchonon Chabad in Los Angeles, who have made this possible, I offer my deepest gratitude and affection.

Mark A. Shaw

Mark Shaw was trapped in Kansas City prior to attending Glamour School (Bennington College) with all the famous people. He is a recipient of a Maryland Individual Artist Award and writes a bi-weekly column for the *Baltimore City Paper*. "Queerbait" is dedicated to Darby Crash of the seminal L.A. punk band the Germs. Many people who knew him believe that Darby killed himself rather than acknowledge his sexuality in the rabidly heterosexual L.A. punk scene.

Matthew Stadler

Matthew Stadler is the author of the novels *Landscape: Memory, The Dissolution of Nicholas Dee, The Sex Offender,* and *Allan Stein.* He lives in Seattle, Washington.

Henri Tran

Henri Tran is a West Coast writer living in Southern California. The genesis of his piece in this collection came to him when, "...I was sitting alone late one night in my apartment, caught in a slow panic. It was the beginning of a new decade. Still, friends had been dying, the enemies remained invisible, and if I but made a false step, crossing the borderline, I would be dying too. The feeling had occurred many times before, except that I now recognized its familiarity with that of living in wartime. It was Saigon all over again during the last years, when we all prayed for our lives. I had thought then that if I ever got out alive, I would go so far away as to forever escape this horrible specter, of death hovering over me; never again, would I have to cry for God's mercy. . . ."

David Vernon

David Vernon's stories have appeared in *Men on Men 4*, *Indivisible*, and *Blood Whispers: L.A. Writers on AIDS*, volumes one and two. He is currently working on a novel and a collection of his short fiction.

"I wrote 'Love Is Thin Ice' at a very peculiar point in my life. I had been asked to write a new story for a reading at A Different Light bookstore entitled 'Boyfriends from Hell.' After the series of events including the riots, the floods, the Menendez trial, and the Northridge earthquake, I felt extremely disenchanted with living in Los Angeles. So even though 'Love Is Thin Ice' contains several honest-to-god 'BFHs' (up to three, depending on your point of view), I wanted to write a story in which the city itself becomes the ultimate boyfriend from hell."

David Watmough

"Horses" is the first of a series that derives inspiration from classical Greek legend but is nevertheless firmly incarnated in a twentieth-century context. My most recent novel, *The Time of the Kingfishers*, also uses Hellenistic myth in its conception. These connecting strands have grown steadily over the quarter century in which I have been writing fiction by the ocean's edge here in Vancouver; in fact, the threads linking my gay protagonist, his Cornish childhood, and subsequent maturity in the U.S. and Canada have been his sense of family, his sense of history, and his homosexual destiny.

This is the first story of childhood I have written in many years and I probably won't write another. But I like to think that all those "marks" that serve an author's signature are present in it. Indeed, it is precisely that which makes me especially content it should appear in this gay anthology.

Acknowledgments

The editors would like to thank Robert Jones, Richard LaBonte, Christopher Schelling and John Talbot for their support and interest in the development of *His* and *Hers*.

We are especially grateful to Betsy Uhrig, who made it all possible. We extend our heartfelt appreciation to Susan Silton, and to Robert Flynt and Connie Imboden.

We are fortunate to have been able to work with the talented writers whose stories are collected in these books. To them, most of all, we offer our gratitude.

All stories are printed by permission of the authors.

About
the
Editors

Robert Drake

Robert Drake is an educator, author, editor, and literary agent. His first novel, *The Man: A Hero For Our Time (Book One: Why?)* was published by Penguin USA/Plume in June 1995. With Terry Wolverton he co-edited the anthology *Indivisible: new short fiction by west coast gay and lesbian writers,* receiving two Lambda Literary Award nominations. He is the book review editor for the *Baltimore Alternative.* He teaches writing at St. John's College and the American University, and resides in Annapolis, Maryland, with his dog, Pudsey Dawson—a white bull terrier with brindle ears, named for a "bully" the English poet Rupert Brooke went swimming with in Byron's pool at Granchester.

Terry Wolverton

Terry Wolverton is the author of *Black Slip,* a Lambda Book Award-nominated collection of poetry from Clothespin Fever Press. Her poems, short fiction, essays, and dramatic texts have been published widely in journals and anthologies. She is the former executive director of the Woman's Building in Los Angeles, and the founder of the Perspectives Writing Program at the Los Angeles Gay and Lesbian Community Services Center.

She has also edited *Harbinger: poetry and fiction by Los Angeles writers* (with Benjamin Weissman, for the 1990 Los Angeles Festival), *Indivisible: new short fiction by west coast gay and lesbian writers* (with Robert Drake), and *Blood Whispers: L.A. Writers on AIDS,* volumes one and two (Silverton Books).

"In my own writing," she says, "I aim to demonstrate that truth is a complex entity. As a teacher and editor, I have two goals: to create opportunities for exceptional writers whose voices might otherwise not be heard, and to help raise the overall standards of craft and quality in the gay and lesbian literary community."